POST-HOLOCAUST FRANCE AND THE JEWS, 1945–1955

Post-Holocaust France and the Jews, 1945–1955

Edited by Seán Hand and Steven T. Katz

NEW YORK UNIVERSITY PRESS
New York and London

NEW YORK UNIVERSITY PRESS
New York and London
www.nyupress.org

References to Internet websites (URLs) were accurate at the time of writing.
Neither the author nor New York University Press is responsible for URLs that
may have expired or changed since the manuscript was prepared.

Library of Congress Cataloging-in-Publication Data

Post-Holocaust France and the Jews, 1945–1955 : edited by Seán Hand and Steven T. Katz.
  pages cm
 Includes bibliographical references and index.
 ISBN 978-1-4798-3504-1 (cl : alk. paper)
 1. Jews—France—History—1945–1958.   2. Jews—France—Social conditions—History—
1945–1958.   3. France—Ethnic relations—History—1945–1958.   4. France—Politics and
government—1945–1958.   I. Hand, Seán, editor.   II. Katz, Steven T., 1944– editor.
 DS135.F83P67 2015
 305.892'404409044—dc23   2014044423

New York University Press books are printed on acid-free paper,
and their binding materials are chosen for strength and durability.
We strive to use environmentally responsible suppliers and materials
to the greatest extent possible in publishing our books.

Manufactured in the United States of America

10 9 8 7 6 5 4 3 2 1

Also available as an ebook

CONTENTS

ACKNOWLEDGMENTS

The editors wish to acknowledge the generous support of the Marilyn and Mike Grossman Conference Fund, housed at the Elie Wiesel Center for Judaic Studies at Boston University, for making possible the international conference held at Boston University in 2011 that inspired the production of this book. The editors also gratefully acknowledge the financial assistance and additional resources given to the production of this book by the Humanities Research Centre and the Department of French Studies, both at the University of Warwick. We wish to thank Dr. Claire Trévien for her translation of one chapter, and Dr. Amanda Hopkins and Holly Langstaff for their editorial assistance with all the chapters. We also thank David Lees for help with indexing. Sincere thanks, in addition, are due to Pagiel Czoka, the former Administrative Assistant at the Elie Wiesel Center, who worked tirelessly to see that everything needed for a successful conference was in place. Thanks also go to Rabbi Joseph Polak, who made the Hillel House available to us for use during the conference and provided our meals. We wish also to acknowledge the expertise, support, and friendship of Jennifer Hammer at NYU Press, and to thank the JDC Archives for permission to reproduce the cover image.

Introduction

SEÁN HAND

This book is concerned with a pivotal moment of history in France, the first ten years of political and social reconstruction after the end of World War II. It is a period that was crucial to the restoration of a Jewish population and cultural presence in France after years of persecution and destruction, and it involved such immediate tasks as the reunification of families and communities, restitution of property and resources, and reestablishment of rescinded rights. But it is equally a decade that involved major developments that came to challenge the very notion of a restoration of order, to the extent that it changed the enshrined and understood relationship between France and Jews. For in betraying Jews in France through the implementation of anti-Semitic policies and the facilitation of murder, the Vichy state also broke the powerful pact of republican assimilation. This pact had distinguished the particular French model of Jewish emancipation sometimes called Franco-Judaism. It conferred on Jews a theoretical equality arising out of secularist and universalist principles that effectively insisted on public invisibility as a distinct grouping.[1] Significantly, however, protection of Jews during the Vichy and occupation period had come overwhelmingly from nonstatist sources, and in the immediate postwar period the particular mistreatment of Jews was subsumed within an official narrative of an indivisible France that remained united in a collective experience and in reconstructive efforts. One observable consequence of this approach was a conscious and isolatable form of public self-organization among Jews in postwar France that was new to the country's modern history. The decade in question therefore saw a rapid proliferation of societies, agencies, and schools of thought devoted to the open articulation of particular visions and community identities for Jews in France, where previously any distinctiveness had been subsumed, more often than not willingly, under the powerful assimilationist ethos of the French republican model. This fundamental shift was thereafter to become further propelled by subsequent postwar events of international significance, and especially those relating to decolonization and to post–Cold War geopolitics, which not only altered France's demographic makeup, including that of its identifiable Jewish population, but also tested again the historical notions of allegiance, loyalty, and cultural affiliation for Jews in France.

Yet, for all the fundamental significance of these changes in the relationship between France and Jews, this is a decade that has often been somewhat overlooked until now. The reasons for this are perhaps obvious: momentous international events take place before and after the period in question, combined with the desire in both political circles and survivors' mentalities to leave behind shameful and traumatic events and focus instead on national reconstruction and hopeful emotions. Unsurprisingly, historical accounts can repeat this effect when they return to the drama and uncertainty of the wartime period. They therefore tend to focus on the treatment of Jews that for so long remained insufficiently acknowledged by official accounts, and then move forward rapidly to review such dramatic moments of change as the significant immigration of North African Jews to France caused by the Algerian war of 1954–62 and more generally by the region's decolonization, or to observe the tense conflict in loyalties and identifications produced by the events of the Six-Day War in 1967, including in reaction to comments made by significant figures such as Charles de Gaulle.[2]

To accept these large historical moments as defining, however, is also to internalize a certain timetable set in motion initially by the very synthesizing Gaullist narrrative of wartime efforts and postwar will, and therefore to overlook those fundamentally significant efforts made in many different quarters to restore the life, culture, and institutions of French Jewry in the immediate postwar period. Indeed, we could say that these movements were themselves to affect subsequent international shifts. It is therefore the aim of this volume to focus on the key relevant activities and ideas relating to the years 1945–55 in order to provide a fuller and truer picture of the relationship between France and the Jews on its soil at a moment of complex renovation.

At the beginning of the occupation, Jews in France numbered over 300,000. Almost two-thirds of them lived in Paris, and 190,000 were French citizens. Of the 76,000 deported from France during the war, fewer than 5 percent were to return. This does leave some 200,000 who did survive the destruction, and their numbers were to be augmented further by refugees immediately after the war, as well as at key moments thereafter. (Polls conducted in 2012 estimated the number of Jews resident in France to be between 483,000 and 600,000, making them the third-largest national grouping after citizens of Israel and the United States.) This is the size of the postwar population, then, that was to be affected by the tasks of wholesale institutional and psychological reconstruction. These tasks were undertaken by a rapidly proliferating number of committees, special operations, and purposeful individuals, whose actions and efforts took place within a period of continuing hardship and competing claims to immediate assistance. By focusing on this time, and especially by highlighting the efforts of significant Jewish organizations, large-scale related planning, and associated intellectual reconstruction, we achieve a much more continuous and informed understanding of the life, contribution, and significance of Jews in France in the postwar era. We can also note immediately that such reconstructive efforts served a difficult dual function in relation to Jewish identity. On the one hand, such identity could be naturally of a wholly practical and concrete nature, concerning, for example, the key issue of saved orphans whose psychological as well as physical welfare was forever affected by their experience. On the other hand, the question of identity effectively also had to assume the equally fundamental task of attempting to conceptualize the events that had taken place, and to propose a range of intellectual and identificatory solutions for Jewish life and culture in France and Europe. This is a task that we see enacted by such influential postwar figures as Emmanuel Levinas, Léon Poliakov, and André Neher. At both levels of activity, this kind of work came to assume a fundamental significance for any continuing sense of French republicanism, since these efforts effectively created a subtle shifting of weight between the coexisting dual identities of Jewish French citizen, on the one hand, and French Jew, on the other hand. This is not at all to suggest that French Jews necessarily abandoned the republican model of assimilationist identity. It is notable that postwar Jews did not relocate in significant numbers from France to Israel; and in seeking to isolate some of the reasons why this was so, we can do no better than to review the position of René Cassin, who provides an unambiguous reassertion of commitment to the traditional French concept of citizenship. But it remains equally true that the assimilationist model was thrown into crisis by the events of the Shoah in France, just as it has been further tested on subsequent occasions when official adherence to republican indivisibility and neutrality momentarily slipped in relation to attitudes toward Jews. In this aspect also, then, the immediate postwar period, in terms of accommodation and reaction, was effectively a foundational one for the contemporary complexities of Jewish identification and affiliation in France.[3]

Organizing Complexity

The focused study of this period, which involved an internationally coordinated approach to recovery and planning, immediately highlights the complexity and interactivity of all sociopolitical renewal in France, including for Jews. The tasks and events reviewed here were also occurring at a time when the end of World War II was widely felt to have inaugurated a potentially more deadly struggle for European domination that eventually was to settle into Cold War vigilance. Our focus therefore has the additional benefit of locating itself at a key moment of urgent and uncertain interactivity affecting not just France's national self-identity but also Europe's new transnational humanitarian and strategic concerns. David Weinberg's chapter makes an essential point when it emphasizes, among other details, how, from the devastation of France's religious and lay leadership, there arose an organizational will. By virtue of having survived the Holocaust in France, and being also at the heart of postwar allied operations with a heightened moral status, this organizational will made France the natural locus for forms of concerted Jewish activism that were also European, North American, and Zionist in their scope, address, and resources. This meant that new forms of French Jewish autonomy and internationalist self-identification arose powerfully in a period of geopolitical flux, wherein traditional structures and allegiances in France nevertheless wished to reassert themselves. The resulting complexity interestingly highlights how the transnational organizations that became important agents during this time were an early instance of the fundamental shifts in power that would begin to develop rapidly in postwar globalizing politics. As a result, we can appreciate how the French-based activities of the Conseil représentatif des israélites de France (CRIF), or the American Jewish Joint Distribution Committee (JDC or "the Joint"), or the American Jewish Committee (AJC) ultimately held ramifications that extended well beyond their precise initial concerns. Such organizational activity therefore certainly affected the self-perceptions of French Jewry, and it arguably affected the broader image of France's exceptionalism. Several of the chapters in this book therefore refer naturally to the existence and activities of such organizations, some of which were financed significantly via the JDC. To isolate just a few examples: the Comité juif d'action sociale et de reconstruction (COJASOR) assisted surviving or returning Jews; the Fonds juif social unifié (FSJU) evolved from initial refugee support to more wholesale orchestration of a French social, educational, and cultural Jewish presence in response to decolonization's effects; the Conseil représentatif du judaïsme traditionaliste de France (CRJTF) looked to create Jewish youth centers, kindergartens, or holiday camps; the Jewish Restitution Successor Organization (JRSO) took an internationalist perspective on restitutions; and the Centre de documentation juive contemporaine (CDJC) during the war itself began to compile documentary evidence of war crimes against Jews that would be cited in the Nuremberg trials, before becoming part of the archives of the Mémorial de la Shoah located in Paris. Such new forms of affiliation and planning were in addition, of course, to the transformed aims of other longestablished organizations. One of the most important of these was undoubtedly the Paris-based Alliance israélite universelle (AIU), founded in 1860 to preserve the rights of Jews throughout the world via education. In the postwar period its politics shifted toward Zionism, even if de Gaulle typically viewed the Middle East presence of the AIU as also serving French colonial interests. A further example is the Oeuvre des secours aux enfants (OSE). Originally founded in 1912 by doctors in St. Petersburg as an organization designed to protect the health of needy Jews, during the war it had housed and assisted Jewish refugee children; but today it works in a much broader arena involving health, sociomedical, and educational support for Jewish populations, and as such works in partnership in several eastern European countries as well as in Israel.

The chapter by Samuel Ghiles-Meilhac detailing the founding fortunes of the CRIF during this period provides one valuable focus on the multiplicity of issues and choices which we can see would have affected the organizational will that emerged at this historical point. From the moment of its wartime inception, which itself was already contextualized by the history of interwar competition for Jewish political affiliation, the CRIF's mission of speaking for all French Jewry instituted a fundamental change in the historical nature of French Jewish identification, in terms of both organization and political univocity. While the Central Consistory, the body governing Jewish congregations, looked at that time to retain internal control (it left the present-day CRIF in 2004), the alliance of often divergent political visions united such different figures as Léon Meiss (then head of the Consistory), Isaac Schneersohn (cofounder of the CDJC), and Robert Gamson (founder of the French Jewish scouting movement) around instances of anti-Semitism. Indeed, one of these instances involved early judgment of the possible moral culpability of the Union générale des israélites de France (UGIF), a wartime French Jewish council or Judenrat recognized by a Vichy law of November 29, 1941. Out of this internal politics, however, and quickly moving beyond judgment of the war years, it found itself adopting international positions on Palestine and Israel, postwar rearmament, and Cold War politics, though without necessarily cohering around one common vision or creating common cause with organizations such as the AIU. The general effect during this decade was therefore to begin a process of shifting the collective voice away from a neutrality in keeping with a French assimilationist instinct, and toward the status of being an official French affiliate to the World Jewish Congress and an influential organ in French political life, a position the CRIF occupies today.

In a similar vein, the chapter by Lisa Leff traces a parallel shift in relations between Jewish organizations and the state during this time, concerning how the postwar insistence on republican "race-blind" policies could also generate major restitutional injustices, including where purloined items such as artworks were treated as national rather than private property. The case of book looting and restoration here provides a particularly fascinating study of the precise mechanisms and decisions that came into play when works were treated simultaneously as French patrimony (irrespective of a work's origins) and as the heart of a particular Jewish community or society. As Leff shows, the interactive and diplomatic nature of much of the expeditionary and attributive work therefore involved the maintenance of a delicate partnership between bodies such as the AIU and the French state, in a way that seemed to maintain the historical assimilated position of Franco-Judaism and yet to acknowledge a cultural particularism whose untypical nature was justified as needs-driven but perhaps signaled a new relationship. In counterpoint to this, Maud Mandel's study of the contemporary tensions and transformations created by immigrant arrivals for the predominant character of Franco-Judaism usefully stresses how the disruptions of the Shoah and World War II did not necessarily overturn all traditional internal notions of difference, but rather perhaps laid the conditions for an accommodation of the equally dramatic development of French Jewry following the further immigrant influx arising in particular from France's decolonizations. Mandel traces all the organizational attempts to articulate and govern these changes in a way that brings out how the Consistory and the CRIF themselves needed to acknowledge entrenched exclusivist attitudes among the historical Jewish population. These attitudes could be seen to reaffirm the national neutralism of Franco-Judaism and simultaneously to betray a snobbery and fear regarding how association with unassimilated groups might undo certain historically acquired benefits. In a fascinating reflection of changes occurring at the national level, this complex reaction produced both a continuing rhetorical adherence to assimilation and the beginnings of a more pluralist sensibility that would, for example, allow consideration of greater institutional decentralization as the price for retaining unity within a broader Consistory. Mandel ultimately isolates two key factors in this transformation which also acted as a profound influence on the entire French nation in the postwar period: the general "Americanization" that was accelerated in this case by JDC funding, and which challenged and overtook older sectarian divisions; and the dramatic revitalization of French Jewish spirituality by North African immigration.

Uses and Abuses of Children

The chapters by Daniella Doron, Susan Suleiman, and Lucille Cairns collectively highlight one exemplary instance of the complex consequences of immediate reconstruction, namely, the operations and aims associated with the plight of Jewish orphans after the war. Approximately 10,000 Jewish children were deprived of one or both of their parents, with as many as 7,000 placed in Jewish children's homes at the Liberation. As 40 percent of these children had one surviving parent, the situation was further complicated by the economic circumstances of surviving relatives.[4] As with other problems, this issue was overdetermined by the specifics of the political context: France had to deal not just with a national version of postwar restoration, but also with the intricacies of simultaneous adherence to anti-Semitic hatred by Vichy and resistance to those operations by ordinary citizens. Given the destruction of families through war, the inclusion of children in round-ups and deportation by Vichy officials, and the concealment by French people of Jewish children under threat, the plight of children was to provide an obvious focal point for multiple and sometimes conflicting thoughts of restorative justice. Inevitably, as Doron discusses, the issue quickly became politicized, with the condition of innocent and vulnerable children being co-opted not just by contesting narratives of martyrdom, but also by broader forms of exculpation and universalization. This was a period marked dramatically by the so-called Finaly affair (1948–53), a legal dispute involving the Consistory that played out against the background of a Vatican instruction, wherein two Jewish boys from Grenoble whose parents had been deported were cared for by a Catholic who initially refused to return the children to their aunts on the grounds that they were now Catholics. In the midst of this instrumentalization, as Suleiman brings out in detail, the French context also entailed the further psychological complications associated with a whole generation of Jewish children who had survived the war by dint of being hidden in France by non-Jewish families, and for whom subsequent conflicts of emotional identification and narrative understanding remained unresolved, sometimes to the present day. Inner conflict and religious identity became intertwined, creating a French Jewish memory that was effectively denied forms of "working through" during the period. Suleiman endorses the view of Annette Wieviorka and other historians that, because of the general public attitude, this situation did not change until after the 1961 trial of Adolf Eichmann. This meant that for these young survivors psychological conflict was to remain as a foundational complex for the postwar era, resulting in later eruptions around such moments as the Six-Day War, where one's French and Jewish identity again became potentially opposed.[5] These unresolved complications, which play out a tension between memory and history that occupied French historiography from the 1970s on, are intimately charted by Lucille Cairns in her reading of personal testimonies by hidden Jewish girls. Both their accounts and the related research highlight the sheer diversity of the problem. Orphanages could have distinct regimes, aims, and therapeutic practices, whether because of a director's personality or because of the different secular, religious, and ideological identities of the organization involved. Beyond this, though, there were also broader implications relating to the source of financial support, such as the JDC, and even to the fact that the French Jewish community, perhaps regarding the orphaned child as an unwelcome link to the past or simply as an impossible additional burden, itself sometimes displayed a dereliction of duty. An associated fact is that approximately 5 percent of the total Jewish population in France between 1947 and 1950 undertook a change of patronymic, a figure that doubles if one includes Jews who adopted a gallicized patronymic on acquiring French citizenship. Such recorded name changing was six times higher in the period 1945–57 than in the whole of the period from 1808 (when Napoleon I decreed that all Jews had to adopt a fixed patronymic) and 1939.[6] Cairns also advances the interesting thesis that the analyzed memoirs seem progressively more generous as the events recede into the past, suggesting a longer-term resolution of trauma that among other things confirms the idea that the immediate postwar period provided no accessible psychological framework for recovery and rehabilitation. By focusing, then, on the hugely compelling cases of the Jewish orphans produced by the persecutions, extermination policy, and war, and by including in their study the continuing conflict generated by subsequent propaganda campaigns, traumatic identity formation, and unresolved tension between personal memory and public history, these chapters underscore powerfully again the key point that this period not only saw the attempted management of immediate concerns, but also anticipated a postwar age of multipolar belonging. The effects of this conflicted sense of allegiance were to be registered belatedly in France by later generations, whether via political adherence or by way of complex narrative constructions that attempted to express the intricacies of "postmemory" identity.[7]

One Nation, One Narrative

The resolutions of Jewish agencies and authorities during this period were fundamentally contextualized by the political and economic problems besetting the French Fourth Republic, which ran constitutionally from 1946 to 1958. From September 1944, when the government assumed the task of rebuilding a nation still at war, and so favored the armaments and associated infrastructural industries over domestic shortages, France used national resurgence to dismiss self-examination. This era was above all to be one of rapid economic and institutional regrowth in both France and Europe. There were some key achievements in the period, notably relating to the establishment of comprehensive social security and health care systems. But the government was also dogged from the beginning by its immediate history, tense relations with General de Gaulle, and an unstable ministerial balancing act that sought to maintain a three-way party alliance. It was also being driven along at the same time by the multiple ideals of European unity and the epochal collapse of colonial empire. In this new landscape, the capacity and will of the government to assume full responsibility for the Shoah, and to confront its profoundly altered relationship with the Jewish population, were arguably already limited by these immediate politicoeconomic priorities, as well as by unwillingness or inability to acknowledge the national nature of betrayal.

One key effect was that the particular treatment of Jews during the Vichy and occupation years became categorized as a precise wartime event that could therefore be addressed and settled by the *épuration* or purging process that largely took place between 1944 and 1945. "Order, efficiency, and justice" were de Gaulle's stated priorities in a liberation speech made at the Palais de Chaillot on September 12, 1944, and at one level this list was clearly being stated in terms of relative importance.[8] Indeed, the prevailing conditions arguably militated against any sympathy for Jewish survivors of France's war record, who in some quarters were still tenaciously identified as entirely foreign, and whose return from the camps or exile could therefore be represented as an added burden rather than as a consequence of the state's culpability. Indirect factors further fueled this sentiment: the resolute Gaullist presentation of France as a unified resistant wartime force that had never betrayed itself even in its darkest moments, and the ambivalence about the assistance and continuing presence of the United States on French soil (which flared up, for example, over military decisions taken at the moment of the recapture of the city of Strasbourg at the beginning of 1945), encouraged and mobilized a general chauvinism that vaguely legitimated dismissal of the treatment of Jews.[9]

These tendencies were already primed, moreover, by the experience of ordinary French citizens during the initial period when prisoners and deportees liberated by Allied forces gradually returned home. The word *experience* is here salient, for plainly the national narrative of united resistance and self-won triumph in the face of external threats was flatly contradicted by the complex and compromised reality that refugees embodied. Of the 5 million people of different categories who had to find their way home and attempt to rebuild lives, 700,000 were actually Service du travail obligatoire (STO) workers, that is, "compulsory work service" laborers who were returning from mostly forced employment in German factories. Their status as a Vichy-requisitioned nonresistant workforce complicated the notion of refugee for state propaganda and ordinary citizen alike. Moreover, the logistics associated with returning prisoners, deportees, workers, and survivors at one level were regarded as hampering the continuing war effort's need to ration resources such as transportation, medical facilities, and liaison work. In addition, attitudes to this situation were made even more conflicted by the requirement to scrutinize returnees for any cases of criminality or collaboration. As de Gaulle suggested in the same Palais de Chaillot liberation speech, anything that was not obviously building for the future was implicitly a "waste."[10] In this context, the situation of those Jews liberated from extermination camps, which could have been acknowledged as irrefutable local evidence of the Holocaust, was instead widely treated as indistinguishable from that of non-Jews returning from concentration camps. As such, the experience of Jews here was treated as one detail of an organizational problem concerning the movements of over a million people, which was dealt with by the significantly named Ministry of Prisoners, Deportees and Refugees over a mere nine months lasting up to June 1945.

From our present perspective, then, a highly significant element of the story of post-Holocaust France and the Jews concerns how even the return of Jewish refugees involved a lack of official or emotional recognition of a specific kind. The stories of surviving deportees, especially Jewish but also non-Jewish, seemed for a long time destined to remain unembraced by national or communal understanding. As a result, the intellectual processing of what had taken place was effectively left in the early years to certain key individuals whose work sometimes was colored by the politicized nature of the Nuremberg trials or the ideological motivations of political groupings. It is a significant fact, for example, that one of the best-known early attempts at a lucid expression of experience, David Rousset's *L'univers concentrationnaire*, is not specifically Jewish in its account of the Nazi extermination machine. Indeed, its insistence on a universalist and antifascist thesis was implicitly the refutation of any specifically Jewish category of genocide. As demonstrated subsequently by the concerted vilification of Rousset as an agent provocateur during the period when he exposed the existence of the Soviet gulags and helped in 1950 to found an international commission against concentration camps, the events related to survival and return were generally subordinated to the political imperatives of the day, which themselves were soon dominated by Cold War realpolitik.[11] In other words, there was no special desire on the part of any major political faction, including the Communist Party, as well as those on the political right or in the Gaullist camp, to highlight the plight of Jewish deportees. The Communists' wish, for example, to exploit the credibility of *résistant* status led them to redefine Auschwitz as an essentially political prison. And it should also be noted in passing that there were certainly anti-Semitic members of the Resistance, just as anti-Semitism had not of itself defined the core political position of the Vichy regime, in contrast to that of the Third Reich.[12] This does not, of course, obscure the fact that, as Michael Marrus and Robert Paxton pointed out to a still recalcitrant French audience, Vichy's anti-Semitic machine gave more support to the German extermination program than did Germany's allies Hungary and Romania.[13]

Thinking beyond the Shoah

The Holocaust has undoubtedly presented the greatest challenge to Western philosophy in its modern history, not only in terms of understanding, but also in terms of the emergence of the events and their justification from within supposedly enlightened cultures. The narrative vacuum in the immediate postwar years in France consequently called forth a variety of key attempts at Jewish intellectual reconstruction that offered both radical revisions of Western philosophical assumptions and a series of equally bold postulations, whether of a philosophical or of a more broadly activist category. The chapters by Bruno Chaouat, Jonathan Judaken, and Edward Kaplan progressively map out for us the broad contemplation of this challenge in the immediate environment by a number of major intellectual figures. As a result of their work, significant developments for a renewed or invented vision of modern French Jewish thought then begin to take place. Chaouat's review of an intense period of intellectual reaction, covering only a few years in the late 1940s, looks at how surviving thinkers such as Rousset set out to understand the problem of evil and to acknowledge how the conditions had also permanently changed for philosophy. His chapter tellingly finishes by noting some of the key innovations in philosophical categories produced by Emmanuel Levinas immediately after the war, when he clearly wishes to unwrite the Heideggerian language of ontology and authenticity that for him has become tainted with Nazi associations. In our present context we can add to this reading how the conclusion to Levinas's *Time and the Other*, originally delivered as lectures shortly after the end of the war, significantly introduces an ethical message of vulnerability or absence of virility, and the almost visionary advent of a new child, which stand as the rekindling of both philosophical and social aspirations. Judaken's account of Léon Poliakov's foundational work of Holocaust studies, the 1951 *Bréviaire de la haine*, also highlights the intertwined nature of intellectual and social reconstruction, pointing up Poliakov's close connections to the industrialist Isaac Schneerson (a founder of the CDJC and instigator of the Paris World Memorial to the Unknown Jewish Martyr), his role as head of research at the CDJC (which published several of Poliakov's works), and his important interactions with emblematic Catholic thinkers such as François Mauriac and Jacques Maritain who sought to promote

Jewish-Christian intellectual and spiritual reconciliation. Judaken more particularly pursues the acute significance of the ambiguous thesis of Christophobia in the *Bréviaire*, showing how intertextually it works with Sigmund Freud, Maritain, and Maurice Samuel in order to achieve a complex articulation of the causes of anti-Semitism that offers postsectarian reconciliation, but also locates Jewish identity within a Christianizing metanarrative. Finally, Kaplan's account of the contribution of André Neher to a renewed Jewish intellectual activism in postwar France details some of the highly significant ideological contests, not least for postwar identification for French Jews, reflected in Neher's 1947 doctoral thesis on the prophet Amos (which was dedicated to friends and teachers who were shot or deported). Here we can see that prophetic action is privileged over finite questions of freedom or justice, and Israel is presented as the nation that is exemplarily marked by a perpetually renewable covenant or *berith*. Kaplan goes on to show how, in this and subsequent works such as the 1956 *Moses and the Vocation of the Jewish People*, Neher sought to generate a vigorously activist response to the Holocaust and to questions of historical continuity for French-language Jews. As part of this mission, Neher therefore promoted the revival of a traditional Judaism via such initiatives as the foundation in 1946 of the Jewish École des cadres Gilbert Bloch at Orsay by Robert Gamzon, Jacob Gordin, and Léon Ashkenazi. Later, Neher was also to be a key founding member of the annual Colloquium of French-Language Jewish Intellectuals, inaugurated in 1957. Levinas and Neher, described as the colloquium's "soul and foundation," each year traditionally contributed a Talmudic reading and a biblical exegesis, respectively.[14] Neher's work here points up for us how the republican existential narrative posed particular problems for a Jewish intellectual response, and how one response to this, which evidently disagreed with a Sartrean solution, but also with Poliakov's more integrated theorizing, was an enthusiastic renewal of tradition. Such a return to sources, adopted as an intellectual as well as an affective solution, also significantly restored an overarching religious perspective, in which even the Shoah could be understood as part of a greater dynamic.[15]

Notwithstanding the production of such core challenges to French Jewish intellectual assimilationism, it is important to note that another conclusion could involve reaffirmation of the republican model. No better representative of this position exists than René Cassin. As Jay Winter shows, Cassin worked not only to develop a postwar internationalist governance epitomized by the Universal Declaration of Human Rights, but also to restore the integrity and confidence of republican assimilationist values. At one level, this was logical, as it was through his wartime work with de Gaulle's France libre that he was asked to assume the presidency of the AIU, along with a series of governmental or international duties. These included being the first president of the Council of the École nationale d'administration, established by de Gaulle in 1945 to train a new meritocratic breed of senior civil servant, and later being president of the European Court of Human Rights. But Winter details Cassin's efforts, over a thirty-three-year period as president, to generate systemic improvement and significant extension of the AIU. Much of this could involve quite detailed operational matters as well as much broader sociopolitical aims; all of it was nonetheless significantly pursued always along secular and republican lines. As Winter puts it, Cassin was effectively the foreign minister of Francophone Jewry, and as such projected a thorough identification with France as a universalist and enlightening instrument, while negotiating with American funders, arguing for preservation of the status of AIU schools in the new State of Israel, or seeking to protect North African Jewry at the time of decolonization. Elie Wiesel notes at one point in "To Be a Jew" that the postwar moment in France seemed to present a Jew with the extreme options of "total commitment or total alienation, unconditional loyalty or repudiation."[16] French Jews had indeed every reason to lose faith in the republican model of integration. But René Cassin's reply to the anguished search for a new narrative of Franco-Judaic identity was to seek to embody everything for which he felt the republican model ultimately still stood.

Surviving Change

In time, the "resistencialist" myth of a France united against an external oppressor was subjected to a critique that itself sometimes proposed an equally extreme contradiction to the Gaullist narrative. Since the publication of Rousso's *Vichy Syndrome*, which presented collusion and guilt as pervasive, this countervailing tendency has become qualified to account better for the various and complex forms of involvement and survival.[17] In keeping with this more nuanced perspective, then, we should note that desire for restorative justice and institutional reestablishment for Jews during the postwar period had to combat not only a political reluctance to acknowledge involvement and the psychological tensions inherent in recollection of persecution and betrayal, but also the general population's basic exhaustion. Conditions for ordinary French citizens continued to be grim after the war. Almost 50 percent of the transport network, involving roads, railways, and bridges, had been destroyed, often by allies and the resistance, and 80 percent of all lorries had been put out of action. Petrol and coal (still France's first fuel) were in short supply and expensive. The accumulated poor diet and bad harvests caused by the terrible winter of 1944–45 combined with a shortage of machinery and fertilizer to make agricultural growth similarly hard, meaning that bread rationing continued until 1949. Added to this was a set of conditions guaranteed to produce both inflation and the "moral destruction" of a flourishing black market that continued with occupation practice.[18] Taken together, these conditions prioritized national infrastructural operations to the detriment of the individual citizen, who was left sometimes malnourished as well as frustrated. This policy was, moreover, endorsed by all the main political factions, including the French Communist Party, which treated increased production as a means to berate and disempower the reactionary political and financial forces rewarded by Vichy. The rapid, almost improvisatory, nationalization of companies such as Renault, or of air traffic companies that eventually became Air France, could be felt to serve both these ends, therefore, since not only could productivity supposedly be centrally controlled, but economic collaboration with the German occupation could also be punished through sequestration. With the speedy nature of this dirigiste increase in production, however, came not just a less controllable inflationary wage-price spiral, but a quick return to reliance on autonomous management, whatever its immediate political past. In fact, this overwhelming drive to increase production via an idiosyncratic nationalization created a fundamental blurring of extreme political objectives, ranging from sovietism to technocratism. The attempt to balance this particular mixture of intervention and liberalism, and to modernize France's economy (in part by acquiring resource-rich German territory, thus again combining restoration with punishment) for the postwar period, was to give rise to the Monnet Plan of 1946–50, in which the structural shortcomings of France's performance were identified via a statistical approach to demography and economics that again relied without irony on the development of such tools under the Vichy regime. The solutions presented involved productivist targets that in addition to use of German coal crucially involved reliance on Marshall Plan aid to hold down inflation, as well as nationalized use of the banks. The benefits flowed primarily to the major industries and capital production, and especially energy and transport services, and much less so to building and agriculture, meaning that continuing shortages and deprivation in housing and food were still experienced by an exhausted and sometimes polarized civilian population. The attempts to survive this period of structural recovery, shortage, and inflation were therefore eventually to replace the collectivist will of the Liberation period with a technocratic economic liberalism.

Some later accounts of this period, themselves a form of counternarrative, were to bitterly denounce how the idealism and goals of the Resistance became so swiftly sidelined. One downbeat truth indirectly acknowledged here is that the Resistance was a narrative construct as well as an actual physical struggle, and as such would be necessarily overtaken and smothered by the Gaullist monologue of postwar reassertion. It is all the same true that the revolutionary potentiality of 1944, with Communism poised for potential takeover, rapidly evaporated, in part as the French Communist Party obediently accepted Moscow's preference for a fundamental defeat of Germany and the quick restoration of a France that could limit postwar Anglo-Saxon dominance. In essence, then, this initial period was not only experienced but was also instantaneously narrated as one of a general ongoing struggle that had to deal with both infrastructural and human damage as well as with emerging geopolitical challenges. It is therefore understandable, however unsatisfying, that a judgment of the collaboration period, let alone France's assistance in the persecution of Jews during that period, might be dispatched in a statist and sometimes cynical manner. Contrary to what some *résistants* hoped, the period did not initiate a wholesale social revolution, for which the situation and treatment of Jews might indeed have acted as a catalyst.

The purges of 1944–45 therefore enacted a determining pragmatism. The Liberation period had naturally unleashed the fears of a civilian population pressurized by occupation and collaboration, which expressed themselves in a wave of furious reprisals conducted against collaborators, informers, traitors, and profiteers. Political feeling was inevitably mixed in with more personal and internecine instances of score settling. Mob rule and summary executions, perhaps amounting to 9,000 cases, occurring in a country still at war, rapidly became a problem for national orchestration. De Gaulle's memos of the day show how seriously destabilizing these uncontrolled outbreaks were felt to be.[19] The government therefore quickly moved to reassure allies and control sentiments by shifting power from military tribunals to civil authority, and by instituting the largely pacifying processes of internship, protective custody, and verification commissions. Beyond the reduction in revenge killings, other consequences of this deliberate restraining included using trials of prominent figures (with a populist focus, for example, on well-known entertainers) as a collective cure. This kind of theater also permitted the relative exculpation of still-useful but nationally irrelevant figures, meaning that punishment was disproportionately meted out to whomever did not fall into an administrative or industrial specialism. And it simultaneously began to demonize stubborn *résistants* as antipatriotic agitators and disrupters. This whole process was intentionally brief as well as slow: by the end of 1948, almost 70 percent of condemned cases had been released, and the dismantling of the courts at the beginning of 1951 passed unnoticed. This had the further effect of defining the crimes of Vichy and collaboration overwhelmingly in terms of isolatable actions and individual allegiances, rather than as instances of a generally sustained context for which France as a whole could be held accountable. In keeping with the republican vision of France as indivisibly resistant to aggression and betrayal from World War I to the moment of its self-liberation in 1944, true recognition of a national crime against Jewish inhabitants therefore became marginalized as antithetical to the story of national renewal, and was dealt with inadequately as one feature of the Vichy aberration. In addition, a strange countertendency even set itself in motion: with the Gaullist narrative insisting that responsibility for wartime atrocities lay only with foreign invaders, the summary punishment that was handed out to French citizens, and especially to those women who had engaged sexually with German soldiers, soon attracted negative public reaction in France and abroad. The often lurid presentation of these individuals as victims of excessive violence certainly helped the governmental desire to control *maquisard* justice. But in the process, it also helped to steer attention away from the victims of state-supported persecution and extermination, and it even hastened the rehabilitation of right-wing factions that in turn depicted themselves graphically as the new victims of injustice.

Finally, it is worth pointing up again how the war campaign, and the insistence that military actions involving American or British forces late in the conflict should always be subordinated to the needs of the French state, gave de Gaulle immense currency at the moment of the country's newly gained independence and of his subsequent temporary resignation. As we have repeatedly stressed, this meant that focus on the state's treatment of Jews was always going to be implicitly categorized as a distracting detail, given de Gaulle's imperious dismissal of all "interests, passions or quarrels which might interfere with the rise of France."[20] De Gaulle's continuing influence would additionally have lasting consequences for the later relationship between post-Holocaust France and its Jewish citizens, given in the short term the waning of more far-reaching social change arising from a combination of socialist idealism, Communist Party credibility, and liberal Catholic political renaissance, and in the longer term such dismaying moments relative to the Six-Day War as de Gaulle's casual depiction of the Jewish people as self-assured and domineering (echoed in former ambassador René Massigli's later repetition of the old insidious claim that French Jews retained double loyalties).[21] In the meantime, however, the immediate tasks of an uncertain interregnum caused by de Gaulle's resignation period at the beginning of 1946, the short-lived nature of simple denunciation, the failed attempt to develop a Resistance Party, the need to involve or contain the Communist Party, and the electorate's apathetic response to a new constitution and national elections all promoted uneasy tripartist cohabitation that swiftly reconstituted politics along recognizable lines and indeed quickly created conditions favorable to the return of right-wing parties whose rhetoric offered apology for the Vichy period. All of these factors were therefore to encourage the continuing emergence of independent Jewish agencies, both at this point and in ensuing decades, in the absence of any real national determination to address specifically Jewish claims.

Framing Presence: From "Silence" to Plurality

The initial postwar period in France therefore gives us simultaneously a lack of official specification of the treatments of Jews and a related growth in Jewish agency and identity. This situation qualifies a still vaguely accepted view that the 1950s and 1960s in France, as well as elsewhere, were a period of silence amounting to a generalized repression of events that had traumatized survivors, revealed suspicion and hatred in implicated societies, and even exposed inherently repressive tendencies in technologized cultures. Such an interpretation, problematically reviewed by Bruno Bettelheim as a kind of autism, became popularly ingrained as a psychologization of the period by Rousso's *Vichy Syndrome*, first published in 1987, which now presented the postwar decade in antipositivist terms as one of an "unfinished mourning" destined to return in the 1970s as an obsessive screen memory against which contemporary anxieties were being projected.[22] This view of a haunting "past that will not pass" seemed to be endorsed by both surviving intellectuals and a postmemory generation of artists. The former mostly recalled a landscape in which nothing was said or heard, while the latter seemed hypnotized by the moral ambiguities of the period.[23] These kinds of fixations coexisted with the multivolume work (produced between 1984 and 1992) of Pierre Nora, which relocated French collective consciousness in monumental "realms of memory." One relevant thought here is that these relocations could absorb specifically Jewish experience within an undisrupted and even consolidated concept of republican singularity and its martyrology.[24] A case in point here is the Paris World Memorial to the Unknown Jewish Martyr. In design and symbolism, this memorial clearly harmonizes with traditional universal and national war monuments, even to the extent of depicting only foreign camp names. It was inaugurated in 1956, at a ceremony opened by André Le Troquer (then president of the National Assembly), attended by military representatives, and accompanied by a rendition of "The Marseillaise," thus giving a controlling and exculpating role to the nation (in the guise of the Vichy state) which had itself sanctioned the martyrdom. The original memorial, incidentally, now finds itself within the premises of the Mémorial de la Shoah, which was itself inaugurated on January 25, 2005, by the then president, Jacques

Chirac. On this occasion, Chirac's discourse offered a psychological vision of the "perversion" of anti-Semitism and the "criminal madness" that had been "seconded" by the French state. This vision was then immediately followed by an expression of French vigilance, responsibility, and duty. His speech obviously recalled and reinforced the one he had famously given in 1995 to mark the fifty-third anniversary of the Vel' d'Hiv roundup, where he had spoken notably of a nation's collective blame. In parallel to the absorption of the memorial here, we can also note how neither Alain Resnais's 1955 film *Nuit et brouillard* nor the contemporary collection of survivor accounts by Henri Michel and Olga Wormser-Migot made reference to the specificity of Jewish victims, and instead employed in largely the same way the homogenizing tones and thematics of tragedy.[25]

Such productions and commemorations could indeed all seem to associate a generalized tragic tenor with a decade locked in individual or national mutism.[26] Yet the analyses supplied by this book point powerfully instead to a very different dynamic. For they emphasize how, throughout the decade in question, the struggle to achieve political and moral recognition for the abundance of testimony, evidence, and analysis is pursued at every level of communal and institutional engagement. This more positive perspective is also arguably endorsed by the emergence of a subsequent key generation of activists and historians. These include the self-described "memory militant" Serge Klarsfeld, who in 1979 founded the Association des fils et filles des déportés juifs de France (Association of the Sons and Daughters of Jews Deported from France) to defend and prosecute on behalf of deportees, who helped to bring Klaus Barbie, Maurice Papon, and others to justice, and whose massive book and database, the *Mémorial de la déportation des Juifs de France*, documenting the core statistics of some 76,000 Jews deported from France, has now itself the status of a national memorialization.[27] They also include the work of postwar historians such as Annette Wieviorka, whose valorization of testimony, from the moment of her doctoral dissertation on deportation and genocide, equally insists on a rebalancing of the competing claims of memory and national history.[28] With the detailed study of the cultural production of "silence" carried out by Hasia Diner in relation to postwar American Jewry in mind, we also note the wealth of other forms of communication during the 1950s in France, including the rapid resurgence of a Jewish press both in French and in Yiddish, newsletters such as *Vendredi Soir* produced by the Consistory, Zionist publications such as the revitalized *La Terre retrouvée*, and the radio program Écoute Israël. In the light of these, and the overwhelming drive and variety of responses detailed by our chapters, we therefore conclude that we should read the period 1945–55 in France not merely as the morose and guilty scene of an unattended crime, but more productively as a deeply foundational process that entails a profoundly transformed status for Jews in France during the twentieth century.[29]

This means that the postwar years in France are not just the post mortem of a relationship that has been destroyed, but that they are equally the establishment of a new relational identity. This identity would shortly after become further transformed by the effects of decolonization, the Cold War, the Six-Day War, and contemporary world politics. The French Empire had already been undermined by World War II and the hopeless conflict in Indochina, yet was still intractably adhered to by almost every major political party, with military expenditure actually increasing from a quarter to a third of the French budget in the period 1952–55. The eventual independence from France of North African countries (Tunisia in 1952–56, Morocco in 1956, Algeria in 1962), combined with the 1948 Arab-Israeli war and the Suez campaign in 1956, also had fundamental and ultimately positive consequences for the relationship between Jews and France, given not least the mass immigration to France from the Maghreb of over 145,000 Jews. In addition to the social and cultural changes that this naturally entailed for a Jewish presence in France, the firm support for Israel from North African Jews and the clear equation made between the Holocaust and fascism by a younger generation of left-wing Jewish intellectuals also injected a further intellectual and political activism into French Jewish identities. The period beyond the postwar decade is therefore one in which a Jewish French presence moves decisively from the traditional homogeneity and invisibility of Franco-Judaism to a greater pluralism and diverging involvement. This evolution has not been slowed or diverted since, even when upsurges of anti-Semitic violence regenerate doubts about integration.[30] This book therefore attests not only to an important moment in the historical relationship between France and

Jews, but also to the future of this relationship. For the efforts of organizations and activists in the first postwar decade both restored a community and its infrastructure and laid the groundwork for a renewed relationship between France and the Jews that continues to the present day.

NOTES

1. For discussion of both the formation of this French model and the challenges it has undergone, see Pierre Birnbaum, *Jewish Destinies: Citizenship, State, and Community in Modern France* (New York: Hill and Wang, 2000).

2. For an energetic commentary on this period, see David Pryce-Jones, *Betrayal: France, the Arabs, and the Jews* (New York: Encounter, 2008).

3. For accounts of more recent moments of tension and discord, see, for example, Henry H. Weinberg, *The Myth of the Jew in France, 1967–82* (Oakville, ON: Mosaic Press, 1989). More recently again, the Jewish Agency for Israel and the Israel Ministry of Immigration and Absorption reported in 2013 a spike in French aliyah rates, attributing this effect both to economic recession and to anti-Semitic outrages such as the killing of schoolchildren and a rabbi in Toulouse by a French Algerian lone terrorist.

4. For details of numbers and circumstances, see Katy Hazan, *Les orphelins de la Shoah* (Paris: Éditions Les Belles Lettres, 2000).

5. See, for example, Annette Wieviorka, *The Era of the Witness* (Ithaca, NY: Cornell University Press, 2006).

6. For details of these changes in patronymic, see Nicole Lapierre, *Changer de nom* (Paris: Stock, 1995).

7. For discussion of the narrative takes of a postmemory generation, see Marianne Hirsch, *Family Frames: Photography, Narrative, and Postmemory* (Cambridge, MA: Harvard University Press, 1997). For Hilberg's eventual conclusion that historiography involves storytelling, see "I Was Not There," in *Writing and the Holocaust*, ed. Berel Lang (New York: Holmes and Meier, 1988), 273.

8. Charles de Gaulle, *War Memoirs: Salvation, 1944–1946; Documents* (London: Weidenfeld and Nicolson, 1960), 22.

9. On this "crisis," see the explanations given in Jean Lacouture, *De Gaulle: The Ruler, 1945–1970* (London: Harvill, 1991), 33–39.

10. De Gaulle, *War Memoirs*, 23.

11. For further details of these tensions, see Pieter Lagrou, *The Legacy of Nazi Occupation: Patriotic Memory and National Recovery in Western Europe, 1945–1965* (Cambridge: Cambridge University Press, 1999). See also comments by Tony Judt, *Reappraisals: Reflections on the Forgotten Twentieth Century* (London: Vintage, 2009), 309–10.

12. In support of this view, see Richard Vinen, *The Unfree French: Life under the Occupation* (London: Penguin, 2006).

13. Michael R. Marrus and Robert O. Paxton, *Vichy France and the Jews* (Stanford, CA: Stanford University Press, 1995), 369.

14. See *La conscience juive: Données et débats; Textes des trois premiers Colloques d'Intellectuels Juifs de Langue Française organisés par la Section Française du Congrès Juif Mondial*, presented and reviewed by Éliane Amado Lévy-Valensi and Jean Halperin, preface by André Néher [sic] (Paris: Presses universitaires de France, 1963), ii.

15. See, for example, Neher's 1979 post-aliyah *They Made Their Souls Anew* (Albany: State University of New York Press, 1990), which describes the Jew as riven and existential, but ends by extolling a "dynamic of the way" (241).

16. Elie Wiesel, "To Be a Jew," in *A Jew Today* (New York: Random House [Vintage], 1979), 15.

17. Henry Rousso, *The Vichy Syndrome: History and Memory in France since 1944* (Cambridge, MA: Harvard University Press, 1991).

18. Keith Lowe, *Savage Continent: Europe in the Aftermath of World War II* (London: Penguin, 2013), 47–48.

19. See, for example, de Gaulle's memo on the subject of summary executions taking place in prisons, on December 30, 1944, in de Gaulle, *War Memoirs*, 144.

20. Speech made by General de Gaulle to the Consultative Assembly, November 9, 1944, in ibid., 66.

21. Massigli wrote about the Jew's "double appartenance" in a piece published in *Le Monde* on February 27, 1970. For a broader exposition of tensions in French discourse during and after the Six-Day War, see Joan B. Wolf, *Harnessing the Holocaust: The Politics of Memory in France* (Stanford, CA: Stanford University Press, 2004), 51–78.

22. See, for example, Bruno Bettelheim, *Surviving and Other Essays* (London: Random House, 1980).

23. See, for example, the account of Simone Veil recorded by Annette Wieviorka as "Une difficile réflexion," *Pardès* 16 (1992), or that of the Communist deportee Pierre Daix in *Bréviaire pour Mauthausen* (Paris: Gallimard, 2005). I am clearly referring to the work of Georges Perec, and especially *W ou le souvenir d'enfance*, which Susan Suleiman isolates; but also to that of Patrick Modiano, including *Dora Bruder* (Paris: Gallimard, 1997).

24. Pierre Nora, *Realms of Memory*, 3 vols. (New York: Columbia University Press, 1996–98).

25. Henri Michel and Olga Wormser-Migot, eds., *La tragédie de la déportation, 1940–1945: Témoignages de survivants de camps de concentration allemands* (Paris: Hachette, 1955).

26. See Henry Greenspan, *The Awakening of Memory: Survivor Testimony in the First Years after the Holocaust* (Washington, DC: United States Holocaust Memorial Museum, 2000).

27. Serge Klarsfeld, *Le Mémorial de la déportation des Juifs de France* (Paris: Beate et Serge Klarsfeld, 1978).

28. Annette Wieviorka, *Déportation et génocide: Mémoire et oubli* (Paris: Plon, 1992).

29. Hasia Diner, *We Remember with Reverence and Love: American Jews and the Myth of Silence after the Holocaust* (New York: New York University Press, 2009).

30. For comments on one atrocity in 1980, when the synagogue in the rue Copernic was bombed, see Shmuel Trigano, *La République et les juifs après Copernic* (Paris: Les Presses d'aujourd'hui, 1982). Most recently, the controversy surrounding the anti-Semitic references embedded in the performances, pronouncements, and associations of the "comedian" Dieudonné has exposed continuing tensions within French society regarding competing testimonies of memory and identity, and in the process has also problematized application of the 1990 Gayssot law, whose first article states that "any discrimination founded on membership or non-membership of an ethnic group, a nation, a race or a religion is prohibited."

1

The Revival of French Jewry in Post-Holocaust France

Challenges and Opportunities

DAVID WEINBERG

In February 1945, six months after the liberation of Paris, a Jewish writer in the French capital described the situation of his fellow Jewish survivors: "We are like the inhabitants of a city that has been devastated by an earthquake; we survey the ruins and do what comes naturally; we utilize that which is still usable in order to organize emergency relief."[1] The comparison of the condition of French Jewry in the immediate postwar period with the aftermath of a natural disaster seemed a particularly apt one, at least in the first months after liberation. The community had lost nearly one-third of its prewar population of 300,000, including 20,000 children, to the ravages of the Final Solution. Of the 76,000 Jews deported from France during the war, the overwhelming majority were east European Jews, and only about 3,500 returned to their homes. The largest and most important French Jewish settlement, that in Paris, which before the war had been a dynamic and at times volatile mixture of over 200,000 native Frenchmen and east European immigrants, was seriously weakened by the loss of approximately 70,000 members. Throughout the country, Jews agonized over the disappearance of hundreds of small communities and the reduction of many others to a mere handful of families.

Included among the murdered thousands was the cream of French Jewry's prewar religious and lay leadership. Of the sixty rabbis who in 1939 were members of the Consistoire central—Judaism's major religious body in France—twenty-three were deported to death camps and two were shot. Influential lay leaders such as Raoul-Raymond Lambert, a central figure in Jewish affairs during the war and a former editor of *L'Univers israélite*, the quasi-official newspaper of prewar French Jewry;

Jacques Helbronner, president of the Consistoire central; and Léonce Bernheim, a socialist activist and noted prewar Zionist spokesman, met their
deaths during the Nazi occupation. Other community leaders had fled
from Nazism and were never to return to France. In addition, many
committed young men and women who had served in Jewish resistance
groups and who had been expected to assume leadership roles in the
community after the war concluded that there was little future for Jews
in France and chose to immigrate to Palestine.

And yet, compared with other European Jewish communities, the situation of French Jewry after liberation was far from hopeless. French
Jews were in a unique position: they had experienced the Holocaust, but
thanks in large part to being protected by their fellow citizens, they
survived in large enough numbers to reassert themselves after the war.
It is estimated that there were 180,000 Jews in France in 1946—160,000
residents and 20,000 refugees from central and eastern Europe. The continuous influx of refugees fleeing displaced persons camps—there
were over 35,000 in the first three years after the war—meant that France
would soon become the second most populous Jewish community outside of the Soviet Union on the European continent and following
subsequent emigration from the Soviet Union would become the largest
European community.

It was not only the size of the French community that made it so central in postwar European Jewish life. In ways that may have not been
immediately apparent in the first few years after 1945, the active compli-
ance of the wartime Vichy regime in the persecution of its Jewish citizens
contributed to the restructuring of the community by breaking the historical reliance of French Jewish organizations on the state.[2] For the first
time since the Napoleonic era and the creation of the quasi-governmental
Consistoire, the Jews of France had an opportunity to reshape their
institutions and policies in order to create a self-sustaining and independent community. At the same time, the fact that Jews had been
active in the anti-Nazi resistance reinforced the community's belief that
it had earned a rightful place in postwar national reconstruction. Shar-
ing in the excitement and enthusiasm generated by the creation of the
Fourth Republic, French Jewry looked hopefully to the future.[3]

Not surprisingly, therefore, French Jewish organizations that arose out
of the Resistance, such as the Conseil représentatif des israélites de France

(Representative Council of Jews of France, or CRIF), were quick to claim leading roles in European Jewish affairs. These claims were strongly supported by international organizations as well as by local activists on the Continent who sought to replicate policies and activities initiated by postwar French Jewish leaders in their own communities.[4] Nor was it coincidental that the World Jewish Congress (WJC), the American Jewish Joint Distribution Committee, the Jewish Agency, and the American Jewish Committee (AJC) established their European offices in Paris after the war. The French capital also hosted major conferences of Zionists, left-wing Jewish movements, and Jewish relief agencies in the postwar period.

Before any plans for reconstruction could be implemented, however, the French community had to address the immediate material needs of survivors. While local philanthropic agencies struggled to provide assistance to the tens of thousands of returnees from camps and those emerging from hiding, the American Jewish Joint Distribution Committee (JDC)—or "the Joint," as it was known in Europe—assumed the major financial burden. In 1944, the Joint spent more than $1.5 million in France on relief. A year later, the figure had increased to nearly $2 million. By 1947 it stood at nearly $6 million, after which it slowly declined.

The impact of the Joint and other international agencies on the lives of the Jews of France would go far beyond the provision of food, shelter, and clothing. As international Jewish agencies gradually realized that the overwhelming majority of survivors in France were intent on reconstructing their lives in their former homeland rather than on migrating to Palestine or elsewhere, they took a keen interest in reshaping the nature and purpose of communal life. In their view, the challenges confronting the Jews in France and in western Europe in general after 1945 demanded innovative responses and broad global and regional strategies that were beyond the capabilities of the local philanthropic and religious organizations that had survived the war. In particular, the lingering social and economic problems brought about by the Holocaust meant that traditional community policies and procedures, which had been based on notions of ethnically and socioeconomically constructed polities, loyalty to specific organizations, and philanthropy, were gradually losing their relevance.[5]

Of the many external Jewish agencies that played a role in aiding in the reconstruction of the French Jewish community after 1945, three stand out. Originally established in 1914 to assist the *yishuv* or Jewish settlement in Palestine, the JDC was primarily responsible for material aid to European survivors of the Holocaust and for their organized exodus to Israel. As it became increasingly clear that most French Jews had no intention of leaving, the Joint assisted in creating a self-sustaining community in France by transforming the nature of communal fund-raising and the delivery of social services. Beginning in the 1950s, the relief agency also worked closely with the Conference on Jewish Material Claims against Germany distributing reparations money to assist in the religious, educational, and cultural revival of the Jews in France and other communities and to aid individual survivors. Less visible was the AJC, which was mainly concerned with the defense of French Jewry's legal and political rights and with the struggle against anti-Semitism. Supported largely by wealthier and more assimilated Jews in the United States, the AJC generally opposed migration to Palestine and encouraged Jews in France and other western European countries to integrate into their own societies. Strongly influenced by Zionist ideology and committed to the democratization of Jewish life, the WJC sought to reintroduce European Jewry into the world Jewish polity. In contrast to the Joint and the AJC, which generally engaged in "quiet diplomacy" in their dealings with government leaders, the WJC insisted that overt political action be an integral part of the activity of French Jewry.[6] In attempting to reinforce notions of Jewish peoplehood and national consciousness among Jews throughout the globe, the WJC also took an active role in assisting French Jews in expanding their educational and cultural programming.

Israeli institutions such as the Jewish Agency also had a visible presence in the community after 1945, most notably in expediting the migration of both native-born Jews and refugees to Palestine and later in the development of financial and political support for Israel. However, with the exception of cultural and educational work, and in particular the exporting of Israeli-trained educators and the promotion of Zionist ideas, these groups took little interest in the reconstitution of French Jewish communal life.[7]

The involvement of American and international Jewish organizations in the reconstruction of French Jewry—and the relatively fluid and open postwar environment that seemed to favor dramatic changes in communal structure—would lead to the creation of four new types of local institutions: a central fund-raising organization that ran coordinated campaigns and that was responsible for the maintenance of communal activities and for the financial support of the State of Israel; social service agencies administered by skilled professionals that provided basic and long-range social, economic, and psychological services for an increasingly diverse community; a federated political organization that defended Jewish interests before government authorities and voiced communal concerns in the public arena; and broad-based cultural and educational organizations that enabled adults and children who had been isolated from Jewish life during the war to reconnect with their heritage.[8] In addition, the Joint introduced long-range planning and professionalism into communal procedures and administration. Both innovations were meant to replace ad hoc decision making and the reliance upon volunteers drawn from the community's elite to deal with immediate needs. The reconfiguration of at least certain aspects of communal life was already evident by the early 1950s as the community stabilized and American and British Jewish relief organizations increasingly diverted their funds and attention to the new Jewish state.

In the immediate postwar period, the fact that French Jews remained dependent upon world and American organizations for assistance and advice meant that decisions over their fate were often made in boardrooms in New York rather than in Paris. Yet the relationship between foreign Jewish agencies and French Jews in the period directly after 1945 was hardly one of munificent and sage donors and advisors on the one hand, and needy and passive recipients on the other. From the inception of their relief campaigns, the JDC and other international Jewish organizations encouraged limited initiatives on the part of the French community itself, if only because they recognized that they could not sustain financial and administrative support indefinitely. At the same time, despite their weakened condition in the immediate postwar period, Jews in France refused to play the role of the "joyous pauper." Though grateful for the aid they received, communal leaders of established organizations resented the efforts by outside agencies to tread on their traditional charitable and social welfare activities. For their part, young Jewish activists in France were angered by the tendency of external organizations to take credit for innovative programs and procedures that had actually originated within local communities either before or shortly after the war. They also were frustrated by the failure of the Joint and the

World Jewish Congress to give them representation on committees and agencies that provided financial and other assistance to European Jewry. And old and new leadership alike were deeply offended by the occasional patronizing and condescending attitudes expressed toward survivors by world Jewish leaders and their local representatives. European Jews were more than merely victims of Nazi oppression, French communal leaders and intellectuals contended; in contrast to the "upstart" and unsophisticated American Jewish community, the Jews of Europe and of France in particular were heirs to a rich and vital heritage spanning hundreds of years. In the immediate postwar period, such attitudes could be dismissed as a defensive posture that betrayed a lack of self-confidence. Yet the reaction was not without significance for the future revival of French Jewry. In ways that neither Americans nor Europeans fully understood at the time, the intervention of outside forces in French Jewish life after 1945 would fuel an emerging self-consciousness and assertiveness.

The recovery of French Jewry after 1945 can be seen most clearly in its response to a series of distinct challenges that can only be briefly examined in this short chapter. The first and most daunting challenge was that of relief and rehabilitation. International organizations and French Jewish leaders understood that they would have to significantly restructure the community in order to ensure its survival. The efforts to meet immediate needs were largely completed by the end of the 1940s. Some issues—such as the recovery of spoliated property, assets, and businesses; the return of children hidden in non-Jewish homes; the tracing of lost relatives; and demands for compensation for acts of brutality and murder committed by the Vichy government—were met with tepid responses from government officials during the first decade after the war. The transformation of communal institutions and polices, which was far more successful, took far longer, and its history extends well beyond the period being examined here. In the first two decades after the war, local leadership often sharply resisted the demands made by external agencies that they create a professional bureaucracy and initiate coordinated and centralized fund-raising. Those that welcomed the changes generally had little previous experience in community administration and labored under extremely trying circumstances.

Three additional challenges, imposed from without, defined French Jewish life in the late 1940s and early 1950s. The first external challenge was the creation of the State of Israel in 1948. For the first time in their modern history, Jews could choose whether or not to live in the Diaspora. There were hundreds of survivors in France who were convinced that the Holocaust had brought an end to organized life in Europe and migrated to Palestine as soon as they could. Those who insisted upon remaining in France rather than making aliyah (that is, settling in Israel) were forced to defend their decision to continue to live among their fellow Frenchmen, some of whom had participated either directly or indirectly in the carrying out of the Final Solution. This debate provided the first indications of a dramatic change in collective behavior and attitudes, including a greater assertiveness in the public arena and a new form of Jewish identification that rested upon spiritual and emotional ties with Israel mingled with deep concerns about the issue of "dual loyalty."

Another challenge was anti-Semitism. Many observers in France had assumed that the defeat of Nazism would spell the end of anti-Jewish propaganda and violence. Though the postwar French government expressly banned overt hate propaganda, neofascist gangs maintained a presence on the streets of Paris and Lyon, occasionally ransacking Jewish-owned businesses, attacking individual Jews, and scrawling anti-Semitic graffiti on the walls of the metro. Influenced by Jewish resistance efforts during the Holocaust and later by the military triumphs of the *yishuv* and the new Jewish state, French Jewish activists insisted upon a more aggressive and assertive response as embodied in the activities of the CRIF. As in the case of the restructuring of communal institutions, they drew upon strategies and programs suggested by outside Jewish organizations, most notably the American Jewish Committee. Unwilling to blindly follow the lead of the latter, however, French Jews also developed their own perspectives on several significant issues relating to their physical safety, which were often in opposition to those of American Jewry. This was especially true in the case of their near-unanimous support of the campaigns against German rearmament and for the aggressive prosecution of war criminals.

Tensions between French Jews and their fellow citizens in the immediate postwar period were not always overt, however. Jews living in the aftermath of the Holocaust could not ignore the striking differences between the way that they and the general populace understood the Nazi occupation and its legacy. However painful, most French viewed their experiences during World War II and under the Vichy regime in particular as aberrations, which were either to be forgotten or to be wished away with exaggerated narratives of collective resistance to Nazi occupation. For survivors in contrast, the war was a searing memory that raised serious questions concerning the viability of their individual and collective future on the European continent. The tensions between French Jews and the larger society were manifested in debates over issues such as the treatment of Jewish deportees and the memorialization of the Jewish victims of Nazism.

A final external challenge was the Cold War, which split the Jews of Europe into two camps. For the Jews in France in particular, Soviet and American threats of unleashing nuclear missiles raised the prospect of a posthumous victory for Adolf Hitler over his ideological and "racial" enemies. Divisions also reached into the community itself; Communism had gained new visibility and respect among those Jews in France who had participated in wartime resistance and in the struggle against neo-Nazism in the postwar period, and among postwar refugees from eastern Europe. In the late 1940s and early 1950s, the divisions between Communists and anti- or non-Communists threatened to undo the fragile unity that leaders had worked so hard to create after 1945.

Yet the French Jewish community was not totally paralyzed by the Cold War. Despite the formidable obstacles, mainstream communal leaders sought to steer a middle path between the demands of local political militants and those of American Jewish officials. While eliminating or at least diminishing the influence of schismatic Communist elements from communal affairs, community leaders—often with the aid of those Communists who had remained within the communal fold—forcefully resisted pressures from the AJC and elements in the Joint to break off all contact with their coreligionists behind the Iron Curtain. Forty years after the end of World War II, such efforts would ease the reintegration of post-Communist Jewish communities into European Jewry as a whole.

Having overcome or at least accommodated themselves to external threats to their survival, the Jews of France in the early 1950s increasingly returned to internal concerns. Of particular importance was their response to the religious, educational, and cultural needs of the community's diverse constituents.

In the first two decades after the war, the gradual withdrawal of American aid, the influx of east European refugees, and later the first trickle of North African Jews to France led to transformations in the nature of the community's religious life. Among the most notable changes were the gradual melding of Sephardic and Ashkenazic liturgy and ritual, the resurgence of Jewish secular culture, and, most importantly, the rejection of the glib association of French Judaism with the norms and values of the host nation that had defined native Jewish identity before the war. The sharp increase in the number of alienated and unaffiliated Jews in France also spurred liturgical changes within established Orthodox institutions and allowed alternative religious movements such as Liberal Judaism to make new inroads in the community.

The attempt to revive Jewish education in the postwar era involved more than the replenishment of library bookshelves and the rebuilding of schoolrooms. Like their coreligionists in the United States, Jews in France soon recognized that the dangers facing their local communities came not only from external physical assault, but also from the erosion of loyalties from within. Many young men and women had lived through the war years in isolation, without any access to Jewish learning or to Jewish communal life. In addressing the needs of this "lost" generation, local educators developed innovative pedagogical techniques, such as informal classes, public lectures and discussion groups, and the use of audiovisual technology. Thanks to funds generated from the German Material Claims Agreement in the early 1950s and with the assistance of teachers and curricula supplied by American and Israeli agencies, local communities began to train a new corps of administrators, spiritual leaders, and schoolteachers. Here too, these early developments would not bear fruit until the 1960s.

Finally, the decimation of the Jewish religious and literary elite during the war in both eastern and western Europe dealt a severe blow to Jewish culture on the Continent. In attempting to formulate a strategy for collective survival, community leaders of all stripes in France recognized that there could be no simple return to the prewar polarities of rigid religious orthodoxy on one hand, and assimilationism on the other. The profound rupture in both Jewish and general life brought about by the war and the physical dislocation that followed the end of hostilities meant that many survivors in France, especially young men and women, had to rediscover or discover for the first time their identities and their place among other Jews and their fellow citizens. With the aid of monies from reparations payments, local leaders created new institutions and expanded old ones, such as community centers, summer camps, and sports clubs, in order to appeal to a mobile and disparate population. What slowly emerged were new forms of consciousness that enabled young men and women to express their commitment to a shared Jewish fate outside the traditional framework of religious and educational institutions.

In their attempts to restructure the French Jewish community, the JDC and the AJC had hoped to apply the practices and perspectives of the Jews of the United States. Yet French Jewish life after 1945 did not become a mirror image of the American community. In many instances, new-comers supported by the Joint and the AJC did gain positions of prominence and attempted to "Americanize" the community. However, several novel experiments introduced by the Joint, such as centralized "umbrella" organizations, professional fund-raising, and Jewish community centers, did not transfer easily to the French Jewish reality and had to be adapted to fit the distinctive profiles of local communities. Other programs, such as children's homes and public demonstrations against anti-Semitism, were initiated by forces within the communities during the war or shortly thereafter.

The result was that in the first decades after the war, the attempt to reshape Jewish communal life in France showed mixed results. Neither frozen irretrievably in the past nor liberated sufficiently to fully control its destiny, the French community presented a complex picture in which newly created institutions and procedures existed alongside more established organizations and policies. It was also an era of numerous stops and starts, of unbounded optimism and deep disillusionment. Local French communities developed innovative projects and created dynamic institutions to ensure their survival, only to see them dissolve or retrench within a few years or months. Decades-old behavioral and structural patterns reflecting divisions between native-born Jews and immigrant Jews, as well as those between Zionists and political militants, continued to hold sway despite the intense efforts of innovators both within and outside the communities to replace them. Many of the new plans and programs to revive Jewish life would ultimately bear fruit in the next generation. Even in the late 1940s when local communities were showing signs of stabilization, French Jewry could not easily overcome the prewar divisions and wartime losses that had weakened it. However, already in the first decade after 1945, the Jews of France would show significant signs of overcoming the brutalization of the Nazi occupation and of being able to confront successfully the failure of established norms and institutions in the larger society.

Almost six decades later and in a dramatically different political and communal context, there is much discussion among Jewish intellectuals in France and in other parts of the Continent about the importance of asserting European Jewry as a "third way," a distinctive voice in world Jewish affairs between what is alleged to be the hedonism and materialism of American Jewry and the isolationism of Israel. Whatever the merits of this view, there can be little question that the origins of this perspective lie in the painful yet courageous steps taken by the members of the Continent's most significant Jewish community—that in France—to reconstruct their personal lives and collective institutions in the first decades after the devastation of the Holocaust.

NOTES

1. J. Jacobs, *L'Unité*, February 23, 1945. Material in this chapter is drawn in large part from my monograph on postwar west European Jewry that will be published by the Littman Library of Jewish Civilization.

2. The French sociologist Pierre Birnbaum describes the response of the postwar French Jewish community to Vichy in the following terms: "Like disappointed lovers, they abandoned the state they had once adored." Birnbaum, *Jewish Destinies: Citizenship, State, and Community in Modern France* (New York: Hill and Wang, 2000), 217.

3. The attitudes of Captain Robert Gamzon, a leader of the Éclaireurs israélites de France (French Jewish Boy Scouts) and a major figure in the Jewish Resistance during the war, were typical of those of many young French Jews in the heady days after the war. In a fund-raising letter addressed to the American Jewish community in 1946, he proclaimed the vitality of the new generation of French Jews. "Our people showed and still show a fighting spirit," Gamzon wrote. He went on to assure his readers that French Jewry "will witness not only the rebuilding of what was, but also the emergence of a new, young and vigorous Judaism which will be our answer to Hitler's destruction." Gamzon, "The Fight for Survival Goes On," press release for an article published in 1946, in 45/54 No. 311 ("France General 1944–1947" folder),

Archives of the American Jewish Joint Distribution Committee in New York (hereafter cited as JDC-NY). It should be noted that Gamzon immigrated to Palestine in 1948.

4. See, for example, the comments by the journalist Josef Hollander in *Unzer vort* 1, May 9, 1947; and "Report of the Reconstruction Committee of the JDC to the Directors' Conference," Paris, October 1949, p. 5, found in 45/54 No. 3467 ("General and Emergency Report Area Directors Conference 1949" folder), JDC-NY. For a typical view of French Jewry in other Continental communities, see the undated letter sent by the Unione delle comunità ebraiche italiane (Union of the Italian Jewish Community) to the CRIF requesting information on laws relating to the French organization's activities in the community; and the letter dated April 27, 1948, from the Unione requesting a copy of the CRIF's statutes. Both letters can be found in the file titled CRIF Correspondance 1948 in the Archives of the Centre de documentation juive contemporaine (CDJC).

5. Daniel Elazar, "The Reconstitution of Jewish Communities in the Post War Period," *Jewish Journal of Sociology* 11, no. 2 (1969): 199.

6. "Executive Officers' Report," National Conference of the World Jewish Congress, London, May 12, 1946 (British Section); "Report of the Executive Officers' Summary of Proceedings," 4; both documents are in file MS239/T34/1, Archives of Southampton University (SH).

7. On the attitudes of *yishuv* officials toward internal communal concerns, see, for example, the letter to Hanan Daichman, a *shaliach* (emissary of the Jewish Agency abroad) in Paris, dated January 5, 1948, in file C2/12, Central Zionist Archives, Jerusalem.

8. For further discussion, see Elazar, "Reconstitution of Jewish Communities," 212.

2

The Encounter between "Native" and "Immigrant" Jews in Post-Holocaust France

Negotiating Difference

MAUD MANDEL

Was World War II a radical break in French Jewish history—a turning point in notions of community, identity, and political expression—or did the restoration of Jewish citizenship and the Fourth Republic's promise to protect and defend all citizens regardless of religion or ethnic origin allow long-standing patterns of Jewish identification to reinstate themselves? This chapter will address this question by turning to an aspect of Jewish communal life that transcended the pre- and postwar years—that of how to integrate incoming Jewish refugees and immigrants into communal institutions and French society more broadly. To be sure, the question of immigrant integration is only one of a wide variety of topics one could investigate to consider the impact of the war on Jewish attitudes and practices, including relationships to Zionism, responses to anti-Semitism, levels of religiosity, communal engagement, and institutional structures. I focus on encounters between native and newly arriving Jews in part because this issue has received less attention to date, and in part because it so clearly highlights the questions of continuity, change, and causality that have informed my interest in postwar French Jewish history.[1]

To frame the subsequent discussion, I shall begin with two citations. The first comes from Jules Meyer, a prominent native Jew, who lamented in 1925 the large numbers of eastern European Jewish migrants who had begun to arrive in Paris by noting, "The walls of Paris must no longer be covered with Hebrew characters; Paris must cease being flooded with Yiddish newspapers, books, films and plays."[2] Calling for the rapid assimilation of his coreligionists from the East, Meyer—and other Parisian

Jewish notables—responded to the tens of thousands of Polish and German Jewish newcomers who came in the interwar years with considerable ambivalence. As David Weinberg, Paula Hyman, and Nancy Green have demonstrated, due to fears that the newcomers' "foreignness" would undermine their *own* position in French society in an atmosphere of economic depression and rising anti-Jewish sentiment, the local Jewish leadership actively worked to encourage the immigrants' acculturation, prevailing upon them to adopt French customs and to shed their "Jewish" traits. Even those most sympathetic to the refugee plight never stopped admonishing the newcomers to acculturate quickly, arguing that in exchange for such transformations, the French government would provide immigrants with citizenship and defend their equality.[3]

The second citation comes from Edmond Dreyfuss, reporting to the Consistoire de Paris, the central institution of Jewish religious life in France, on the state of their community in 1946: "All children of Israel are our spiritual brothers," he remarked, "those who claim the Torah, those who speak French, Yiddish, or Hebrew as well as the peaceful Parisian merchant or the heroic Palestinian soldier. . . . We listen to the opinions of these spiritual brothers to the same extent as those of the original members of our community. Because the solidarity of Israel endures beyond persecution. We did not need the ashes of Auschwitz to teach us that."[4]

The juxtaposition of these two citations suggests that the French Jewish leadership had undergone a rapid realignment from the mid-1920s to the mid-1940s regarding their attitudes toward diversity. The purpose of this chapter is to explore the origins and depth of this transformation. I shall argue, perhaps unsurprisingly, that the war had much to do with changing the French Jewish establishment's attitudes toward pluralism within their community and toward increasing willingness to welcome Jewish newcomers into their institutions. Indeed, the war's targeting of all Jews regardless of level of integration or assimilation challenged long-standing beliefs in republican democracy's promise to eliminate differences between peoples. One result was that French Jews began articulating a new appreciation for those differences.

And yet, as we shall see, the Holocaust and its related persecutions did not completely dismantle long-standing paternalistic attitudes of French Jewish communal leaders toward their coreligionists from other lands.[5]

Rather, while the war created the context for new attitudes to emerge, *postwar* developments were crucial in institutionalizing the shift and thus rendering it more permanent. Put differently, the *process of rebuilding*— that is to say the widespread structural changes of the postwar years, particularly American philanthropic intervention and the decolonization of North Africa—was at least as influential as Vichy in establishing new attitudes toward incoming Jewish migrants. Thus, as we shall see, while World War II had a significant impact on communal attitudes, it did not single-handedly or immediately upend all prior ways of understanding communal differences. Moreover, as those who have studied the arrival of Jewish migrants to France after the decolonization of North Africa have made clear, the rhetoric of Jewish unity could at times fail to transcend the differences that emerged when diverse Jewish populations encountered one another in the metropole.[6] We must be cautious, therefore, in assuming that the disruptions and traumas of the Holocaust immediately challenged the entrenched positions toward difference. A watershed moment to be sure, the Vichy anti-Jewish aggressions were certainly transformative, but as in all moments of great historical change, continuities linked beliefs and practices over this momentous event.[7]

As noted in other chapters in this volume, Vichy's attack against French Jews impoverished the community, destroyed religious and cultural life, and stripped individuals of their status, their professional stability, and—often—their lives. Of the 76,000 deported from the country, only about 3 percent returned, the rest perishing in transports and camps in eastern Europe.[8] Rabbis and communal leaders had often been deported, and synagogues, libraries, and schools dismantled, leaving few institutional structures or leaders in place to facilitate rebuilding. Jewish immigrant neighborhoods were hit particularly hard due to Vichy policies that targeted them much more heavily than their French Jewish neighbors, meaning entire congregations simply disappeared from Paris and other large French cities.[9]

Despite the extent of the destruction, however, approximately 200,000 French Jews survived the war, many of whom went to work rebuilding their devastated communities.[10] To these numbers were added large incoming Jewish populations who began arriving almost as soon as the war had ended. Given that France was one of the few countries open to Jewish refugees before 1948, this influx is not surprising. While some hoped to stay, others were passing through en route to Palestine or else-where.[11] Even those hoping to leave, however, often remained for several years and sometimes permanently thanks to the aid and support they received from Jewish welfare agencies.[12] In the calculations of Doris Ben-simon and Sergio Della Pergola, approximately 37,000 Jews took up residence in France from 1944 to 1949, mostly from displaced persons camps or from inhospitable eastern European nations.[13] The Comité juif d'action sociale et de reconstruction (COJASOR), created in 1945 with funding from the American Jewish Joint Distribution Committee (AJDC or "the Joint") to centralize all assistance to Jews hurt by the war and deportations, estimated that 75,000 Jews passed through their services between 1946 and 1950, with some 40,000 ultimately moving on to other destinations.[14] The numbers of Jews living in France increased again in the latter half of the 1950s, as several thousand Egyptian Jews sought ref-uge from the Suez crisis (during which France, Britain, and Israel bombarded Egyptian air bases and military installations along the Suez Canal) and as Jews from Hungary and Romania fled new waves of per-secution. Tens of thousands more came from the mid-1950s through the mid-1960s during and following France's decolonization of North Africa, and particularly during the Algerian war. During this "massive, tumul-tuous stampede," as one Joint official described the flight, over 925,000 French, Spanish, Italian, Maltese, and Algerian Muslims came to France, as did 140,000 Jews.[15] In addition, while many Moroccan and Tunisian Jews went to Israel, nearly 65,000 migrated to France.[16]

The arrival of so many Jewish immigrants on the heels of the wartime destruction had a tremendous impact on Jewish life in the metropole.[17] As during the prewar decades, the newcomers taxed the financial and structural resources of the already settled population, forcing communal leaders to make difficult decisions regarding the allocation of funds, the organization of communal services, and the development of religious and cultural bodies. The processes through which these decisions were made, however, seemed to reflect a new attitude toward incoming Jews. In May 1962, the central Jewish philanthropic body, the Fonds social juif unifié (FSJU), established in 1949 through the efforts of the Joint, held a confer-ence on the settlement of North African Jews in France. At that event, Guy de Rothschild, the FSJU's president, told attendees that financially sup-porting the newcomers was not their sole responsibility: "Simultaneously, we should assist them morally, we should assist them intellectually, we should assist them culturally *without thoughts of superiority*, of course, but providing them with the guidance that they require to assist them in being themselves, to assist them in adapting to the milieu in which they find themselves."[18]

While Rothschild may not have spoken for all French Jews, as president of the central Jewish fund-raising and social organization, he influenced and reflected the outlook of much of the Jewish leadership. His remarks suggest that attitudes among such communal directors had changed dramatically since the 1920s and 1930s, when their predecessors sought to assimilate eastern European Jews to French cultural norms. Certainly in both cases, the leadership saw its role as establishing the appropriate setting into which newcomers could and should integrate. In addition, like his predecessors, Rothschild stressed that Jewish institutions had a responsibility to the government to prevent the newcomers from becoming social charges. During remarks made to the FSJU's annual meeting in 1960, Rothschild proclaimed that if Jewish institutions did not welcome and guide the new refugees, they could become socially ill-adapted and create problems for France. According to him, it was up to French Jews to "bridge the gap" between the newcomers' old life in North Africa and their new life in Europe.

Yet, if in some notable ways Rothschild's views mirrored those of earlier years, his approach also reflected the shifts that had taken place in the French Jewish leadership in the period between the end of the war and France's decolonization of North Africa. Most importantly, while Jewish leaders may have wanted to prevent incoming Jews from becoming charges of the French state and in that sense wished to integrate them, they did not necessarily hope to fashion the newcomers in their own image. During his speech, Rothschild repeatedly stressed that the new arrivals were not inferior in any way. Indeed, it is notable that Rothschild entitled his remarks "Pour un judaïsme ouvert," reflecting his views that French Jews should welcome different forms of Judaism. Solidarity and tolerance among Jews, he believed, would guarantee the North Africans' successful integration.[19]

Such an attitude change, while most cogently articulated in response to the arrival of the North African Jews, was born in the aftermath of the Vichy years as the native communal leadership attempted to come to terms with their losses. Indeed, immediately following the war, the Consistoire, home to some of the strongest criticism of eastern European Jewish immigrants during the interwar years, began stressing the importance of diversity and the sense that the war had united all Jews in a common fate.[20] As one Consistoire official commented of his internment at Drancy, no distinction had been made between Jews of different rites: "They were Jews; that was all."[21] Echoing similar sentiments, Georges Wormser, Consistoire president, wrote in a 1946 pamphlet on postwar Parisian Jewish life that a common enemy had tied all Jews together, including the disbelievers, the disaffected, and the detached. "We will stand close together," he insisted. "Racism made no distinctions between us, destroying the illusions that, one has to admit, were nursed in some of our consciences."[22]

Such comments suggest that the Consistoire leadership, aware of the attitudes that had created divisions in previous decades, were now prepared to adopt a new outlook toward divisions in France's Jewish population. For many, the war's greatest lesson was that solidarity among Jews must prevail. Assimilating newcomers to Consistorial norms, as had been the preference in the past, would have to give way to an acceptance of difference as permanent and even beneficial to organized religious life. While the Consistoire de Paris still considered its main constituency to be the upper-middle-class Jews of France as well as all "assimilated" immigrants, it attempted to broaden its base, not by encouraging conformity among all Jews but by accepting their differences. As Edmond Dreyfuss—cited at the outset of this chapter—noted, "We must persist in working towards a spiritual reconciliation between all congregations with the purpose of forming a union but not becoming uniform." By stressing that Jews must form alliances with one another without melding into one indistinguishable whole, Dreyfuss voiced the dramatically different postwar attitude of many Consistoire officials. "Uniformity is impossible," he proclaimed, "but union is a duty."[23] While Dreyfuss believed that the Consistoire should avoid any action that would encourage French citizens to view Jews as foreigners, he also insisted on a greater tolerance of those who manifested their faith differently from what had previously been considered acceptable. Georges Wormser advocated similar views: "As we attempt to regroup all Parisian Jews around us, we have no desire for exclusivism or intolerance. The Consistoire must serve as a bond between the different religious denominations and the diverse groups."[24] Solidarity without eliminating difference became the Consistoire's postwar mantra.

This call for unity found institutional form toward the end of the war when Consistoire representatives agreed to work with immigrant Jewish Zionists, Communists, and Bundists to create a new umbrella organization, the Conseil représentatif des israélites de France (CRIF).[25] The organization's goal was to study political questions, particularly those raised in regard to restitution, to articulate a united public voice against further anti-Semitism, and to provide a unified front to the government on Jewish issues.[26] Such cooperation between immigrant and native leaders was rare in the years before the occupation due to an inability to agree upon a common communal agenda. Moreover, faith in the state had long prevented native Jews from organizing to publicly safeguard their political rights. Because the CRIF defended Jewish rights in the public square and represented all political, religious, and social tendencies, its birth was unprecedented. If, despite its lofty goals, the CRIF's ability to effect change was limited, and if the much-heralded unity broke down when splits between Communists and their opponents prevented the organization from maintaining a single voice with regard to political questions, the attempt to cooperate nonetheless shows the powerful drive to bridge some of the divisions preventing joint political action in the interwar years.[27]

Additional signs of a change in Consistorial attitudes emerged in discussions among its leaders over encouraging a new pluralism within their *own* ranks as they struggled to decentralize, giving more autonomy to individual communities throughout France. Historically, the Consistoire had been a highly centralized body. When originally constructed under Napoleon, power lay in Paris with a small group of rabbinical and lay leaders. While departmental consistories (next in the chain of command) contested the decisions of the Parisian elite and sought more autonomy over local religious affairs, the Consistoire de Paris fought to maintain control of the periphery.[28] Following World War II, however, various Consistoire members, both religious and lay, began discussing the pros and cons of increased local autonomy. Such independence, some hoped, would inspire a more active participation in Jewish life by providing more breadth to organized Judaism.[29] As Rabbi Maurice

Liber noted at a 1949 Consistoire meeting, "The day when decentralization creates new communities in Paris, they will assume very diverse forms and this pluralism is desirable."[30] Decentralization, then, while seemingly far removed from the Consistoire's overall goal of solidarity, actually remained intrinsically linked to it. As one of the Consistoire members reminded his colleagues at the 1957 Assises du judaïsme, "In order for diversity to prosper, it is also necessary that underneath it shared aspects be integrated, larger currents brought together or juxtaposed in a constantly widening frame, failing which the ensemble will split up infinitely until each isolated cell disappears forever."[31] By diversifying and broadening its base, then, Consistoire leaders hoped to promote greater unity.

Despite the new rhetoric of solidarity, however, we should be cautious about seeing the Holocaust as a watershed after which all prior perspectives changed.[32] While the Consistoire de Paris took an active part in aiding eastern European Jewish migration to France in the late 1940s, certain members insisted that only those who would "benefit" the French Jewish community should be encouraged to migrate. Others could come if they were "useful" and would assimilate rapidly into French society.[33] Moreover, coordinated activities between immigrant and native Jewish organizations did not always go smoothly. For example, in 1947, members of the Consistoire de Paris expressed concern when Chief Rabbi Jacob Kaplan lent his name to a summer camp fund-raising drive by the Fédération des sociétés juives de France (FSJF), an umbrella organization originally formed in 1913 to coordinate the activities of immigrant Jewish groups. Concerned that their own organization would not get the appropriate credit or, perhaps more importantly, the financial benefit of this joint appeal, certain members complained that the rabbi should have consulted them first. Others worried that the summer camps would not stringently enforce religious practices. Wormser, despite his previous rhetoric of unity, refused to sign his name to any FSJF document written in Yiddish. Nevertheless, other Consistoire members were pleased to know that their organization and the FSJF could work together and voiced hopes that such cooperation would continue.[34]

As is clear here, the divisions of the past did not disappear as a result of a few well-meaning speeches. While the war had made its mark, long-standing patterns and attitudes were not immediately transformed. Moreover, if, as Mônica Raisa Schpun has shown, French Jews went to tremendous lengths to ensure that incoming Jewish war refugees received administrative, medical, and professional aid, allowing many of those passing through the country to remain, some of the prior ambivalence expressed toward eastern European Jewish immigrants was now directed toward their arriving North African coreligionists, whose numbers began growing in the late 1940s just as the eastern European influx began to abate.[35] These Algerian, Moroccan, and Tunisian Jewish families looked and sounded different from the migrants of the previous several years. While those who worked in Jewish social services were often Yiddish or Polish speakers and shared a background with the World War II refugees passing through their agencies, they had little in common with the very poor, often Arabic-speaking North African Jewish families arriving in the late 1940s. To cite one example of the biases that could accompany the encounter: in June 1948, the Comité de bienfaisance israélite parisienne (CBIP), a philanthropic body founded in the nineteenth century and associated with the Consistoire, recorded discomfort over the "delicate problem" posed by increasing numbers of North Africans in Paris. Describing many of the newcomers as "quarrelsome, vindictive and unwilling to earn a living through regular work," CBIP officials displayed many of the prejudices common among the prewar Jewish leadership toward incoming migrants, and initially, at least, CBIP officials did what they could to encourage the repatriation of these North African Jews, many of whom were transients either seeking to travel to Israel or to return after having fought in the war there.[36] Similarly, the Consistoire de Paris addressed the problem of North Africans in June 1949, on the one hand proposing a meeting of various communal leaders interested in helping the new refugees, while on the other seeking to stem the tide. The chief rabbi of Paris thus noted that in order to prevent such a flow of poor Jews to France "under very precarious conditions," he had asked the grand rabbin de France, Isaïe Schwartz, to intervene with the North African rabbinate.[37]

Whatever reticence to the newcomers was reflected in such discussions, however, key developments in France *after* World War II created the context in which the newer ideologies toward incoming Jews could take hold. Here I refer to two developments in particular that shifted the ground for French Jewish elites. The first was French Jewry's dependence on American Jewish philanthropy to rebuild their devastated communities, largely in the form of contributions from the Joint. As I have discussed at length elsewhere, this money not only provided essential resources for all aspects of Jewish institutional life—including orphanages, old age homes, welfare agencies, relocation agencies, vocational education, and religious institutions—but gave American Jewish welfare workers significant power to shape local institutional life around their own priorities. Jewish fund-raising practices, social welfare techniques, and Jewish community centers were all imported through these processes to France, where they left a permanent imprint on communal development. While scholars have begun to debate how deeply this "Americanization" penetrated, there is little doubt that the Joint sought to encourage French Jews to build structures that would transcend the sectarian divisions of the past.[38] Thus the FSJU and new communal centers, both established with Joint money, were meant to create spaces in which Jews of different religious, political, linguistic, and national backgrounds could come together. Likewise, immigrant aid organizations, for which the Joint carried the full financial weight for years, were shaped very much by American social work practices taught in a Joint-run school founded to educate French employees in the most up-to-date practices. Until the early 1960s, then, the CBIP, the COJASOR, and the FSJU relied almost entirely on Joint resources and methods to provide aid to incoming immigrants.[39] In December 1956, for example, the COJASOR worked with the Joint to create a placement office for Egyptian Jews, while the FSJU organized housing aid and established links between the new arrivals and various Jewish cultural programs.[40] Indeed, the FSJU's various subventioned agencies provided some sort of aid to 50,000 new arrivals between 1954 and 1959 primarily thanks to American Jewish philanthropic aid.[41] Given how profoundly American Jewish philanthropy was linked to a particular nonsectarian and centralizing model of communal development, its vision bolstered those parts of Jewish communal life in France already inclined to favor a broader appreciation of diversity.

A second postwar factor shaping the French Jewish establishment's perspectives on diversity was the nature of the North African migration itself, which, unlike earlier migration waves, proved relatively familiar.[42] Indeed, the fact that so many of the newcomers were Algerian, meaning that they held French citizenship (granted to them with the 1870

Crémieux Decree), spoke French, and had been educated in French schools, allowed Jewish communal leaders to view them as part and parcel of French Jewry, thereby removing some of the distinctions that had prevented a sense of solidarity with previous new arrivals. In 1956, for example, just as the influx of Algerian Jews was beginning to gather steam, Henri Levy, the secretary of the Consistoire, had already identified the newcomers as "an important part of French Judaism." Moreover, insofar as they were different, he stressed the benefits of North African Jewish spirituality on French Judaism: "We are pleased to see in them a lively source of piety and fidelity to our traditions, which, thanks to a daily increasing interpenetration, is infusing new blood into our communities."[43] Thus, not only were the newcomers not really "new," but they were more observant, a fact that simply made them more palatable to religious leaders. The result of such attitudes meant that the Consistoire devoted significant energy in the 1950s and 1960s to building synagogues, oratories, and communal centers for North African Jews in Paris and its suburbs, where many incoming migrants were settling.[44]

Arriving Jews also helped emphasize the connection among those in France and those from the Maghreb. Emile Touati, for example, an Algerian Jewish journalist and editor for the journal *L'Information juive* who became actively involved in the Consistoire upon coming to France, reminded readers in 1953 that North African Jews, and particularly those from Algeria, were already part of the French Jewish community: "We cannot really speak of an upheaval or a revolution," he noted of the immigration waves. "In reality, the Jewish community of Algeria was already part of official French Judaism. Through its language, spirit, and institutions, it was one of the 'provinces,' and the symbiosis on the two sides of the Mediterranean, except in terms of rites, was almost perfect, practically organic."[45] Nevertheless, he also encouraged French Jewish institutions to make "a large space in the mosaic of French Judaism." Solidarity could not rest on conformity: "No group can claim to possess the exclusive truth to which others must necessarily adhere," he admonished. "Without mutual respect, without reciprocal concessions, the failure will be fatal—and fatal for everyone. French Judaism, just restored, can no longer be *synthetic*. Each group has its own eminently respectable traditions. It is not a question of sacrificing them on the altar of an illusive uniformity." Yet autonomy, he insisted, should not prevent cooperation, coordination, and even a certain centralization of Jewish life. In this way, individuals with different origins or ideological beliefs could work, fight, and create together.[46]

Such views, echoing those circulating among the Jewish leadership since World War II, became more prominent as the numbers of North African Jews grew. Whether communal leaders viewed repatriating North Africans as a source of religious rejuvenation, "new blood" for a decimated community, or simply an integral part of French Judaism defined broadly, they repeatedly stressed the importance of providing a welcoming and warm atmosphere for the new arrivals. In addition, while previous generations had doubted the ability or desire of immigrants to blend into the larger society, leaders of the 1950s and 1960s now worried that the North Africans might rapidly assimilate.[47] Algerians, in particular, having already acquired French citizenship, education, and cultural standards, were at risk of blending into the larger society.[48] Even Tunisians and Moroccans, however, dispersed throughout the country with no link to organized Jewry, might become alienated from their roots.[49] As Consistoire officials noted in the mid-1960s, "Without a great communal effort, families, [and especially] children isolated in the large suburban communities, will be given over to assimilation and to a moral and social disaggregation."[50] Similarly, in a 1960 article in *L'Arche* (the FSJU's newspaper), the caption to a photograph of three teenage North African Jewish immigrants read, "In the absence of a Judaic-French structure, these young immigrants from North Africa remain exposed to the powerful solicitations of political assimilation."[51] Such fears stood in direct contrast to the decades preceding World War II when the Jewish leadership encouraged such assimilation. As *Univers israélite* (a newspaper closely connected to the Consistoire de Paris) reported in 1906: "[The East European Jewish immigrants'] mentality seems to us to be insufficiently adapted to ours. But we forget that we did not require less than a century to attain the *assimilation of which we are proud* and which was made impossible for them in their country of origin."[52]

Whereas during the interwar years native French Jewish leaders hoped that new immigrants would rapidly shed all distinctive traits, in the late 1950s youth movements, women's clubs, and the like sent teams of volunteers to establish systematic contact with incoming Jewish populations to prevent such processes from taking root. As Pierre Kaufman, director

of the Bureau d'information et d'orientation pour les réfugiés et rapatriés d'Afrique du Nord (an emergency reception center established by
the Union des israélites nord-africaines and the FSJU in 1961) noted
after bemoaning the fact that only 50 percent of the new arrivals had
passed through the bureau or any other communal institution, "If they
do not come to us, it is up to us to go to them."[53] In cities throughout
France, representatives traveled to the surrounding suburbs where
incoming repatriates had congregated. In Nice, for example, repatriates
living on the outskirts of town had difficulty attending religious functions. To prevent their disengagement with Jewish life, young volunteers
under rabbinical direction went into the suburbs in search of Jewish students, organizing their transportation to supplementary religious
schools every Thursday and Sunday.[54] The Conseil représentatif du
judaïsme traditionaliste de France (CRJTF) also made tremendous
efforts in this regard. By the early 1960s, the CRJTF had thirty-six organizations in Paris and the provinces, including youth centers, kindergartens,
educational facilities, and *colonies de vacances.* In an effort to spread
their religious fervor and to prevent new arrivals from feeling cut off from
Jewish life, the CRJTF organized groups of young missionaries who
contacted new arrivals, created courses in religious instruction, and
organized Friday night services in suburbs with significant Jewish
populations.[55]

Clearly, whatever problems communal organizers predicted would
arise from the influx of North African migration—whether it be lack of
funds to settle them properly or their massive disaffiliation from communal life—most did not fear the growing pluralism of Jewish life in
France. At the conference considering how North African refugees and
repatriates would affect French Jewry, Emile Toutati explained that the
immigration would give a new dimension to their postwar needs. In
other words, the problems had changed in degree but not in form.[56] As
the Jewish sociologist Wladimir Rabinovitch (otherwise known as Rabi)
noted in 1962: "Until now, integration or co-existence has been accom-
plished without any major incidents. The former conflict between natives
and immigrants has been solved by time and common trials. Having
learned from our experiences, we cannot permit it to resurge."[57]

Of course, a migration this large was not problem free, and the rhetoric of solidarity and tolerance within the national leadership was not

always shared by the wider community. Indeed, while many believed that in the post-Holocaust world Jewish solidarity could no longer be denied, this sense of solidarity could not smooth over the numerous transitional problems that such a massive migration brought in its wake. Thus, tensions between Ashkenazim and arriving Jews from North Africa, between "newcomers" and those already in France, erupted over religious differences, control over communal institutions, and insufficient resources.[58] In some areas, the newcomers felt as if the settled population was not doing enough to ease their settlement. Likewise, the settled French Jewish population occasionally accused its leadership of abandoning general programs in favor of those for North Africans.[59] Moreover, French Jews were confronted, once again, with an influx of immigrants who were Jewish in name but who remained culturally and ethnically distinct. As a result, conflicts arose particularly over shared synagogues and differences in rites and religious practices. As Rabbi Meyer Jais described the problem in 1964: "The fact that there are more than 200,000 North African Jews, the fact that the Jews are spread out all over, the fact that we cannot create communities in certain locations that are exclusively Ashkenazic or exclusively Sephardic, the fact that often the same Ashkenazic synagogue houses an immense majority of Sephardim, all this poses extremely unfortunate problems."[60] Such problems could lead to schisms. Moreover, as work on recent French Jewish communities has made clear, the economic, social, and cultural differences separating native French Jews from those originating in North Africa are still salient.[61]

And yet we cannot overlook the shift in attitude at the heart of established Jewish institutional life by the early 1960s. As M. C. Kelman, vice president of the FSJU, argued in 1962, the path bringing North African Jews to France was "providential." Of eastern European origin himself, Kelman stressed that French Jews must work to integrate them rapidly and harmoniously. "It took thirty years and Hitler's cataclysm," he remarked during a conference on North African Jewish repatriates and refugees, "to integrate men [hommes] of my background and generation into the community. Those of us who escaped an unprecedented genocide have neither the time nor strength to wait." For Kelman, it was the responsibility of Jewish intellectuals and communal leaders of every background to prepare "spirits and hearts for the necessary amalgam."

For him, a harmonious settlement process was essential to communal survival: "What differentiates us deserves cultivating, deserves a mutual respect. No one is interested in the loss of a group's identity. This would, in the end, be a loss for the ensemble. From now on, everyone should come to terms with the recognition that the future of French Judaism will be profoundly influenced by the original contribution of North African Judaism."[62]

Similarly, Rabbi Simon Schwarzfuchs worried that any effort to turn North African children into Ashkenazim and that ignored the "specific character, the sensibility of Sephardic Judaism," would alienate the new population. While Schwarzfuchs noted that time might bring some kind of fusion between the new and old, such amalgamation should not be forced.[63]

Such ideas, born of the persecutions of World War II but institutionalized in the period thereafter, radically reoriented the French Jewish leadership as the Jewish population began to expand dramatically at the end of the 1950s. Although France's decolonization of Algeria was yet another tumultuous turning point in French Jewish history, the structures and ideologies that shaped the integration of the newcomers were forged in the prior period—both during the Holocaust and, perhaps more interestingly, in the intervening years, as new structures and ways of thinking reshaped the Jewish leadership once again.

NOTES

1. I have covered some of these issues in my book *In the Aftermath of Genocide: Armenians and Jews in Twentieth-Century France* (Durham, NC: Duke University Press, 2003).

2. Cited in Paula Hyman, *From Dreyfus to Vichy: The Remaking of French Jewry, 1906–1939* (New York: Columbia University Press, 1979), 118.

3. Nancy Green, *The Pletzl of Paris: Jewish Immigrant Workers in the Belle Epoque* (New York: Holmes and Meier, 1986); Hyman, *From Dreyfus to Vichy*; and David H. Weinberg, *A Community on Trial: The Jews of Paris in the 1930s* (Chicago: University of Chicago Press, 1977). Vicki Caron, "Loyalties in Conflict: French Jewry and the Refugee Crisis, 1933–1935," *Leo Baeck Institute Yearbook* 36 (1991): 336, argues that there was not one single native French Jewish voice on the refugee issue. Rather, members of the Jewish leadership debated whether their primary loyalties should lie with the refugees or the French state. Even those most sympathetic to the refugee plight, however, "vehemently opposed mass colonization, fearing that the creation of

unassimilated ethnic enclaves would prevent the successful integration of the refugees and would offend French sensibilities."

4. Edmond Dreyfuss, "Rapport au Consistoire de Paris sur les mesures à prendre en vue de remédier à la désaffection pour le culte," Minutes, May 5, 1946, AA27, Consistoire de Paris.

5. As Aron Rodrigue, *French Jews, Turkish Jews: The Alliance Israélite Universelle and the Politics of Jewish Schooling in Turkey, 1960–1925* (Bloomington: Indiana University Press, 1990), and Lisa Moses Leff, *Sacred Bonds of Solidarity: The Rise of Jewish Internationalism in Nineteenth-Century France* (Stanford, CA: Stanford University Press 2006), have shown, French Jewish paternalism toward their Ottoman and North African coreligionists helped shape their international commitments.

6. See, most notably, Sarah Sussman, "Changing Lands, Changing Identities: The Migration of Algerian Jewry to France, 1954–1967" (PhD diss., Stanford University, 2002), 304–64, and Véronique Poirier, *Ashkénazes et séfarades: Une étude comparée de leurs relations en France et en Israël (années 1950–1990)* (Paris: Cerf, 1998), 69–80.

7. Joan Wolf, *Harnessing the Holocaust: The Politics of Memory in France* (Stanford, CA: Stanford University Press, 2004), makes the case that long-term communal trauma became evident only in 1967 when the attack on Israel gave rise to new fears of Jewish extinction.

8. Michael Marrus and Robert Paxton, *Vichy France and the Jews* (New York: Basic Books, 1981), 343.

9. Mandel, *In the Aftermath of Genocide*, 91–92.

10. Annette Wieviorka, "Despoliation, Reparation, Compensation," in *Starting the Twenty-First Century: Sociological Reflections and Challenges*, ed. Ernest Krausz and Gitta Tulea (New Brunswick, NJ: Transaction Publishers, 2002), 205.

11. Idith Zertal, *From Catastrophe to Power: Holocaust Survivors and the Emergence of Israel* (Berkeley: University of California Press, 1998), 52–92, documents disagreements in the French administration over allowing Jews to pass through en route to Palestine, with those in the Ministry of Interior often turning a blind eye to these activities.

12. Mônica Riasa Schpun, "L'immigration juive dans la France de l'après guerre," in *Terre d'exil, terre d'asile: Migrations juives en France aux XIXe et XXe siècles*, ed. Collette Zytnicki (Paris: Editions de l'éclat, 2010), 115–31.

13. Eighteen thousand of all new arrivals ultimately left for Israel. Doris Bensimon and Sergio Della Pergola, *La population juive de France: Socio-démographie et identité* (Jerusalem: Institute of Contemporary Jewry; Paris: Centre national de la recherche scientifique, 1984), 36.

14. Schpun, "L'immigration juive," 115, 119. The 40,000 figure referred specifically to the years 1946–48.

15. "The North African Influx—A New Crisis for the French Jewish Community," prepared by J[ulian] Breen for the American Joint Distribution Committee (hereafter AJDC), September 5, 1963, 328.

16. Jewish figures are from Sussman, "Changing Lands," 1. The wider figure is from Jacques Fremeaux, "Le reflux des français d'Afrique du Nord 1956–1962," in *Marseille et le choc des décolonisations*, ed. Jean-Jacques Jordi and Emile Temime (Aix-en-Provence: Edisud, 1996), 15.

17. For works tracing the impact of North African Jews on French Jewish life, see Joëlle Bahloul, *Parenté et ethnicité: La famille juive nord-africaine en France* (Paris: Mission du patrimoine ethnologique de la France, 1984); Doris Bensimon-Donath, *L'intégration des juifs nord-africains en France* (Paris: Mouton, 1971); Poirier, *Ashkénazes et séfarades*; Sussman, "Changing Lands"; Claude Tapia, *Les juifs sépharades en France (1965–1985): Études psycholosociologiques et historiques* (Paris: Éditions l'Harmattan, 1986).

18. Guy de Rothschild, "Allocution de M. Guy de Rothschild," in *XIIIe Assemblée générale du FSJU: Journée d'études des problèmes des réfugiés et rapatriées d'Afrique du Nord* (Paris: Fonds social juif unifié, 1962). Emphasis mine.

19. Guy de Rothschild, "Pour un judaïsme ouvert," in *Assemblée générale du Xe anniversaire du Fonds social juif unifié* (Paris: Fonds social juif unifié, 1960).

20. The native Jewish leadership did not come to this position at the outset of World War II, spending the better part of the war years insisting that their fate was different from that of eastern European Jewish immigrants. Richard Cohen, *The Burden of Conscience: French Jewish Leadership during the Holocaust* (Bloomington: Indiana University Press, 1987).

21. *Bulletin quotidien d'information de l'agence télégraphique juive*, 28ème année, 307 (May 7, 1946), French Jewish Communities, 13/2–1, Jewish Theological Seminary.

22. Georges Wormser, "La leçon des évenements," introduction to *La communauté de Paris après la libération* (Paris: Consistoire israélite de Paris, 1946), 6–7.

23. Edmond Dreyfuss, "Rapport au Consistoire de Paris sur les mesures à prendre en vue de remédier à la désaffection pour le culte," Minutes, May 5, 1946, AA27, Consistoire de Paris.

24. Minutes, February 7, 1946, AA26, Consistoire de Paris.

25. For the origins of the CRIF, see Adam Rayski, *Le choix des juifs sous Vichy: Entre soumission et résistance* (Paris: Le Seuil, 1991); Annette Wieviorka, *Déportation et génocide* (Paris: Hachette, 2008).

26. Conseil représentatif des juifs de France, no date (received at the Board of Deputies on December 18, 1944), C11/7/3b/1, Greater London Record Office (hereafter GLRO). Also see CRIF archives at the Centre de documentation juive contemporaine.

27. For the CRIF's marginality, see Annette Wieviorka, "Les juifs en France au lendemain de la guerre: État des lieux," *Archives juives: Revue d'Histoire des Juifs de France* 28, no. 1 (1er semestre 1995): 9. Also see Samuel Ghiles-Meilhac, "From an Unsolvable Dispute to a Unifying Compromise: Zionism at the Heart of the Debates Underlying the Creation of the French Jewish Umbrella Organization, the CRIF," *Bulletin du Centre de recherché français à Jérusalem* 20 (2009), accessed June 26, 2012, http://bcrfj.revues.org/6196, which shows the CRIF's insignificant role in French

diplomacy. For the breakdown in unity, see *European Jewry Ten Years after the War: An Account of the Development and Present Status of the Decimated Jewish Communities of Europe* (New York: Institute of Jewish Affairs of the World Jewish Congress, 1956), 209.

28. Phyllis Cohen Albert, *The Modernization of French Jewry: Consistory and Community in the Nineteenth Century* (Hanover, NH: Brandeis University Press, 1977), 45; chap 8.

29. Minutes, May 5, 1948, AA27, Consistoire de Paris. While many favored increased decentralization, others feared that it would threaten the Consistoire's ability to communicate with and direct those on the periphery. On July 7, 1948, therefore, they agreed to table the issue. Nevertheless, the issue resurfaced repeatedly throughout the next several years. Minutes, July 7, 1948, AA27, Consistoire de Paris.

30. Minutes, June 14, 1949, AA28, Consistoire de Paris. Liber's call for pluralism is all the more surprising when one considers his adamant "assimilationist" stance prior to the war, when he feared that the newcomers' distinctiveness would call undue attention to the native Jewish population. Interestingly, Liber himself was foreign-born. Having come to Paris in 1888 at the age of four from Poland, he was educated in French Jewish schools and was a naturalized citizen. Rejecting the position of chief rabbi in 1935 because he believed it too perilous for a foreign-born rabbi to lead the Consistoire in a period of mounting anti-Semitism, he took the position of chief rabbi for the provinces. Robert Sommer, "La doctrine politique et l'action religieuse du Grand-Rabbin Maurice Liber," *Revue des Études juives* 125 (January–September 1966): 9–20. See also Weinberg, *Community on Trial*, 138; Hyman, *From Dreyfus to Vichy*, 123–24.

31. Untitled report, Assises du judaïsme, 1957, Consistoire de Paris.

32. In 1948, the leadership of the Consistoire de Paris refused to modify its statutes to provide full membership for women. Minutes, May 5, 1948, AA27, Consistoire de Paris.

33. Minutes, December 4, 1946, AA26, Consistoire de Paris.

34. Minutes, June 4, 1947, AA26, Consistoire de Paris.

35. For social service efforts on behalf of incoming Jewish refugees, see Schpun, "L'immigration juive."

36. Mônica Riasa Schpun, "Les premiers migrants juifs d'Afrique du Nord dans la France de l'après guerre: Une découverte pour les services sociaux," *Archives juives* 45, no. 1 (2012): 61–73; citation is from page 71.

37. It is not clear whether Consistoire officials considered arriving North African Jews to be a religious or a social problem, although some indications suggest both. Minutes, June 1, 1949, AA28, Consistoire de Paris.

38. Mandel, *In the Aftermath of Genocide* and "Philanthropy or Cultural Imperialism? The Impact of American Jewish Aid in Post-Holocaust France," *Jewish Social Studies* 9, no. 1 (Fall 2002): 53–94. For an assertion of French Jewish efforts to counter Americanization, see Laura Hobson Faure, "Un 'Plan Marshall juif': La présence juive américaine en France après la Shoah, 1944–54" (PhD diss., École des hautes

études en sciences sociales, 2009). See Sussman, "Changing Lands," 271–75, for the establishment of communal centers for incoming North African Jews.

39. Julian Breen, "Sources of Financing for the Principal Relief and Rehabilitation Programs in France in 1962," AJDC, July 29, 1963, 309. For the transition to FSJU financial control, see Laura Hobson Faure, "Le travail social dans les organizations juives françaises après le Shoah: Création Made in France ou importation américaine," *Archives juives* 42, no. 1 (2012): 43–60; she notes on page 55 that the Joint covered over 55 percent of the FSJU budget until 1961.

40. Rapport de M. Hassid sur l'accueil en France des refugiés juifs d'Egypte, Assises du judaïsme, 1958, Consistoire de Paris.

41. Julien Samuel, "Rapport moral: Regard sur 10 années d'activité du Fonds social juif unifié," in *Assemblée générale du Xe anniversaire du Fonds social juif unifié*, 5.

42. Sussman, "Changing Lands," chap. 6.

43. Henri Levy, untitled report, Assises du judaïsme, 1956, Consistoire de Paris.

44. Sussman, "Changing Lands," 278, 282, 298–303.

45. Emile Touati, "Migrations nord-africaines," *Evidences* 35 (November 1953): 10.

46. Ibid.

47. As early as 1949 certain Consistoire officials began voicing fears that North African refugees were blending too rapidly into the non-Jewish population. One, concerned that poor North African refugees were turning to Christian organizations for aid, complained, "We are not doing anything to assist them; it is normal that they are losing their foothold." Minutes, December 21, 1949, A A28, Consistoire de Paris.

48. Some Algerians feared a similar process. Henri Chemouilli, "Le judaïsme français change de visage," *Evidences* 94 (September/October 1962): 5, posed the problem in the following terms: "Before planning our future in the heart of France's Jewish community, it is advisable not to blind ourselves to a danger that threatens us. The danger of a complete integration into our new life, the danger of an assimilation that will make us into good average French men, indiscernible under the pretext of not colliding with the good people surrounding us."

49. In response, one organization opened a boarding school to train teachers, spiritual leaders, and rabbis to be sent into the various communities. Centre traditionnaire de formation des enfants réfugiées d'Algérie, "Eschel" to Chief Rabbi Brodie, May 27, 1964, papers of the Chief Rabbinate, E1196, GLRO.

50. Association consistoriale israélite de Paris, *Bâtir de nouvelles communautés* (Paris: ACIP, 1966).

51. Alex Derjanski, "Immigrés et autochtones," *L'Arche* 44 (1960): 51. Fears that young North African Jews were vulnerable to a massive disaffiliation from Jewish life dictated many of the FSJU's programs. When Edgard Guedj ("Programme d'action pour la jeunesse," *XIIIe Assemblée générale du FSJU*) laid out the FSJU's program for North African youth, he remarked that these newcomers were importing new blood into French Judaism; it was up to the community to support them and provide continuity to their former lives. Without such support, French Jewry would be responsible for their disaffiliation and assimilation into "inferior social categories."

52. B.I., "La tolérance ne suffit pas," *Univers israélite*, September 21, 1906, 10, cited in Hyman, *From Dreyfus to Vichy*, 117 (emphasis mine).

53. Pierre Kaufman, "Rapport sur les problèmes d'accueil et la coordination des activités à Paris et en Province," *XIIIe Assemblée générale du FSJU*. For information on the Bureau d'information, see Sussman, "Changing Lands," 221–23, and Maud Mandel, "In the Aftermath of Genocide: Armenians and Jews in 20th Century France" (PhD diss., University of Michigan, 1998), chap. 8.

54. Report on situation in Nice, Théodore Khan, June 14, 1964, *Session ordinaire, Assemblée générale ordinaire: Assises du judaïsme française* (Paris: A. Schipper, 1966). Such methods were not always used to ease the newcomers' transition to France. In Toulouse, for example, the director of the local chapter of the Jewish Agency sent students from door to door in highly concentrated Jewish neighborhoods to encourage aliyah. E. O. Kremsdorf, "Visite à Toulouse les 21 et 22 Novembre 1962," AJDC, 346.

55. Rabi, *Anatomie du judaïsme français* (Paris: Éditions de Minuit, 1962), 157. See Sussman, "Changing Lands," 252–319, for a broader discussion of Consistorial and FSJU efforts to reach out to Algerian Jews.

56. Cited in M. C. Kelman, "Rapport de synthèse présenté à la journée d'étude," *XIIIe Assemblée générale du FSJU*.

57. Rabi, *Anatomie du judaïsme français*, 150.

58. Sussman, "Changing Lands," chap. 6; Mandel, "In the Aftermath of Genocide," chap. 8; Poirier, *Ashkénazes et séfarades*, 69–80.

59. Minutes, AJDC and FSJU, February 5, 1962, 357, AJDC.

60. Grand Rabbin Meyer Jais, June 15, 1964, *Session ordinaire, Assemblée générale ordinaire: Assises du judaïsme française*.

61. Kimberly Arkin, " 'It's the French and the Arabs against the Jews': Identity Politics and the Construction of Adolescent Jewishness in France" (PhD diss., University of Chicago, 2008).

62. Kelman, "Rapport de synthèse présenté à la journée d'étude."

63. Rabbi Simon Schwarzfuchs, "Aspects culturels et éducatifs du problème des réfugiés et rapatriés," *XIIIe Assemblée générale du FSJU*.

3

Centralizing the Political Jewish Voice in Post-Holocaust France

Discretion and Development

SAMUEL GHILES-MEILHAC

Anti-Semitic persecutions targeting French and foreign Jews in France from 1940 to 1944 had deep consequences when it came to Jewish political organization. This chapter focuses on one of the most striking of these consequences: the creation in the winter of 1943–44 of the Conseil représentatif des israélites de France (Representative Council of French Israelites, CRIF). This organization symbolized unification of the different cultural and political Jewish groups that were active illegally under German occupation. The chapter therefore presents the events leading to this revolution and focuses on the political life of this new organization in postwar France.

From Forced to Autonomous Political Centralization

In the interwar period, Jewish political life in France was the scene of a competition between the Zionists—divided among themselves— advocating the creation of a Jewish state in Palestine, the socialists of the Bund, and the Communists. These three groups addressed their political propaganda primarily to those Jews who had arrived from eastern and central Europe. The "native" French Jews, citizens since the Revolution—the Israélites, as they were called by others and themselves— had one centralized body representing them on a neutral and purely religious level: the Consistoire. Established in 1808 by Napoleon I, it defended a policy of public assimilation which implied the total absence of any collective political orientation in the name of the Jews. The war, anti-Semitic laws and decrees from Vichy, the pro-German regime in

France, and the presence and influence of German forces profoundly altered conditions for all Jews in France. However, in spite of being progressively excluded from society, many resisted, while some also decided that circumstances called for a profound political transformation.

The creation, in the underground, of the CRIF followed the establishment in July 1943, in Grenoble, of the Jewish General Defense Committee, which consisted of the Communist Union des juifs pour la résistance et l'entraide (Union of Jews for Resistance and Assistance, UJRE), Zionists of the Fédération des sociétés juives de France, and the Bundists. These groups represented the political diversity that characterized the Jewish immigrants who actively took part in the fight against the Nazis and Vichy. The establishment of the General Defense Committee was the first step in the integration of Jewish Communists at the heart of French Judaism. This was a decisive development. Indeed, following the signing of the Molotov-Ribbentrop Pact in the summer of 1939, the critical distance adopted by Jewish institutions toward their Communist coreligionists had become transformed into anger and rejection. Adam Rayski, a Jewish Communist leader, wrote several decades later of the divisive effect this decision by the Soviet Union had on Jewish Communists.[1] The German invasion of the USSR in June 1941 and other evolutions in France and the rest of Europe, in particular the union of Jewish factions during the insurrection of the Warsaw ghetto in the spring of 1943, created a new political situation enabling the creation of coalitions previously thought impossible.

With the General Defense Committee, the political Yiddishland of France became united in a fight against extermination. During the occupation, these groups led many of the Resistance's illegal activities. A number of these acts were nonviolent in their nature, such as the creation of false identification documents. Their constant aim was to protect and rescue Jews, particularly children, who were hidden in families or, when possible, transferred to Switzerland. Clandestine Jewish organizations were also at the origin of armed operations against the Nazis and their collaborators. Jewish Communists were very present in these fights, which enabled them to ally themselves with other Jewish political movements.

The CRIF was the result of the union between the clandestine movements of Jewish resistant immigrants and the Consistoire. The creation of a collective structure whose raison d'être was to be the sole legitimate voice of French Jewry constituted a revolution. The birth of the CRIF can be seen as an act of self-defense and autonomy; self-defense because it united groups from the Jewish underground with the Consistoire, and autonomy because the shift to illegal activities was a reaction to the failure of the Union générale des israélites de France (UGIF), a body founded in December 1941 by the Germans and a Vichy law. Resulting from a compulsory conflation of Jewish institutions, it played a role in supplying social assistance to Jews, but it also simultaneously served as an instrument in the policy of targeting and persecution.[2]

The formation of the CRIF was therefore the beginning of a new chapter in the political history of Jews in France. In 1943 and 1944, the delegates of the founding groups of the CRIF wrote and debated their first charter, which constituted a political platform.[3]

Who were the essential actors in the creation of this unprecedented political umbrella group in the history of Jews in France? Knowing the origins and journeys of the main protagonists of the CRIF sheds light on the significance of its creation. Indeed, these men represent, in numerous ways, the diversity of the Jewish groups that came together to create a unique alliance. The first of these, Léon Meiss, epitomized the typical Alsatian Israélite, a stereotype that has not evolved much since the nineteenth century. Born in 1896 in the Alsatian village of Sarrebourg, he studied law at Strasbourg, a town that became French again after the German defeat of 1918. A religious Jew and a member of the Consistoire, he was a magistrate in Nancy. He saw commitment to the Jewish community and participation in wider public life as being perfectly compatible. During the war, Meiss lived in the large southeastern town of Lyon, where he was the vice president of the Consistoire. He visited the large Synagogue of Lyon, which was situated on the Quai Tilsitt by the Saône River. He became the de facto president of the Consistoire when Jacques Helbronner was arrested and deported. The birth of the CRIF owes much to this man, who represents a double compromise. First, there was a compromise established between Israélites thought of as old-stock French and more recently immigrated Jews. Second, a compromise arose in relation to the determining role played by the Consistoire, which accepted the creation of a political structure only if it retained its dominance. Indeed, it was agreed upon from the start that the Consistoire would decide who would be the president of the CRIF.

Negotiating with Léon Meiss was a group of Jewish militants. These representatives of Jewish political parties (Zionists, Communists, and Bundists) all originated from the Yiddishland. One such, Joseph Fisher, was born in 1893 in Odessa, which was then part of tsarist Russia. During the 1920s he immigrated to France, where he played an active role in Zionist movements. He was the founder and director of the Zionist bimonthly *La Terre retrouvée*.[4] Another, Fajvel Shrager, was one of the French representatives of the Bund, a Socialist, Jewish, and revolutionary movement founded in 1897 in Vilna (present-day Vilnius, Lithuania), whose name is a Yiddish acronym for the General Alliance of Jewish Workers of Russia, Lithuania, and Poland. Two others, Adam Rayski and Charles Lederman, both Communists from the UJRE, were likewise born in Lithuania, a country which, up until World War II, had the largest Jewish community in the world.

The Quest for Visibility and Mobilization on Urgent Issues

We turn now to focus on the internal life and political visibility of this new organization, eager to speak in the name of French Jewry, which was shattered by the loss of more than 70,000 of its members. The first public and legal meeting of the CRIF took place in Lyon on September 5, 1944, just two days after the city's liberation by the American army. While there had been ambiguity regarding the use of the term "Israélite" or "Jew" during negotiations over the charter, it was now decided that the organization would be known as the Representative Council of French Jews. Misunderstandings, distrust, and divisions between native and immigrant Jews were no longer relevant, since the suffering and despair shared by all Jews in France created a new situation. The CRIF's members held several meetings per month, a sign of their strong motivation and their determination to become an active federation.

How visible was the CRIF in the first years following the Liberation? Was it recognized as the centralized voice of organized Jewry? In the first weeks of its legal existence, the new institution acted quickly in the hope of obtaining external recognition in French society. It did this by sending messages out to the press and multiplying its approaches to reach members of political parties and the new, powerful man of liberated France: General de Gaulle, the head of the Provisional Government of the

French Republic. International actors were also contacted, and a message was even sent to the pope in Rome. However, there is no evidence in the archives to show that the CRIF received any answer from these two figures.

Yosef Hayim Yerushalmi has depicted the quest for a relationship with public authorities as the cornerstone of political life in Jewish communities for centuries. The creation of the CRIF in postwar France followed this tradition. In terms of organization, the CRIF maintained the vertical relationship that was the tradition of Jewish leadership in the Diaspora, which meant that it was not possible for an individual to become a direct member of the CRIF. Its name said that the body was the voice of the Jews of France, but its meetings could be attended only by delegates of associations. However, leading figures of Jewish national life did attend some meetings of the new organization; these included people such as Isaac Schneersohn, rabbi, historian, and founder of the Centre de documentation juive contemporaine; and Robert Gamzon, who in 1923 established the Éclaireurs israélites, the Jewish branch of the scout movement in France.

Struggling against Anti-Semitism and Judging the Immediate Past

The loss of tens of thousands of Jews during the deportations fundamentally affected French Judaism. Many leaders of the CRIF were directly marked by the genocide. Jeanne Levy-Meiss, sister of the CRIF's first president, Léon Meiss, was deported along with her husband and children in convoy number sixty-six. It departed from Drancy for Auschwitz, where they were assassinated. Several members from fellow organizations of the General Defense Committee were also assassinated, such as Léo Glaeser, who had notably participated in discussions during the editing of the CRIF's charter. Glaeser was executed by a militia firing squad on June 29, 1944.

The end of four years of state-sponsored attacks against the Jews did not mean that this issue had vanished; on the contrary, one immediate task consisted in monitoring and reacting to any sign of anti-Semitism in France, such as attacks on the Jews in the press, or violent reactions in society against the restitution of stolen Jewish property. But even with the help of the American Jewish Joint Distribution Committee (the Joint), the CRIF had very limited financial resources in those years and managed to hire only a part-time secretary, which meant that the fight against anti-Semitism depended mainly on the voluntary vigilance of its members and that the reaction to anti-Semitism would often simply consist in sending a letter of protest. The reintegration of Jews into society was not a high priority for the government, and the distinctiveness of the discriminations imposed on them was not recognized.

Moreover, the first moves of the CRIF were also meant to look back at the internal Jewish controversies concerning the years of the occupation and of Vichy. In the summer of 1944, still meeting illegally, members of the new umbrella organization took the opportunity to examine the consequences of decisions made by some Jewish leaders between 1940 and 1944. One issue that tested the viability of the CRIF was how they should respond to the UGIF, the Jewish structure created by the Vichy regime in 1941 which was, after the war, at the heart of violent controversies among Jews. The CRIF decided in October 1944, in the first weeks of its legal existence, to establish a commission of inquiry whose mission was "to examine and judge from a political and moral point of view the action of the UGIF and its leaders." The main question that needed to be explored was Jewish responsibility in the German roundup of children on July 24, 1944, from a children's home run by the UGIF in Neuilly-sur-Seine, a western suburb of Paris. These Jewish children were arrested and sent to the death camps, and the Jewish administrators of the home were accused of having helped the Nazis in their mission through their total respect for legalism.[5] On October 15, 1945, a year after the establishment of the commission, Léon Meir stated his opposition to "a moral condemnation" of the Jews who worked for the UGIF, putting a temporary end to a historical introspection that would really only be concluded decades later. In the same period, the CRIF helped to transfer evidence of anti-Semitic persecutions to the French delegates at the Nuremberg trials where Nazi war criminals were being judged. These documents came from the Centre de documentation juive contemporaine. Léon Meiss, in his capacity as president of the CRIF, even spent a few days in Nuremberg and witnessed a session of the tribunal, but did not participate in any way.

A Jewish French Voice on International Affairs?

Dealing with the immediate and traumatic past was one part of the CRIF's agenda. Another concern was to define the scope of its activities, especially when it came to matters outside of metropolitan France. Should French Jews defend a common platform on foreign issues, and how should this be articulated in relation to French diplomacy? One situation in particular illustrates this dilemma and the challenges it posed for French Jewry. A major Jewish institution, the Alliance israélite universelle, was left out of the process that led to the creation of a new political body of French Jews. The Alliance, historically opposed to Zionism, saw itself as the sole French Jewish body with the ability to take action in diplomatic matters such as the question of Palestine or the protection of Jews overseas. But the CRIF's charter was very explicit: the new umbrella group would speak in the name of all French Jews to public authorities and would act on the international scene. Writing about the postwar situation of the Alliance, the French historian Catherine Nicault notes that the body feared that a challenge was being made to its historical missions, and key members of the organization, such as Maurice Leven, viewed the CRIF's position on Palestine as being too close to that of the Zionists.[6] Leven believed that there was a high risk that such a position would give the French public "the impression of serving the interests of an ethnic group different from the rest of the French [national] community." The debate about whether or not the Alliance should join the CRIF began at the end of 1944 and continued for several months. CRIF members, such as the group's first president, Léon Meiss, and their counterparts from the Alliance, knew each other well and were aware that it made little sense for the Alliance not to take part in a Jewish umbrella organization that had succeeded, during the dark days of the war, in overcoming political rivalries. René Cassin, president of the Alliance, met on several occasions with his counterpart, Meiss, in order to reach an agreement. He won the assurance that the CRIF would not be seen as a pro-Zionist group and, most importantly, he obtained a guarantee that the Alliance would keep its prerogative in diplomatic affairs, as per its historical tradition. In a letter to the Alliance, the CRIF stated that the Alliance would remain in charge of all matters "concerning Jews outside France's borders." The Alliance voted to join the CRIF on July 25, 1945.

The bitter debate over Zionism during the drafting of the CRIF's charter and the difficulty on the part of the Alliance to adjust to the new institution shows that the issue of defining the nature of their relationship with a Jewish homeland in Palestine was not a simple matter for French Jews. However, the period of time we are focusing on (1945–55) cannot be analyzed as a monolithic block when it comes to French Jewish organizations' attitudes to the question of Palestine. As Maud Mandel has written, "Like Jewish organization throughout the Western world, which at early points in the century had publicly declared their hostility to Zionist goals, French Jewish organizations became actively involved in the Zionist cause."[7] The best illustration of this phenomenon was the shift in the position of the Alliance israélite universelle, which in 1947 began to defend the rights of Jews to create a national home in Palestine. This was also true for the CRIF, but without such a clear pro-Zionist shift.

The evolution of the political views of President Léon Meiss is a good example. While he was not known for having any strong sympathy toward Zionism before World War II, the shock of the destruction of European Jews modified his views and explained why he endorsed the CRIF's founding charter, which included support for the goals of the Jewish agency. Then, in the spring of 1946, Meiss visited Palestine along with André Blumel, a Socialist politician and former secretary of Léon Blum when he headed the government in 1936 and 1937. Blumel was a passionate advocate of the Zionist cause. They met local Jewish leaders, such as Yitzhak Ben-Zvi, president of the National Council, the shadow government of the Jewish community in Mandatory Palestine. This journey would have an impact on Meiss.

On his return, he spoke at a meeting of the CRIF of his great admiration for the political, institutional, and cultural achievements of the Yishuv; but he did not take a stand on the political future of the territory, nor did he see his presentation as the opportunity to start a debate within the organization he headed. He appeared to believe that neutrality was the only way to maintain the fragile unity of the federation. On the one hand, in 1946 and 1947, he was pressured by the Zionists, represented by Joseph Fisher, to support adoption by the CRIF of a clear position in favor of the creation of a Jewish state in Palestine. On the other hand, the Communists were also pressuring him not to publicly act on this issue in the name of the umbrella organization. Another factor explaining the low profile of the CRIF on this issue was its very weak internal organization. In the summer of 1947, when French opinion, as in many other parts of the world, followed with passion the developments of the Exodus crisis, the CRIF did not take a stance, simply because it did not meet during the summer holidays.

This refusal of the CRIF to implicate itself was also apparent after Israel's proclamation of independence on May 14, 1948. While Paris voted in favor of the division of Palestine adopted by the United Nations General Assembly on November 29, 1947, its attitude remained ambiguous toward the Jewish state for several months. French diplomacy was divided on whether to acknowledge Israel as a state. Israel was only officially recognized by France in May 1949. On that particular topic, family ties deserve a mention. The representative of the Jewish Agency in Paris, who then became the first Israeli ambassador to France, was none other than Maurice Fisher, whose brother Joseph played a key role in the creation and early years of the CRIF. Yet, the archives of the CRIF, as well as publications on France and the birth of Israel, give no indication that this family tie served to shake the CRIF out of its neutrality or to try to intercede with the policy makers of the Quai d'Orsay on behalf of the Jewish state.[8]

By 1954 the CRIF had evolved in various political ways, but its position on Zionism and support for the new State of Israel was still very limited. Jacob Tsur, the Israeli ambassador to Paris from 1953 to 1959, experienced a cold welcome from Jewish leaders who wanted to keep their distance from Israeli diplomats. On November 11, 1953, when attending a service in remembrance of the 1918 armistice at the Victoire synagogue in Paris, he was shocked by his reception. As he later recorded, "It was as if my first encounter with the Jewish elite of Paris had been turned into an opportunity to make me understand that French Judaism was determined not to be dragged into too much intimacy with Israel." A few months later, he got the same impression in Strasbourg, where he was told, "You know, we are French citizens and you are the envoy of a foreign state."[9] Previously mentioned documentation would suggest, however, that the CRIF's position was not always as hostile as these episodes might suggest. So in 1954, for example, in its official declaration made at the Paris Prefecture, the CRIF stated that its duty was to "defend the rights of the Jewish community and its members in France." But while it felt able to affirm a "sympathy towards the state of Israel," this sympathy was cautiously expressed and consciously intended to be limited.

A further cause of great concern in France in the early 1950s was the issue of West German rearmament. The CRIF voted in October 1950 and again in November 1953 to waive their firm opposition to this international decision. Less than a decade after the capitulation of the Third Reich, Germany was seen as a potential threat, and the possibility of its rearming rekindled fresh traumas for Jews. All the political factions within the CRIF shared this fear and opposed this development, but they differed on the political strategy that the CRIF should adopt. The essential question was, Should the Jewish umbrella organization do more than publish a press release to voice its opposition to West German remilitarization, and, if so, what more should it do?

The Communists adopted the same position as the Parti communiste français (PCF) on a national level and pushed for more energetic action by the CRIF against the rearming, which they portrayed as an imperialistic move by the United States against the Soviet bloc. However, most members of other Jewish organizations believed that the CRIF was powerless and could only lose credibility while wasting its time. Perhaps, as its leaders feared, it would put at risk its fragile and limited legitimacy in a battle that involved European powers and the United States through NATO. As a consequence, in 1954, the Jewish institution limited its public action to a press release where it reaffirmed "its emotion" on the issue. Unity was maintained at the price of invisibility.

The progression of the Cold War had direct consequences within the CRIF. The beginning of the 1950s saw a growing political gap between the Communists and all the other group members of the CRIF due to the fact that they acted as the voluntary Jewish fig leaf of the French Communist Party, even providing unconditional support for the Soviet Union at the time of the so-called doctors' plot.[10] As a result, the voice of the Union des juifs pour la Résistance et l'entraide, a key founder of the CRIF in the underground Resistance, lost its influence permanently.

The Strong Limits of Ethnic Politics

André Fontaine, in Le Monde on October 5–6, 1947, mentioned the CRIF in a series of articles presenting the situation of "churches in France." He wrote: "This union is unique in the world and there is little chance that it will exist after having achieved the goals that led to its creation: restitution of the properties seized, pensions, distribution of the help from the American Joint Jewish Committee or the World Jewish Congress." The journalist was right in highlighting the exceptional political reality that the CRIF represented. However, his prediction that the committee only had a purpose when linked to the emergency management of postwar issues proved false. Ten years after the full liberation of France, the CRIF survived despite the departure of key figures who were instrumental in its creation during the war. Léon Meiss resigned in 1949–50 despite months of pressure from all members of the institution to keep his position. Having become an Israeli citizen, Joseph Fisher changed his name to Joseph Ariel. He was an Israeli diplomat in Belgium at the start of 1950s, before becoming the director of international relations of Yad Vashem from 1960 onward. He died in February 1965 in Israel. His analysis of Jewish self-defense acts in France and the creation of the CRIF was penned in 1963 and published in 1967.[11] Adam Rayski went to Poland to work for the Communist government. However, at the same time, new members strengthened the CRIF's representativeness. After the Alliance joined the CRIF in 1945, the Jewish student organization Union des étudiants juifs de France became a full member in 1947 and was represented by its president, Theo Klein. Then came the B'nai B'rith in May 1948, followed by other political cultural Jewish associations.

This first decade of the CRIF's life represents an important element and a halfway revolution in the political organization of French Jewry. The very creation of such a body illustrates a will to reconfigure the old neutralist system and the belief that political oppositions would not prevent the Jews of France from acting in public in their common interest. But this desire still did not modify the way Jewish institutions decided to act in the public sphere. Whether against the rearmament of West Germany or with regard to full French recognition of Israel, the CRIF never considered the opportunity of taking to the streets as a strategy to pressure the government or to alert public opinion. There was no place in French society or among the Jews of the Fourth Republic for the recognition of a visible advocacy group representing a minority.

In this respect, French society and its political elite certainly maintained the vision that had led to the emancipation of Jews. French collective identity recognized Jews only as individuals. That logic is highly visible in Stanislas de Clermont-Tonnerre's speech on December 23, 1789, to the Constitutional Assembly during the debate on the emancipation of Jews. It illustrates the mind-set of those who voted in favor of their citizenship: "We must deny everything to Jews as a nation, and grant everything to Jews as individuals; we must not recognize their judges. . . . We must refuse to give legal protection to the so-called laws of their Judaic organization; they should not become a separate political body or class within the State; they must be individually citizens."

As the product of the extreme violence against the Jews and the ability of different political organizations to fight for their survival and develop a common political platform, the CRIF faced an environment, both inside the French Jewish community and in society in general, that drastically limited its options. Its leaders had no common vision for the role they should play.

Postwar Jewish politics focused, at least in part, on maintaining the habits of French Judaism since the emancipation. This is illustrated by the supremacy maintained by the Consistoire, which kept the right to decide who should be the president of the CRIF. In the 1950s, headed by Vidal Modiano, a doctor with Greek origins who succeeded Léon Meiss, the CRIF continued to exist in relative obscurity. It was still very far from creating a direct relationship with the "Jewish masses," a concern repeatedly raised in the minutes of its meetings. It also failed to be recognized by high-ranking officials as a regular interlocutor that should be consulted on all political issues related to French Jews. But in spite of difficulties and disagreements, the creation of a political structure common to all Jewish dispositions and their postwar activities was nonetheless a turning point in French Jewish institutional life. During the years of reconstruction, therefore, while the country celebrated the Liberation, all political topics, both national and international, that could directly concern French Jews—the responsibilities of the UGIF, the restitution of Jewish property, the Nuremberg trials, the rearmament of West Germany, the question of Palestine, followed by the birth of the State of Israel—were at the heart of debates within the CRIF. This does not necessarily mean that these debates led to visible or effective political action. Neither a "revolution" nor a "back to normal" situation, the late 1940s and early 1950s nevertheless witnessed the consolidation of an organization whose role became crucial in the decades that followed.

NOTES

1. Adam Rayski, *The Choice of the Jews under Vichy: Between Submission and Resistance*, trans. Will Sayers (Notre Dame, IN: University of Notre Dame Press, 2005).

2. Michel Laffite, "Was the UGIF an Obstacle to the Rescue of the Jews?," in *Resisting Genocide: The Multiple Forms of Rescue*, ed. Jacques Sémelin, Claire Andrieu, and Sarah Gensburger (New York: Columbia University Press, 2011).

3. Samuel Ghiles-Meilhac, "From an Unsolvable Dispute to a Unifying Compromise," *Bulletin du Centre de recherche français à Jérusalem* 20 (2009), http://bcrfj .revues.org/index6196.html (accessed March 28, 2012).

4. Catherine Poujol, "The Daily Life of a Propagandist at the Paris Bureau of the Jewish National Fund (K.K.L.)," *Bulletin du Centre de recherche français à Jérusalem* 8 (2001), http://bcrfj.revues.org/index2132.html (accessed March 27, 2012).

5. Michel, Lafitte, *Un engrenage fatal: L'UGIF face aux réalités de la Shoah* (Paris: Liana Levi, 2003); and Lafitte, "Was the UGIF an Obstacle to the Rescue of the Jews?"

6. Catherine Nicault, "L'alliance au lendemain de la Seconde Guerre mondiale: Ruptures et continuités idéologiques," *Archives juives* 34, no. 1 (2001): 23–53.

7. Maud Mandel, *In the Aftermath of Genocide: Armenians and Jews in Twentieth-Century France* (Durham, NC: Duke University Press, 2003), 137–38.

8. Frédérique Schillo, *La France et la création de l'État d'Israël, 18 février 1947–11 mai 1949* (Paris: Éditions Artcom, 1997).

9. Jacob Tsur, *Prélude à Suez: Journal d'une ambassade 1953–1956* (Paris: Presses de la Cité, 1968), 67.

10. In January 1953, the official newspaper *Pravda* announced that a group of doctors, most of them Jewish, had been arrested and accused of having assassinated high-ranking officials. They were presented as spies working for the Joint (American Jewish Joint Distribution Committee). This "doctors' plot" is seen as the climax of state anti-Semitism in the post-war Soviet Union. After Stalin's death on March 5, 1953, the charges were dismissed and the doctors exonerated.

11. CRIF files, 1944–1954, MDI, Centre de documentation juive contemporaine, Paris. The archives deposited by Joseph Fisher in Jerusalem are available at the Yad Vashem Holocaust Resource Center. The classification mark of these files is O.9/297.

4

Post-Holocaust Book Restitutions

How One State Agency Helped Revive Republican Franco-Judaism

LISA MOSES LEFF

Recent studies about Jews in postwar France have shown that, for the most part, the newly reestablished republican state treated Jewish citizens in much the same way that they had been treated in the Third Republic, and indeed, in all French regimes since Napoleon. That is, Jews were not singled out for special treatment but were rather considered citizens indistinguishable from their fellow Frenchmen. For Jews, this reestablishment of republicanism was a "liberation" indeed, since it signaled an end to the anti-Semitic persecution of the war years. Yet it also brought with it a certain forgetting, making it difficult for there to be public recognition of the special suffering Jews had faced during the war. As Maud Mandel has written, "A commitment to republican government that since the Revolution had de-emphasized all cultural pluralism in the public sphere . . . led [French officials] to treat Jews as *one among many* of Vichy's numerous victims."[1] The contrast was stark. Under the occupation, Vichy and German authorities targeted Jews explicitly on racial grounds for discrimination, expropriation, incarceration, and, eventually, deportation; in contrast, in the war's aftermath, republican state officials were hesitant to write race into official policies in any explicit way, and thus rarely acknowledged this special history, even for the sake of memorialization or redress.

By once again adopting a republican model that relegated Jewishness to the purely private sphere, postwar republicans inflicted certain kinds of unintended harm on Jewish life. Beyond the spiritual terms of "unfinished memory" that Henry Rousso has written about, the postwar erasure of Jewish life from public view was also felt in very concrete terms. When French republican officials refused to recognize that Jews had suffered differently, this meant, in practice, that they did not address Jews' special needs when it came to reconstructing Jewish communal life. Indeed, Jews had suffered disproportionately during the war, and their suffering was ultimately due to official state policy and the conditions it created. Of these affected Jews, 76,000 were deported eastward to Nazi camps on racial grounds; only about 3,500 would return. In the immediate postwar years, recognition of Jews' losses as distinct would have meant recognizing that those deportations were fundamentally different from the deportation of non-Jewish resistance fighters and required at the very least a different kind of commemoration.

This return to race-blind policies also affected the restitution of property. During the war, Jews had been subject quite legally to unprecedented seizures of their property, including businesses, apartments, furniture, household goods, art, books, and papers. In addition, when Jews went into hiding, fearing for their lives, many abandoned their apartments and household property in the process, and while they were gone, their apartments and household goods were appropriated by others who sometimes refused to give them back when the owners returned. Authorities hesitant about creating special policies for addressing these problems were often less than helpful, and this made rebuilding Jewish life in postwar France unnecessarily difficult. As a result of that hesitance, many Jews—David Weinberg tells us as many as half of those who reported having had their household property looted—were unable to get their property back by 1951.[2] Jews faced similar problems when they sought to get their apartments back after the war; here too, authorities balanced the needs of the new occupants against the needs of the returning Jews, without acknowledging what those Jews had suffered at the hands of the state and why they had abandoned their apartments.[3] And while the art restitution authorities worked tirelessly to get back the many paintings and sculptures the Nazis had looted and sent east, few of these items were in fact restored to their original Jewish owners, as the authorities saw them not so much as the personal property of Jewish individuals, but rather as part of the general "French patrimony." This meant that if the original owners did not know to take the initiative to approach the restitution authorities themselves, the works of art they had lost would remain under custodianship in the Musées nationaux system for decades, until this system came to be seen as scandalous in the late 1990s.[4] Taking these different types of cases together, a clear pattern emerges: the consequences of the return to the republican model were thus quite serious for Jews seeking to rebuild their lives.

And yet, one arm of the French restitution authority seems to have operated a little differently from the others. This chapter examines the work of this restitution agency, the Sous-Commission des livres, the arm of the Commission de récupération artistique that handled the restitution of the estimated 10 million books that the Germans had looted in France during the war.[5] Like the larger organization of which it was a part, the leaders of the book restitution authority were imbued with a republican spirit; indeed, the hundreds of reports archived in their files at the Archives nationales testify that they made no explicit distinction between "Jewish books" and "non-Jewish books," and certainly no distinction whatsoever between Jewish book owners and non-Jewish book owners. Nevertheless, largely because of the practical issues involved in the restitution of books, these French authorities wound up doing much that would ultimately help Jewish libraries rebuild after the war in ways that would prove beneficial for rebuilding French Jewish cultural life.

To understand the particular circumstances that made the book restitution authority somewhat different from its sister agencies, we must first understand how the Nazi looting of books had taken place during the war. Under the authority of Nazi ideologue Alfred Rosenberg's Einsatzstab Reichsleiter Rosenberg (ERR), thousands of public, private, and individual libraries were looted from enemies of the Reich beginning in July 1940. The looted collections included a number of Jewish libraries. The largest was that of the Alliance israélite universelle, which had 50,000 volumes, and the second largest was the library of the École rabbinique, which had 10,000 volumes. Smaller collections were also looted, including those of the Fédération des sociétés juives de France, the Paris Consistory, the Paris branch of the Vilna-based Yiddish Scientific Institute (YIVO), the Paris branch of the World Jewish Congress, the Palestine Jewish Colonization Association, the Dubnow Association, and the Éclaireurs israélites de France (the Jewish Scouts). The Jewish-owned Librairie Lipschutz lost 20,000 books in this operation as well. Important collections were also looted from Jewish individuals, such as that of the Rothschild family, which lost 20,000 volumes, including many of great value. The libraries of professors like Marc Bloch and Maurice Halbwachs were also looted, as were those of politicians like Léon Blum and Georges Mandel and religious leaders like Rabbis Jacob Kaplan and Maurice Liber, to name just a few.[6] Jewish libraries were not the only ones looted; Slavic libraries like the Turgenev Library, full of rare Russian literature banned since the revolution in the Soviet Union, as well as Masonic libraries, were also looted, since these too were deemed "enemy" collections. In addition to these printed books, the Nazis also looted rare manuscripts and documents of strategic importance from public libraries and public archives across France.[7]

The Nazis quickly developed a system for book looting in Paris. Beginning in summer 1940, they turned the Alliance israélite universelle's library into a gathering point for books looted in the city. This was done largely for practical reasons: the Alliance's library was among the first to be looted, its collection sent to Germany in August 1940. Its emptied stacks were newly built, since the organization had just moved into a new building; the facility was large and modern; and with the invasion of the Germans, almost all its personnel had fled (with the exception of a trusty concierge), leaving it empty for the Germans to use. In short, it was a perfect place to collect and sort the books to be sent on to the Reich. From there, most of the Judaica was sent to the newly established Institut zur Erforschung der Judenfrage (Institute for the Study of the Jewish Question), a Nazi scientific center in Frankfurt. This was envisioned by its founders to become the preeminent center for Alfred Rosenberg's Hohe Schule, or center for Nazi Jewish studies, a field central to the development of Nazi ideology. By April 1943, the Frankfurt Institute alone had amassed the largest Judaica library in history, with over 550,000 volumes that had been looted across Europe. In 1945, when the Americans found this collection in Hungen, where the Nazis had moved it for safekeeping, it comprised over a million books, although some of them may not have been part of the institute originally.[8] Smaller quantities of Judaica were sent to other branches of the Hohe Schule in the eastern part of the Reich. These were not the only destinations for looted books: books that had no Jewish content, such as French literature, were sent to other centers, including public library collections, throughout the Reich.

Even before liberation, French authorities were extremely concerned with finding their looted cultural property. As early as 1943, they took the lead in pushing the Allies to develop a coordinated policy on how such property would be treated during and especially at the end of the war. By the time the Allied forces entered the Reich, policies were in place that were intended to protect all cultural property found there. Because the 1907 Hague Convention had deemed the long-standing practice of pillage to be a war crime, Allied authorities condemned Nazi looting, and the Americans, the British, and the French—if not, in the end, the Soviets—committed themselves to the arduous task of restituting the property they found. Of course, they made this commitment long before they became aware of the unprecedented scope of Nazi plunder. As Allied armies made their way to Berlin, they found cache after cache of looted cultural treasures that fell into the category of property they had pledged to protect and restore to its rightful prewar owners.[9]

In the aftermath of the war, it was the Americans who organized the largest restitution effort in conquered Germany. Policy held that all looted cultural property found in Germany was to be turned over to commanding officers, who would in turn send on the property to collection points in the country. From the collection points, Allied personnel would attempt to identify the original owners and manage restitutions. When it came to the looted books, starting in February 1946, Judaica that had been found in Germany was centralized in a single collection point, an abandoned warehouse of the I. G. Farben chemical company in Offenbach, near Frankfurt. From here, Americans faced the daunting task of processing over 3 million volumes of Judaica as well as many other Jewish cultural items, such as Torah scrolls, that they found in Germany.[10]

Though American authorities intended to return all the items they collected in Offenbach, it quickly became apparent that this would be impossible, because so many of the books were unidentifiable and, they presumed, so many of the prewar owners had perished in the war. This led policy makers to entertain a variety of suggestions about what to do with such "heirless" items, the largest portion of the property. General Lucius Clay, military governor of the American Zone in Germany, initially favored returning looted books to their country of origin. But American Jewish groups quickly caught wind of this and protested vigorously. Arguing that Jewish books looted from Poland and Lithuania, for example, did not belong in those countries now that their Jewish populations had disappeared, a group of Jewish intellectuals based in New

York organized to put pressure on Clay to develop a policy in which heirless Jewish books would be distributed by a designated Jewish authority. In the minds of these intellectuals, including Columbia University historian Salo Baron, librarian Theodore Gaster of the Library of Congress, and the Columbia University law professor Jerome Michael, Jewish books, like Jewish displaced persons, needed to be treated differently, given what they had been through. And, they argued, Jewish organizations should play a special role in this process.[11]

Responding to their request, in June 1948, Clay established the Jewish Restitution Successor Organization (JRSO), a body with representatives from Jewish communities in Palestine, Europe, and the United States but incorporated in New York State. The JRSO was empowered to claim all Jewish property deemed heirless and to dispose of it as it wished. For books, the JRSO created an organization called Jewish Cultural Reconstruction (JCR), led by Baron and Hannah Arendt, to distribute the heirless books to Jewish libraries, primarily in the United States and Israel, beginning in 1949. Though Jewish communities did remain behind in Europe, the JCR's work was guided by a vision that Jewish books no longer belonged in Europe. Arendt, who ran the day-to-day operations, was well aware that there were German Jews remaining behind, but her correspondence reveals that she saw their days as numbered. Jewish books, she told them, belonged where large populations of Jews could make use of them, and this was in Israel and the United States, not Europe.[12]

The French faced a formidable task when it came to restitutions, including those of books. Many French private citizens and public institutions had been plundered, and much of the property was no longer in France. Yet as early as summer 1944, the forces that would come together to create the new state were setting the wheels of the restitution process in motion. Restitutions as a whole fell under the administrative jurisdiction of the Office de biens et intérêts privés (OBIP), a preexisting agency within the Ministry of Foreign Affairs, originally created in 1919 to handle German payment of reparations.[13] By a decree of November 24, 1944, a separate Commission de récupération artistique (CRA) was created to handle the restitution of archives, art, books, and manuscripts, to be run by cultural authorities such as museum and public library administrators. The CRA functioned semi-independently of the OBIP until 1949, when most of its operations had been completed and it was dissolved; after that time, the OBIP would handle any additional restitution issues that might come up. Within the CRA, a Sous-Commission des livres (SCL) handled the restitution of books. In the five years of its operation, the SCL had able leadership in Camille Bloch, the inspector general of libraries; but its guiding force was in fact in its day-to-day leadership, entrusted to the skillful hands of Jenny Delsaux, a former Sorbonne librarian.[14]

It was in large part due to Delsaux's vision, as well as her skillful problem solving, that book restitutions were handled so differently from other restitution enterprises. Her memoir, written years after the fact, makes it clear that she saw all the looted books as part of the French cultural patrimony. Yet much of her work involved delicate international diplomacy. To accomplish her task, she had to deal with the occupation authorities in Germany, where so many French books were found; in this, she was largely dependent on the goodwill of the Americans, since most of the restitution activity was taking place in their zone of Germany. Across the board and from the very start, French restitution authorities were suspicious of American restitutions, and when it came to book restitutions, the story was no different. Delsaux suspected that Americans were lax in their policies and that many items had been stolen under their watch. In fact, this does seem to have been the case. As with the looted art that was collected in Munich, many books had disappeared from the American collection point in Offenbach before the French could get there. Among the stolen books were some that were taken to Palestine to the Hebrew University. Others were sent with official approval to the Library of Congress, although this was technically a breach of policy. And while she and her counterparts in the other restitution agencies were consistently suspicious that some books were being lost under the American watch, this situation was far better than what they faced in the Soviet Zone, where no restitutions were being attempted and where, for the most part, French officials were not even given permission to search.[15]

In addition to the SCL's dependence on the Americans, it faced other important challenges in the book restitutions. Many books looted by the Nazis had never left France at all, and after the Germans fled, 1.2 million volumes were found abandoned in depots across France. In Paris alone, 60,000 books were found on the shelves of the Alliance library, and these did not include any of the books originally in the Alliance's own collection, which had been sent in its entirety to Frankfurt in 1940. At the Foire de Paris, near the Porte de Versailles, another 300,000 books were found on makeshift shelving. In a garage on the rue de Richelieu, 150,000 more volumes were found stacked haphazardly in piles against the walls. When Jenny Delsaux first visited this depot in June 1945, before she could introduce herself to the military guard watching over the books there, he told her very cheerfully that she could take whatever she pleased as long as it wasn't more than a few books. In this way, she learned that books were disappearing by the day from the depot, and that others had been destroyed by trucks and gasoline, since the depot was also an active military garage.[16]

Nonetheless, under Delsaux's direction, the book restitution commission made every attempt to restitute the books it found in France and the additional books—estimated at 773,000—that it was able to find in Germany, including 323,000 in Offenbach. The initial part of the process was in line with what was being done by the other restitution authorities. In a first period, those whose property had been looted could come to the SCL to find their lost books. As was the case in the parallel restitution processes, this method had only limited success; only a small portion—342,000 books, or 17 percent—were restituted in this way.

Then, the remaining books were deemed heirless. At this point, the book restitution authority acted differently than the other restitution authorities. First, it developed an "attributions" process. Here, books were given to individuals and institutions according to their need, as determined by the SCL. As part of this process, individuals who had filed claims that could not be fulfilled were given heirless books as a substitute for their lost books. This included, for example, professionals such as doctors and lawyers who had lost reference works. It also included public libraries that had their collections destroyed by the Allied bombing at the end of the war. In addition, attributions of Yiddish books were made to Jewish orphanages and hospitals whose charges had lost everything in the war. After this process was over, the SCL sold off the remaining books at very low prices, primarily to public collections; the proceeds of those sales went to the state.[17]

Looking through the records of the SCL, it is clear that an individual's or institution's Jewishness played no explicit role in the process of restitution. More importantly, it also played no role in the attributions or sales processes. Individuals were deemed worthy of attributions according to what they had lost and what they needed, and even in the case of the Yiddish books attributed to Jewish institutions, there was no discussion of the Jewishness of the needy children, just of their losses; it was probably also obvious to Delsaux that Yiddish books were of more use in these institutions than they would be in public libraries. The policy did provoke some dissent among the authorities. Marcel Bouteron, administrator at the Bibliothèque nationale and former *résistant*, protested that the agency had no business acting like a charity.[18] It also annoyed some Jewish groups, who complained that, unlike the process followed by the Americans, the proceeds from the sales went to the state rather than to them, at a moment when communal funds were most needed.[19] From Delsaux's own memoir, it is clear that a race-blind republicanism was the rule here in a way that set this commission's work apart from its counterpart among the American authorities in occupied Germany. Need, not Jewishness, was determinant in the attributions and sales processes.[20]

And yet, unlike in the restitution of art and household goods, even as Jewishness was not an explicit category for the SCL, Jewish cultural experts and Jewish cultural institutions played an important role. This happened for practical reasons rather than due to any ideological commitments on the part of its leadership. First, the SCL used a series of Jewish book experts, all of whom were associated with Jewish institutions that had been looted in the war, to help them identify materials that had been looted from French Jews by the Nazis. Since so many of the books in the American depot in Offenbach were in Hebrew, the SCL sent Rabbi Maurice Liber, head of the École rabbinique, there in spring 1946, together with his student André Chekroum. There, they found and identified some missing French items, including rare manuscripts looted from the Alliance israélite universelle. They also helped the Americans read book titles, since, according to their report, no personnel in the depot at that time read Hebrew. They also showed the Americans how to identify French bindings, to facilitate future restitutions.[21] A second mission to Offenbach was undertaken in September 1946 by Paul Klein, the Hebraica librarian at the Bibliothèque nationale, and a third and final mission was undertaken in 1948 by the head of the YIVO committee in Paris, Gershon Epstein. Epstein's mission was most productive;

he sent back to France 40,000 volumes he found in the depot, although some were lost in transit.[22] As a result of these three missions by these Hebraica experts, the Alliance israélite universelle was able to recover its entire looted collection, and the École rabbinique recovered a good portion of its collection as well. In total, these experts facilitated the return of over 323,000 books to France from Offenbach.[23] Clearly, the decision to make Jewish librarians into restitution officers representing the French state proved beneficial to French Jewish cultural institutions, since it facilitated the return of the collections of the looted Jewish libraries that would have otherwise been lost forever.

In addition, the Alliance israélite universelle functioned as a partner in the restitution of looted books found in France itself. Here too, practical reasons seem to have guided the SCL in its decision to partner with a Jewish institution. Since from the outset the SCL lacked sufficient funding, it took months before adequate space was found for its work, and in the meantime, winter weather was threatening the collections housed outdoors at the Foire de Paris. For that reason, Delsaux decided that rather than moving them to the Foire, she would leave the books found on the Alliance's shelves where they were, and empowered Edmond-Maurice Lévy and Rose Feingold, the Alliance's librarian and secretary, to carry out restitutions of these books on their own. Although they were instructed in and ostensibly followed the SCL's restitution policies, this partnership placed the Alliance library in a privileged position vis-à-vis the SCL. This in turn meant that when the time came for attributions, they were well positioned to ask that once they had finished restituting what they could, the remaining 30,000 heirless volumes of Judaica and Hebraica left on the shelves be attributed to the library so that the books could be made available to the public.[24] In this way, it was with the support of the state that the Alliance was able to rebuild its library, making it stronger than ever in spite of having been emptied entirely during the war.

Through the partnership with the Alliance and the employment of Liber, Klein, and Epstein, the SCL effectively helped some of the most important French Jewish institutions rebuild and, just as importantly, restored their legitimacy. Though it would take the Alliance over a decade to reconstruct its card catalogue, which had not been found in Germany, its active partnership with the book restitution authority made it possible for this library to once again emerge as the preeminent Judaica library in France, and would make Jewish scholarship possible in France once again.

Furthermore, through its attributions process, the SCL effectively eased some of the suffering of many Jewish individuals who had lost their property more than the sister agencies handling art and furniture were able to do, and far more than city authorities handling the return of occupied apartments were doing. As one family wrote to the service after receiving an attribution:

> Madame, it is impossible to express all that my family felt when we received the attribution of the books. We were so very surprised at its contents, containing as they did a good number of the books that we had lost, and the rest were an exact replication of the spirit of the rest of the lost collection. Such [an] effort on your part is confusing to me; I can't tell you how much admiration you inspire in me with this action. We lost everything, furniture, rugs, paintings, our apartment; nothing mattered more to us than our library . . . and now . . . a miracle has happened, you've given us back part of it.[25]

To some, it also felt like justice was being served. As Marie Lahy-Hollobecque, a Jewish writer who received an attribution, wrote to the SCL in 1948: "[Looking through the books you just sent me] gives me such a strong emotion. From the bottom of my heart, I thank you for the . . . help you offered in my great distress. . . . [You] did more than I can tell you to accomplish the impossible. [You] redeemed the injustice that had been committed.[26] In this way, largely because of the nature of the materials it was dealing with, the book restitution authority operated quite differently from the other restitution authorities that have been studied. Certainly, in all of the restitutions processes, most individuals did not get their lost possessions back. Yet ultimately, Jewish individuals and especially Jewish institutions benefited from book restitutions in ways that they did not in the other processes. The contrast with the art restitution authority is particularly instructive. Whereas the ultimate beneficiary in that process was the public Musées nationaux system, which maintained guardianship of unclaimed art indefinitely, the book restitution authority decided to give out all the books. Moreover, the book restitution agency did not neglect Jewish institutions and individuals who had been looted in the process, all the while maintaining policies that remained race-blind. This was far from typical for a state agency in this period.

So to conclude: Does the claim that the French returned to a republican model of Franco-Judaism after the war need to be altered in the light of the evidence presented here about the restitution of books? On the one hand, no, it does not. A comparison with the American restitution process, which we have also examined here, is instructive. Unlike the Americans, the French book restitution commission never imagined a Jewish cultural patrimony separate from the French one. Indeed, even as the French sent Rabbi Liber to Germany to find looted books, it sent him as a *French* restitution officer rather than as a *Jewish* cultural authority. This was more than mere semantics. Unlike the Jewish leaders of Jewish Cultural Reconstruction who partnered with the Americans in their book restitution process, these French Jewish leaders always operated within the framework of the French state, and never supported sending Jewish books outside of France. Indeed, when the Hebrew University of Jerusalem asked for an attribution of books from the French, their request did not bear the stamp of approval of any French Jewish institution. Moreover, since the Hebrew University was never pillaged by the Germans in France and thus did not meet the criteria for attributions, its request was ultimately denied.[27] As in the art restitutions, a strong notion of French patrimony was clearly operative in this agency in a way that was decidedly absent on the American end.

On the other hand, this look at the work of the French Sous-Commission des livres forces us in certain ways to nuance our picture of so-called republican Franco-Judaism. In the end, this authority managed a difficult achievement, helping a number of Jewish cultural institutions to begin to rebuild. The Alliance israélite universelle would serve as an important resource for future Jewish scholarship, and the école rabbinique would be able to rebuild the rabbinate. More importantly, the book restitution authority relegitimated Jewish institutions— particularly the Alliance—by making them partners of the state. This does not seem to fit our caricature of republican Franco-Judaism.

And yet, perhaps it should. If we keep in mind that nineteenth-century Franco-Judaism had always legitimated the Jewish institutions (such as the Alliance and the Consistory) by placing them in a sort of partnership with the state, even as it officially ignored the Jewishness of individuals, perhaps this was indeed a return to a traditional model of Franco-Judaism.

NOTES

1. Maud Mandel, *In the Aftermath of Genocide: Armenians and Jews in Twentieth-Century France* (Durham, NC: Duke University Press, 2003), 83. Emphasis mine.

2. David Weinberg, "The Reconstruction of the French Jewish Community after World War II," paper presented at the Sixth Yad Vashem International Congress, She'erit Hapletah, 1944–48: Rehabilitation and Political Struggle (Jerusalem: Yad Vashem, 1990), 171.

3. See Mandel, *Aftermath of Genocide*, chap. 2.

4. See Elizabeth Karlsgodt, *Defending National Treasures* (Stanford, CA: Stanford University Press, 2011).

5. Numbers are estimates from Martine Poulain, *Livres pillés, lectures surveillées: Les bibliothèques françaises sous l'occupation* (Paris: Gallimard, 2008), 419.

6. Nicholas Reymes, "Le pillage des bibliothèques appartenant à des juifs pendant l'occupation: Les livres dans la tourmente," *Revue de l'Histoire de la Shoah: Le Monde juif* 168 (2000): 31–56.

7. On which libraries were looted, see Poulain, *Livres pillés*, chap. 1; on archival looting, see Sophie Coeuré, *La mémoire spoliée: Les archives des français, butin de guerre nazi puis soviétique* (Paris: Payot, 2007).

8. See Jean-Claude Kuperminc, "The Return of Looted French Archives," in *Returned from Russia: Nazi Archival Plunder in Western Europe and Recent Restitution Issues*, ed. Patricia Kennedy Grimsted, F. J. Hoogewoud, and Eric Ketelaar (Builth Wells, UK: Institute for Art and Law, 2007), 138–39.

9. See Michael Kurtz, *America and the Return of Nazi Contraband: The Recovery of Europe's Cultural Treasures* (New York: Cambridge University Press, 2006), and Lynn H. Nicholas, *The Rape of Europa: The Fate of Europe's Treasures in the Third Reich and the Second World War* (New York: Vintage, 1994).

10. See Robert Waite, "Returning Jewish Cultural Property: The Handling of Books Looted by the Nazis in the American Zone of Occupation, 1945–1952," *Libraries and Culture* 37, no. 3 (2002): 213–18.

11. See Dana Herman, "Hashavat Avedah: A History of Jewish Cultural Reconstruction, Inc." (PhD thesis, McGill University, 2008).

12. Ibid., and Kurtz, *America and the Return of Nazi Contraband*, chaps. 7 and 8.

13. Karlsgodt, *Defending National Treasures*, 350n55.

14. Reymes, "Le pillage," 47.

15. Jenny Delsaux, *La Sous-Commission des livres à la Récupération artistique, 1944–1950* (Ruoms: Ancienne cure Balazue, 1976).

16. Ibid., 5–6. Story also told in the archives of the Sous-Commission des livres itself, held at the Archives nationales (Paris) (hereafter AN), F 17/17977.

17. See Delsaux, *Sous-Commission*, and Reymes, "Le pillage." Attributions to Jewish institutions can be found in AN F17/17981.

18. His term was actually "entraide," referring more to what public social service agencies provide, rather than private organizations or individuals.

19. Reymes, "Le pillage," 54.

20. Delsaux, *Sous-Commission*.

21. Folder "Mission Liber," in AN F/17/17980.

22. Delsaux, *Sous-Commission*, 16.

23. From Kuperminc, "Return," 142.

24. Letter from Edmond-Maurice Lévy to the Sous-Commission des livres, November 26, 1945, in AN F17/17977.

25. Letter to Jenny Delsaux from Sam. Katz, November 17, 1947, in AN F17/17992.

26. Letter to Jenny Delsaux from Mme. Marie Lahy-Hollebeque, October 13, 1948, in AN F17/17992.

27. Request of May 12, 1950, from Dr. Baruk, of the faculté de médecine in Paris, in AN F17/17992.

5

Lost Children and Lost Childhoods

Memory in Post-Holocaust France

DANIELLA DORON

In the wake of World War II, politicians and parents alike proclaimed that they had just endured "a war against children." In the war's aftermath, the consequences of Nazi violence, Allied air bombings, and family separations were most commonly presented in terms of the suffering endured by Europe's youngest citizens.[1] While this concern for children was genuine and eminently reasonable, it also served a political agenda. This chapter therefore traces how the symbol of the child victim aggravated a case of formidable historical amnesia among postwar Europeans who preferred to divert attention from guilt and complicity toward the far more comfortable subject of victimhood.[2] With their own innocence and suffering at center stage, Europeans in 1945 seemed transfixed by the fate of their youth. Children's raw suffering exposed the indiscriminate cruelty of the Nazis, and the category of victim that they inhabited cast a long shadow to include entire families that had been torn asunder by the war. For these reasons nations across the Continent clamored for victim status by harnessing the image of the child victim as a metaphor for all they had suffered and endured. The chapter shows how Europeans thus found themselves not united by their wartime experiences, but still at odds and building competing hierarchies of victimhood with their own children reigning at the top.

France was not immune from the tendency to harness the forceful symbol of the child war victim to justify nationalist aspirations and articulate nascent wartime memories in the reconfigured postwar European politics. However, invocations of children's suffering unleashed a conflict in immediate post-Liberation France about the historical significance of the war against children for French memory and national identity. After a particularly divisive war, the newly resurrected French Republic, then under the leadership of General Charles de Gaulle, sought to shape emerging memories of the occupation into a shared narrative of wartime suffering, heroic resistance, and unwavering republicanism that could imaginatively embrace all French people.[3] In this atmosphere of healing and national reunification, Jews were encouraged to remain silent about the genocidal nature of their losses.[4] But to instantly accept the Provisional Government's position that nearly all had stood united in (Gaullist) resistance would have required an impressive case of "amnesia," as historian Megan Koreman has noted in relation to regional perspectives on the war in France.[5] The harsh truth was that for those who collaborated with the Nazis life was sweet, whereas for those who lay on the wrong side of the national community life was exceedingly bitter. For postgenocide Jews, as this chapter will demonstrate, no other historical fact more forcefully conveyed the genocidal plans of the Nazis and the ahistorical nature of French claims to equal victimhood than the systematic murder of their children.

Yet the history of the evolution of Holocaust memory in France (and elsewhere) has been framed in terms of silence.[6] In this common historical narrative, French Jews accepted the terms of this emerging wartime memory, burying their recollections of persecution and their distinct collective needs in a desperate attempt to return to a normal life as quickly and as inconspicuously as possible. Though memory of the war was still a raw and fraught subject, scholars have argued that neither French Jews nor non-Jews recognized the Jewish experience as constituting genocide. Both groups fiercely adhered to the republican paradigm and considered their differing wartime experiences as "quantitative but not qualitative."[7] With scant attention paid to the immediate postwar era, most scholars have maintained that it was only in the 1960s that Holocaust memory emerged on the French national and international stage. By focusing on the liminal postwar period and by writing the history of childhood into postwar French history, this chapter challenges the assumptions underlying this narrative. Far from acquiescing to the universalizing force of the French state, French Jewry mobilized around the cause of lost children and lost childhoods with particular vigor. Youth functioned as forceful and protean symbols of loss: their innocent deaths highlighted the cruel and specific nature of genocide, while fears about their baptism by Christian rescuers served as a metaphor for Nazi attempts to stamp out Jewish life in Europe.

In these attempts to launch an early conversation about the Holocaust, the symbol of the Jewish child victim represented a seemingly safe entry point. For one, the subject of children's victimhood emerged as a common theme in postwar European discussions about national victimhood under the Nazis, and thus French Jews were simply joining a larger European conversation. Furthermore, as Mark Anderson aptly notes, the trope of child victim facilitates a certain "easy empathy" with Holocaust victims that enables the public to avoid confronting, as Anderson puts it, the "rougher edges" of the millions of other Holocaust victims: eastern European Hasidim, Zionists, or Jewish bankers. Jewish children operated as a convenient synecdoche for the murder of 6 million Jews.[8] But even if the child victim seemed an obvious metaphor for the Holocaust, this chapter will trace how it nonetheless proved frustratingly problematic and slippery. The danger lay in the fact that the image of the Jewish child victim was vulnerable to being sacralized, depoliticized, or universalized by competing interest groups. Thus, even as some French Jews focused on the child victim to signify the singularity of the Jewish experience, French republicans could employ that very symbol to universalize the Holocaust, and French Catholics could harness it to advance Christian themes of sacrifice and redemption. The fierce resistance of the French state and society to alternative memories of the war helps explain why these early efforts at articulating a memory of the Jewish genocide were eventually suppressed, only to be unearthed again in later decades, the era that putatively gave birth to Holocaust memory.

"The Race for the Children"

The often-invoked "war against children" was not mere hyperbole. Postwar Europeans recognized a fact that historians have recently begun to document—children were part of Nazi geopolitics. World War II, in some senses, represented both a war *for* and a war *against* children: those who were damned stood outside the Nazi racial order, while those who were saved lay at its center. The Nazis instituted a series of programs in an attempt to shelter German "Aryan" children from the war's violence: they prioritized supplementing food rations, hesitated about separating families in compulsory evacuation schemes, and enlisted "Aryan" Polish, Czech, and Norwegian children into the Lebensborn program, uprooting them from their families and nations of origin to reside safely within the Reich.[9] However, those outside the national community—such as Jewish, Roma, and Sinti, and handicapped children—were ruthlessly hunted down and systematically murdered in an attempt to racially purify the Volksgemeinschaft.[10] Wartime nation-states and organizations adjusted their policies accordingly, depending on where their children stood in the Nazi racial hierarchy. Resistance and Jewish agencies attempted to shelter Jewish youth from the Nazi onslaught by hiding them with Christian families and religious institutions across the Continent. These efforts saved thousands of children from probable death, but also meant that many Jewish youth were raised in ignorance about their families and communities of origin.[11] Jewish children were not the only ones denationalized and orphaned by the war. As Europeans attempted to flee the aerial bombings and the shifting front lines, thousands of children found themselves uprooted from their homes and severed from their families. Thus, at the war's end, no matter their original place on the Nazi racial hierarchy, millions of European children found themselves rendered parentless and homeless.[12]

The moment that official military hostilities ceased, European nations, child welfare organizations, and parents scrambled to reclaim their "lost children." These efforts were born of the genuine desire to ameliorate the plight of their youngest citizens but also of the perceived need to reconstitute national communities in the wake of Nazi imperialism.[13] Among Jewish circles, lost children likewise governed the policies of Jewish agencies and fueled the imagination of Holocaust survivors. Soon after the war, international Jewish agencies launched into the task of locating traces of their own "lost children": youth who had been hidden with non-Jewish families throughout the theater of war, sometimes in abusive and sometimes in loving circumstances.[14] Though grateful for the heroism displayed by countless individuals who had sheltered and saved these children, even at risk to their own lives, Jewish agencies feared the influence of Christianity on Europe's youngest Jewish survivors. The possibility that, having just been saved from Hitler, the children might now be lost to Catholicism seemed too cruel an irony to passively bear. Reflecting the intense concern of international Jewry, the Zionist Jewish agency the World Jewish Congress (WJC) observed that the "wish to put a stop" to the children's exposure to Christianity propelled this "race for the children."[15] Another activist echoed sentiments shared throughout Europe when he asserted that the "future of the Jewish race" depended upon pursuing a "war without mercy against converters" of Jewish youth.[16]

In France, the sheer lack of information about the whereabouts of the "lost children" fed popular anxiety. By current estimates, 30,000 Jewish children were living in France after the war, approximately a third of whom had been hidden with Christian institutions or individuals during the occupation.[17] French Jewish organizations simply did not know where many of these children had been hidden or if their parents had survived to reclaim them. French Jewish agencies estimated the number of "lost children" at 3,000. Outside France, estimates varied wildly: the WJC put the number at about 5,000; American Zionist Jews working for the American Jewish Congress lamented that 20,000 youth could be lost to Christianity; Israeli agents noted that Christian families housed 1,500 children, but feared that the number could be in the thousands; and British Jewish organizations speculated that 750 children still resided with non-Jews.[18] Historians can never accurately estimate the number of children, but they speculate that these cases were probably quite rare.[19]

Ignorance about numbers did not deter French Jews from their mission. One rabbi organized a virtual one-man operation, sending 36,000 circulars to village mayors in search of French Jewish orphans.[20] When his efforts failed, the American Joint Distribution Committee (an American Jewish relief and rehabilitation agency) began to seek more efficient means to locate these youths, and in May 1945, in a rare moment of Jewish communal collaboration, eleven Jewish child welfare organizations came together to establish the Comité supérieur de l'enfance juive (High Committee on Jewish Children). Though originally set up as a Jewish liaison with the French public, in 1948 it began to search for French Jewish orphans through an "investigative commission" (*commission de dépistage*) composed of three social workers, a lawyer, and young adults hired to spend their vacations locating Jewish children.[21] Between July 1948 and March 1949, the investigators traversed the countryside, visiting seventy-eight departments, examining thousands of lists of displaced children, and finding fifty-nine "certain"—as well as twenty-four questionable—cases of French Jewish children living in non-Jewish settings.[22] That for more than three years after the Liberation Jewish agencies continued to pursue the search for orphans illustrates the perceived urgency of the matter.

The Jewish press did nothing to quell the hysteria. In 1945, the Jewish Communist journal *Droit et Liberté* accused French foster mothers—in its words, "professional nannies"—of child abuse.[23] As late as 1950 the Yiddish daily *Der Tog* claimed that French peasants had enslaved 300 Jewish children in the French countryside.[24] But though physical conditions remained a concern, the majority of articles invoked the threat of baptism looming over vulnerable and impressionable orphans. Articles across the Jewish political spectrum repeatedly questioned how many "unknown" children, victims of Christian zealotry, remained "lost" to Judaism.[25] Max Loiret, writing for a Jewish Communist journal, proclaimed the detention of Jewish children by Catholic priests and nuns a challenge to "religious freedom."[26] The image of Jewish children being lured into Christianity proved particularly tenacious, still emerging in articles into the late 1940s and 1950s. In 1949, the journalist Paul Giniewski suggested that gaining souls for Catholicism had been the primary motivation for Catholic rescue work. Giniewski proclaimed it only fair that the United Nations devote the same attention that they currently devoted to locating Lebensborn children to finding baptized Jewish children. Surely, in his opinion, the two forms of kidnapping represented equivalent offenses and required commensurate organizational attention.[27]

A certain anticlerical sentiment ran through these discussions as postwar Jews struggled to reclaim surviving Jewish children and resurrect a secular republic. Rumors about lost and baptized children did nothing to calm fears about the state of Jewish demography after the Holocaust. As one Jewish communal leader asserted about reclaiming surviving children, "There can be no compromise on the matter—every Jewish child is needed."[28] At the same time, the fever pitch of anxiety over baptized children actually harkened back to nineteenth-century struggles over clericalism and republicanism in shaping modern France. The mid-nineteenth century, in fact, witnessed a series of sensational "affairs" that involved the kidnapping of Jewish children in the name of Christ. In the Mortara affair of 1858, a Jewish family from the papal state of Bologna permanently lost their son to the pope after their nurse baptized the child during a bout of severe illness. When the Holy See learned that a Jewish child had joined the faith, the pope ordered the abduction of the child so that he might be raised in Catholicism.[29] Following on the heels of the Mortara affair, in 1861 three Jewish girls were forcibly converted to Catholicism and secreted away from their parents in an incident (referred to as the Bluth or Mallet case) that was closely followed by the French reading public.[30] Both of these cases failed to culminate in a satisfactory conclusion—the Mortara boy never reunited with his family, and scholars have claimed that two of the Bluth girls apparently became deranged as a result of their ordeal. More importantly, these incidents scandalized the French Jewish and non-Jewish reading public, leading to the establishment of an international Jewish defense league, the Alliance israélite universelle. In the eyes of nineteenth-century Jewish and non-Jewish republicans, these affairs embodied the threat that the Church posed to patriarchal and familial rights and the republican ideal of secularism. These cases, as well as other scandals over forced claustration and religious seduction of women, fed anticlerical sentiments and eventually resulted in efforts to cement *laïcité* as an inviolable ideal of the French Republic.[31] Thus, when a century later fears about the baptism of Jewish children reemerged on the French national stage, Fourth Republic citizens of all faiths were actually participating in a century-long French tradition of considering the Roman Catholic Church as a formidable threat to patriarchy, the family, and the secular Republic.

Rumors about Jewish children languishing in convents and enslaved in the countryside found a receptive audience among segments of the disconcerted French Jewish public. For these individuals, the legacy of losing 75,000 individuals to the Nazis meant that every surviving Jewish child needed to be raised within the Jewish community. Moussa Abadi, a social worker for Oeuvre des secours aux enfants (Children's Relief Agency, or OSE), commented that at the Liberation "we all trembled" at the idea that social workers and families would encounter formidable resistance retrieving the children they had labored to save.[32] In later years, by then convinced of the hyperbolic nature of rumors about baptism, Abadi wrote with irritation of being constantly bombarded by Jews anxious about the well-being of orphans.[33] Arthur Greenleigh of the American Joint Distribution Committee's Paris branch sent letters to American and French Jews assuring them that finding Jewish children—and preserving them for the faith—remained the Joint's "A-1 priority."[34] As far away as the United States, family members wrote to the New York Yiddish language daily *The Forward* asking for legal advice. H.Z., for instance, complained in 1945 in the daily's "Bintel Brief" section of his "heartache" that his nephew had been converted to Christianity. Assuming that the "German beasts" had murdered the rest of his family, H.Z. asked for legal counsel on how to "rescue at least this one child for our people."[35] Saving "our people"—and in particular "our children"— thus figured as an imperative for both ordinary French Jews and French Jewish agencies as they worked toward the intertwined goals of reasserting French Jewish life and memory in the aftermath of the Holocaust.

Lost Children and Holocaust Memory

In addition to asserting Jewish communal continuity in the present, a commemorative impulse also factored as a consideration in Jewish associational policies. In particular, a well-intentioned desire to remain faithful to the memory of the dead largely propelled the "race for the children," despite the anguish it created among families and the political confrontations that inevitably erupted with governmental and ecclesiastical officials. Memoirs written by individuals actively engaged in the work of preserving Jewish children for the Jewish community reveal the motivations driving their efforts. Former general director of the OSE, Georges Garel, for instance, recalled that "the parents had perished because they were Jews" and, as such, he and his colleagues felt obligated to remain faithful to the memories of their lives and deaths.[36] In this context, French Jewish agencies and individuals typically described the effort to gather all surviving children Jewish under Jewish organizational auspices as a resounding refutation of Nazi efforts to put an end to Jewish life in Europe. In turn, any efforts that impeded this goal, from baptism to hiding Jewish children from Jewish agencies, were denounced as a synecdoche for Nazi genocide. Claude Kelman's speech at the first post-Liberation meeting of the Fédération des sociétés juives de France (Federation of Jewish Societies of France, FSJF) thus called for vengeance: the children, he asserted, "constitute our hope for survival, they are our avengers. They assure the continuity [*pérennité*] of Judaism so that the last vestiges of the ideology of their parents' barbarous murderers will be effaced."[37] In the following years, French Jews repeatedly returned to the disconcerting similarities between Nazi efforts at exter-mination and baptism's threat to Jewish regeneration. In 1949, in a sermon on Yom Kippur—Judaism's most solemn occasion of atonement and memory—Chief Rabbi Jacob Kaplan raised the indelible link between Holocaust memory and lost children. Published in the press and in book formats, the sermon exhorted congregants to ensure the religious edu-cation of their own children and reminded them of the frustratingly persistent problem of baptized youth: "Where are they? How many are there? We cannot know. What a tragedy this represents! . . . Nazism snatched them from their parents and now converters don't hesitate to complete the work of persecution—they have turned them away from the religion of Israel." Kaplan and other communal leaders were not alone in remaining convinced that the baptism of Jewish children was akin to persecution.[38] Ordinary individuals also had the deportations on their minds as they followed custody disputes over orphaned and baptized Jewish youth in the pages of the French press. The Finaly affair of 1953 illuminates how memory of the Nazi genocide lingered in the conscious-ness of those not part of the Jewish communal leadership. In this well-publicized case, a French woman, Madame Brun, sheltered two young Jewish boys, Robert and Gérald Finaly, during the occupation. When their relatives living abroad began clamoring for their custody after the war, Brun had the boys baptized and kidnapped to Spain. Unlike earlier, largely speculative discussions, this case, which was closely fol-lowed in the pages of the French press, made the issue of forced baptism concrete and public.

For those French Jews observing another flagrant injustice in 1953, Rabbi Kaplan's 1949 warning that conversion amounted to persecution by another means suddenly seemed prescient. One woman wrote to Kaplan that the children's ordeal reminded her of "*Hitler*-deportation, illegal detention."[39] The Haut Rhin Consistoire declared the Finaly affair an offense not only to the Jewish parents and to their surviving relatives but also to "the memory of innocent dead martyrs for their faith."[40] Rabbi Jaïs (leader of the French Jewish liberal synagogue) and another rabbi equated the Church's subterfuge to genocide: "With this action, the church has evidently only one aim . . . just like Hitlerism, although by different means, the disappearance of Judaism."[41] These statements offer a window into how ordinary individuals internalized a discourse emanating from the highest communal echelons. The Finaly affair foregrounded the fragility of law and order in postwar France and raised troubling questions that cut to the core of the Republic. It is for this reason that French journalists and commentators commonly invoked the Dreyfus affair, the Declaration of the Rights of Man, and the perils of clerical fanaticism in their heated discussions about the safety of the two young boys. Many French Jews were equally passionate about the Finaly case and likewise understood it as an affront to the Republic. However, in their private and public discussions they additionally mentioned— along with Hitler—the faith and deaths of the deceased parents, and the Mortara affair. To those French Jews with the persecutions on their mind, the kidnapping and baptism of Jewish orphans smelled of previous attempts to end Jewish life in Europe and represented yet another blow to the memory of the dead.

Despite the fever pitch of anxiety over lost children, as exemplified by the Finaly affair, organized searches for traces of their whereabouts unearthed far less than a hundred children. In the meantime, rumors about the fate of Jewish lost and baptized children enjoyed an afterlife in the Jewish communal imagination. But even once children were located and "redeemed" for the French Jewish community, the matter of the formerly hidden failed to disappear. Rather, Jewish communal leaders and child welfare organizations labored to keep the issue of Jewish children in the spotlight through public programs, articles, radio broadcasts, and a wide range of mass media appeals. The matter was indeed urgent, as Jewish child welfare agencies depended on public support to fund their children's homes and other child welfare programs. But Jewish child welfare agencies faced a challenging economic climate in the postwar years—after years of persecution and expropriation, only a minority of French Jews enjoyed sufficient discretionary funds to donate to charitable causes. And yet Jewish activists pressed on, invoking the Jewish genocide as cause for popular participation in postwar child welfare work. In short, they positioned support of surviving orphaned children as an act of commemoration. The annual calendar published by the Jewish Communist agency the Commission centrale de l'enfance (Central Commission for Children, CCE), with its images of blue-eyed little girls and healthy adolescents, illustrates alternative—indeed pragmatic— forms of commemoration. The CCE's 1947 calendar departed from the implicit agenda of most calendars: marking the year to come. Rather than noting the French national or Jewish religious holidays of 1947, it instead commemorated the stages of persecution and deportation of French Jews. The Vel' d'Hiv *rafle* of 1942 received particular attention: on July 16, the fifth anniversary of the arrests of nearly 13,000 Parisian Jews, the calendar proclaimed, "We Remember July 16th 1942." The calendar provided explanations for the other significant dates, but the CCE assumed that all would recall the first massive arrests of Parisian Jews.[42] A collective "We Remember" sufficed.

In the immediate wake of the Liberation, the interim chief rabbi, Jacob Kaplan, took to the airwaves to urge French Jews to memorialize the dead by supporting their offspring. Already in October 1945 Kaplan drew upon his considerable communal authority to persuade French Jews to come to the aid of the community's youngest grief-stricken survivors. Kaplan used his weekly radio program to exhort the now safe "brothers and sisters of Israel" to fulfill the "important work that falls upon you. On us, on you, to raise them, to assure their future, to give them the religious education . . . that their parents, gone today, had dreamed for them."[43] The themes of Jewish children, religious education, and memory in fact figured as a leitmotif in Kaplan's sermons and radio broadcasts in succeeding years. At the FSJF annual conference in 1947, Kaplan again addressed the numerous proposals circulating in French Jewish circles regarding how best to "perpetuate the memory" of the dead. Though he conceded that planting trees in Palestine or constructing a monument in France effectively memorialized "our martyrs," he suggested a more enduring memorial: "our children." Met with applause, Kaplan informed his audience that "the real perpetuation of our martyrs will be that which we would ensure for ourselves, our children, [and] our grandchildren. . . . We will be inspired by the Judaism for which they have suffered and for which they have died."[44] The orphans of France seemed a worthier site of commemoration than the distant forests of Israel.

Kaplan was not alone in linking memory of the dead to collective responsibility for the living. In calling on surviving Jews to parent parentless youth, Jewish agencies typically framed the task as a debt that the "survivors of the massacre" owed to the fallen.[45] Jewish organizations regularly positioned potential donors as the lucky "survivors" of the "Nazi deluge" or the "massacre." As one Oeuvre de protection de l'enfance juive

(OPEJ) brochure explicitly suggested, "It is for them that we have, by miracle, survived . . . we must pay an offering to the memory of our dearly departed."[46] In 1946 the French Jewish child welfare organization La Colonie scolaire attempted to link the tangible bodies of Jewish orphans to the intangible memory of the recent dead. Appealing to French Jewry's noblesse, the organization suggested that "no monument" could better "perpetuate" the memory of the dead than homes for the living. In exchange for a few hundred francs, La Colonie scolaire promised to engrave an orphan's bed with the name of the contributor's "dearly departed."[47] Reminding potential sponsors that "the future of their children is the responsibility of the collective survivors of the massacre," the FSJF suggested that they had the power to "replace the [children's] parents."[48] Jewish activists thus encouraged Jews in France to ameliorate the plight of orphans: the rabbinate beseeched French Jews to temporarily house orphaned youth,[49] the familialist organization Karen Hatoldoth urged community members to consider adoption, and nearly all child welfare organizations established sponsorship programs. These injunctions inspired one poet to pen an ode, "Their Children? Our Children!"[50]

The emotional resonance of the obligation to the dead—or in the words of one article, "the sacred work of all Jewish women towards our martyrs"—did not fall on deaf ears.[51] In the first years following the war, the Jewish press published impressive lists of donations and urged others to participate in the cause. Local chapters of Jewish organizations and concerned individuals held fund-raising galas and concerts; youth groups organized collection drives and bought gifts; and labor unions visited the orphanages bearing presents and promises of future contributions.[52] This campaign was so successful that certain Jews in France began to celebrate life cycle events with contributions to orphanages that commemorated the genocide.[53] One couple celebrated the baptism of their child by making a donation to Jewish orphans; in all likelihood, this baptismal celebration was not exactly what Jewish communal leaders had envisioned.[54] Upon learning from his parents of the fate of orphaned Jews, Lucienne Nadzeija in 1946 offered his saved allowance of 300 francs.[55] That same year, the *amicale* (association) of the Ebensee Camp deportees organized a banquet that raised 5,000 francs for Jewish children's homes. In memory of her deceased husband, Mrs. Rosenthal of Valenciennes collected 2,000 francs at a meeting held in her home in 1947 for Jewish orphans. Robert Bruder—a self-described "*déporté* of Auschwitz and Mauthausen"—agreed to donate 200 francs per month as a contribution to the "well-being and happiness of the children of these sad coreligionists and departed comrades."[56] Many ordinary French Jews explicitly tied their financial contributions to the memory of their dead. One woman, for example, cited "the memory of my husband" as the catalyst for her participation in La Colonie scolaire's sponsorship program; another woman drew upon her "spirit of recognition" at having survived with her entire family as cause for her willingness to host an orphaned child during the summer holidays.[57]

The War against Children

Emotional pleas to raise funds for Jewish orphans positioned children as the inheritors of a nearly destroyed past. But attention to Jewish children focused not just on those possibly "lost" to the Jewish community through baptism, but also on those youth forever lost to their families and to French Jewry through Nazism. The murder of their innocent children remained a raw and repeatedly invoked subject among French Jews still reeling from the scale of their personal and collective losses. In the years following the war, French Jewish agencies and the Jewish press produced an endless homage to the 11,000 young French Jews murdered by the Nazis. These initiatives embodied in striking terms the distinctive experiences of Hitler's youngest victims, and thus attempted to disabuse non-Jews of the idea that all of France's citizens had endured the same lot under the Nazis.

Immediately after the war in 1945, journalist, former resister, and child advocate Jacqueline Mesnil-Amar began ruminating on the role of Jewish child war victims in the French experience of war and occupation. On first hearing de Gaulle's now nearly canonical 1945 "not a tear will be forgotten" speech, Mesnil-Amar took offense at the general's attempt to insist that the dead had been sacrificed in defense of republicanism. His celebration of the war dead led her to accuse the general of insensitivity in the face of arbitrary suffering: "*All the children* . . . so many children, massacred because they couldn't work, thrown in the ovens with their mothers because they didn't want to leave them? . . . All this wasn't in vain? Is there some sense in such suffering?"[58] This formerly assimilated and wealthy French Jew now felt alienated from the nation precisely at its moment of national glory.[59] Evidence suggests that others harbored similar sentiments, even if they did not publicly voice their feelings in the Jewish press. One French Jewish adolescent directed her indignation at Rabbi Jacob Kaplan after hearing his assertion that the persecutions had fortified Judaism. Myriam Jurovics wrote to Kaplan, "Our heroes, our saints have uselessly died—our ordeal has been in vain."[60] Both Mesnil-Amar and Jurovics failed to find reason and redemption in senseless murder.

Mesnil-Amar's postwar essays represent rare introspective ruminations on the significance for French Jews of the genocide of children, but they also perhaps signal a disjuncture between private sentiments and public pronouncements. Whereas individuals like Mesnil-Amar and others may have interpreted the victims' suffering as futile, Jewish agencies typically presented children's experiences in a linear narrative that began with suffering under the Nazis and culminated in redemption under the restored Republic. The 1949 public exhibit of Jewish children's artwork held at Paris's Musée pédagogique and organized by the CCE typifies efforts to represent the healing powers of French national identity for orphaned and formerly denationalized youth.[61] The 1949 French event was not the first of its kind to feature children's drawings to visualize national martyrdom and celebrate collective rejuvenation. Earlier, in October 1945, the Berlin suburb of Reinickendorm had held a similar exhibit, and the next year the Polish magazine *Przekój* published children's drawings that depicted the violence of total war experienced by Polish children.[62] The teenage Holocaust survivor Ruth Kluger, who would later become a noted literary scholar, had her early postwar poems about Auschwitz first published in a regional German newspaper; they then circulated (without her consent) in several postwar German publications.[63] Standing in stark contrast to these Polish and German publications that featured raw wartime events, the 1949 French exhibit reflected upon the startling transformation of Jewish children from child victims to carefree children. In the triumphant language of one CCE bulletin, the crisp colors of the artwork from 1948 heralded the children's "return to life."[64] In conveying this important message, the exhibition's organizers aspired to extend beyond the relatively insulated Jewish or

Communist circles to the French public at large to enlighten them on the emotional pain inflicted upon Jewish youth by the Nazis. If children's disturbing etchings did not accomplish this task, these exhibits also found other forums to render visual and public the inner lives of Jewish youth. For instance, one 1950 exhibit was kicked off with a conference presided over by two well-regarded French child psychologists. All together, claimed the CCE, 5,000 individuals eventually visited the event.[65] The themes of survival and memory could not have been more transparent: the 1949 exhibit capped its inaugural conference with a 1946 film about Jewish orphans entitled *We Will Continue.*[66]

By publicly invoking the symbol of the Jewish child war victim, Jewish agencies and individuals joined in the broader national effort to reconcile the ideal of French republicanism with the brutal reality of Vichy. Despite a range of interpretations about French culpability and the fate of Jews in France, the majority of French Jewish agencies publicly blamed the persecution they had suffered squarely on the German Nazis. In evading a discussion about Vichy, they avoided a serious reconsideration of the promises of equality and safety that French republicanism ostensibly offered. The majority of French Jewish agencies in fact sought to reaffirm their place in France and to create a language for healing between Jews and non-Jews. Thus, as the French state and segments of society sought to buoy French republicanism and nationalism after a demoralizing occupation and collaboration, Jews in France did the same. They did not, however, buy into the Gaullist myth that all French citizens equally suffered and died.

At the very moment when some Jewish organizations and individuals harnessed the specificity of the Jewish experience to fortify national commitment, so too did French journals. The daily Resistance journal *Libération* published a two-week series detailing the persecution of young Jews, and the regional paper *Nice Matin* ran a series on the rescue and experiences of Jewish youth entitled "Investigation on Martyred Jewish Children."[67] Through these narratives, the French nation as a whole embodied the noblest sentiments of republicanism through its experience of the suffering and saving of Jewish youth. The arrival in France of half of "the Buchenwald Boys," the 1,000 Jewish teenagers discovered when the camp was liberated, thus sparked extensive reporting and intense public interest. In this well-publicized case, the French press bemoaned the collective and individual fate of children robbed not only of a family, a past, and a nation, but whose unimaginably horrific childhoods symbolized ultimate victimhood and the restorative powers of nationalism.[68]

The Buchenwald Boys' dramatic pasts and their embrace of the birthplace of the Declaration of the Rights of Man elicited popular interest among the French, Jews and non-Jews alike.[69] Publications ranging from the French national *Le Monde* and the regional *Nice Matin* to the small Jewish circular *Bulletin des Services israélite et déporté* reported on—even heralded—the children's excited arrival in France, their rendition of "The Marseillaise" on the train across Germany, and their awe at the City of Lights. In these narratives, the children's suffering and their admittance into France signified the nation's long-awaited return to liberal political values. As one article asked on V-E Day: "Where are the children? In a happier time, this question would come to mothers. . . . Today, it is the entire nation that takes up this question with anguish."[70]

Despite this sense of republican national duty, reporting on the Buchenwald Boys within the French press reflected the limits of republican universalism in the first days of the Fourth Republic. Even reputable journals mistakenly reported that the boys were of French origin, thereby appropriating the children as symbols of the nation and ensuring readers' empathy. *Ce Soir* reported that the Americans had discovered amid the atrocious conditions of the camps a thousand "kids . . . for the most part of our origin," between three and fourteen years old. Confronted with the blatant misery of the children, *Ce Soir* complained, the French government had still not decided whether to repatriate these "young martyrs."[71] In reality, the teenagers originated almost exclusively from eastern Europe, and were of largely Orthodox Jewish backgrounds. On the one hand, such sentiments might seem to reflect the best tradition of republican liberalism. Articles that appropriated the Buchenwald Boys as symbols of the French nation or proclaimed that the "entire nation took up the question [of Jewish children] with anguish" implied that the murder of Jewish children deeply affected all French citizens.[72] On the other hand, by interpreting their persecution as a defense of French republicanism, such reports also implicitly robbed the Holocaust of Jewish specificity. This type of rhetoric placed yet another hurdle in front of Jews as they struggled to disentangle Jewish from non-Jewish wartime suffering. As postwar Jews attempted to describe their particular "martyrdom," they faced either the universalization of their experiences or deaf ears.

Evidence suggests that this process of suppression and denial that we can document on an organizational level was likewise experienced by ordinary French Jews as they struggled to organize their memories of suffering and loss. Serge Knabel, a child victim himself, recalled how he learned to bury his memories of extermination upon his liberation from Auschwitz at the tender age of seventeen. Once safely back in Paris, as the images of Auschwitz leaked to the pages of the French press, friends and acquaintances asked Knabel to describe the dog-eat-dog world of the camps. At first, still reeling from the violence he had just survived, Knabel was grateful for the opportunity to share his personal suffering and bear witness to the mechanics of Nazi murder. But these queries largely produced awkward exchanges between the young Holocaust survivor and even well-intentioned French citizens: some called him a liar, others expressed genuine confusion, and the majority simply remained silent. These conversations proved frustrating for Knabel, who eventually concluded that the French preferred to shroud themselves in ignorance about the qualitative difference between Jewish extermination and general concentration camps. He attributed their inability to, in his words, "imagine the monstrosity of Hitlerian genocide" to the national mood already besetting postwar France. "When speaking about the policies of the Vichy government during those few years, a lot of people didn't want to talk about it any longer—the page had turned. De Gaulle had saved the honor of France, [and] we must forget what had been done in his absence. I was surprised and hurt by this widespread incomprehension, and I later took refuge in privacy, only responding to the questions that were posed to me with, 'it was very hard.'"[73] Knabel's testimony tellingly and poignantly reveals how a child victim himself—not just a symbol of a child victim—learned to suppress his own anguish and pain when confronted with an inhospitable public.

French Jews largely embraced this national attempt to rehabilitate French republicanism, if not the concomitant "inability to imagine the monstrosity of Hitlerian genocide," as Knabel phrased it. The friction created between clashing perspectives on the Nazi occupation is evidenced by the fact that books published in the 1940s that denied the Holocaust found a receptive audience among the French reading public. Maurice Bardèche's *Letters to François Mauriac* and *Nuremberg, or The Promised Land* as well as Paul Rassiner's 1948 *Le passage de la ligne*, an account of his detention in Buchenwald, called into question Jewish claims to specific suffering. Rassiner would later be known as the father of Holocaust denial, but in the 1940s his work found commercial and critical success.[74] These books were not written or read in a vacuum. That they even came into existence suggests they were composed in reaction to Jewish efforts to voice particular victimhood. It is thereby no surprise that Jews eventually buried their memories in the immediate postwar era, only to recover them in later decades. Yet, as Renée Poznanski notes in her study about the wartime policies of the Jewish elite, historians "confuse the outcome with the process" when they find a glaring absence of Holocaust memory in the aftermath of the Shoah in France.[75] A close analysis of postwar Jewish sources reveals a flourishing Holocaust memory—as well as formidable opposition from the state and partial resistance from segments of French society. The failure to arrive at a consensus about the meaning of children's victimization speaks to how deeply ideas about past suffering and the future of French Jewry were contested in postwar France, as Jews and non-Jews laid claim to shifting narratives of loss.

The Week of the Martyred Jewish Child

The Week of the Martyred Jewish Child—initially born of the desire to cement unity—ironically reveals how wartime memory worked to divide French Jews and non-Jews at the Liberation. First conceived soon after the Liberation by Jewish organizations and scheduled for October 1945, the event was intended to join the major Jewish child welfare organizations, representatives of the Catholic, Jewish, and Protestant communities, and French bureaucrats to dramatize the particular wartime martyrdom of Jewish children, as well as their postwar needs. In regard to the latter, the event aimed to raise 20 million francs for the rapidly depleting coffers of Jewish child welfare agencies. The organizers thus planned a week of coordinated events for publicizing the martyrdom of Jewish children: a public exhibit at the Palais de Chaillot (one of Paris's largest theaters), posters throughout France, galas, clothing and fund-raising drives in smaller French cities, and a brochure dramatizing the "odious" treatment of Jewish children in the concentration camps and the "miracle" of having saved a portion of them from the Nazis.[76]

The Week of the Martyred Jewish Child quickly faltered. Plans had progressed and significant sums of money had been invested when the Comité national de l'enfance (National Committee on Children, referred to here as the Comité national), a group charged with the care and needs of *all* French children, decided to stage its own week in February 1946 on behalf of child war victims.[77] The occasionally vicious and always ideological debates surrounding the Week of the Child Victims of War and Nazism versus the Week of the Martyred Jewish Child pivoted around the memory of the persecutions, the specificity of the Jewish experience, and the proper role of Jews within the nation.

The dispute first erupted when the Comité national made overtures to the Jewish agencies involved in the earlier effort.[78] Proclaiming it impossible to "disassociate Jewish youth from French youth," the Comité national invited the Jewish organizations to join its national week and thereby align the experiences of Jewish children with those of all young victims.[79] The Jewish Communist organization the Union des juifs pour la résistance et l'entraide (Union of Jews for Resistance and Mutual Aid, UJRE) seized this opportunity to display solidarity with all French youth (and by extension the entire French nation) and jumped ship. Soon thereafter, stinging ripostes and recriminatory letters bounced back and forth between the once united but now divided Jewish organizations. According to UJRE leader Joseph Minc, the obstinacy of the Zionist FSJF in persisting with the Jewish week represented "sectarian politics" at its very worst.[80] The Zionists countered by claiming that the Communists' position merely represented "disguised Jewish resignation," whereas they remained motivated "above all by Jewish unity."[81] The OSE concurred on the pressing need to draw "the world's attention to the fate of Jewish children, their past suffering, miserable present, and uncertain future." Nonetheless, the OSE (on the national level) dropped its participation in the now floundering Week of the Martyred Jewish Child, citing its skepticism that the event would succeed in raising significant sums of money and its fears about inciting anti-Semitism.[82] The worthy cause of Jewish children thus failed to serve as an effective rallying cry, even among Jews.

The prospects for the Week of the Martyred Jewish Child continued to deteriorate throughout the late summer and early fall of 1945. The minister of health, François Billoux, a Communist leader, retracted his support on the grounds that "all French children are equal"; the Jewish representative body the Conseil représentatif des israélites de France (CRIF) refused to publicly arbitrate the internecine conflict; and the Comité national attempted to undermine its competition by distributing a press release outlining the two agencies' ideological differences, and accused the FSJF of callously refusing to show "solidarity" with the "unfortunate children of France."[83] Finally the Jewish Communist UJRE launched a "press campaign" decrying the "racism" that undergirded the Jewish week.[84]

Remarkably, the Week of the Martyred Jewish Child took place, nearly as planned, in the last week of October 1945. Prominent religious leaders, such as Chief Rabbi Jacob Kaplan and the bishop of Nice, Paul Remond, featured the event on their respective weekly radio broadcasts; posters featuring hands outstretched toward waifish, ill-clad, sickly children were plastered throughout France; a gala was held in the Palais de Chaillot; and articles advertised the event in the Jewish press.[85] In addition, evidence suggests that towns and cities throughout France organized their own events in conjunction with the national week. One Jewish man from Lille wrote of the moving religious ceremony he attended in honor of Jewish "martyred children."[86]

Annette Wieviorka has argued that the week highlighted the problems French Jewry encountered in articulating "the specificity of its martyrs. This Week of the Martyred Jewish Child was the only large-scale public event organized by Jewish organizations. For the rest, the community assumed in silence responsibilities that it considered its own vis-à-vis the children."[87] On the one hand, Wieviorka correctly highlights the formidable internal and external obstacles confronting postwar Jews as they attempted to publicly insist upon their distinct memories. The OSE's assumption that neither week would succeed financially and its explicit fear of inciting a resurgence of anti-Semitism reflected the potentially hostile political climate in which French Jews operated.[88] The OSE, for its part, presciently appraised the public mood: although the campaign initially set a goal of 20 million francs, the week ultimately only netted a tenth of that ambitious sum.[89] Moreover, the refusal on the part of François Billoux, the minister of health, and the Comité national to differentiate between Jewish and non-Jewish children reveals the force of myths about universal suffering as a basis for recreating a French national identity. The French Communists, for example, sought to cement their influence in French political life by plotting a careful strategy of integrating rather than alienating broad segments of the French population. In the immediate aftermath of the war, Communist Jews and non-Jews could have legitimately drawn upon their leadership in the French Resistance to justify their dominance in the political leadership of the newly reconfigured French government. Instead, they opted for an alternative strategy. The Communists labored to departicularize French wartime memory, ahistorically casting the French nation as equal participants in their valiant struggle to shake off the Nazi yoke. The perspective of Billoux and the UJRE thus testifies to their deep investment in the universal project and reveals their early efforts to set the ground rules for their emerging wartime memory and rebuilt national identity.

But French Jews did not "remain silent" about lost children and lost childhoods. Jewish leaders visited the highest ecclesiastical officials in the name of Jewish orphans, engaged in public and private custody disputes, and held public exhibits visualizing children's suffering. Furthermore, the advocates of the Week of the Martyred Jewish Child remained doggedly convinced, no matter the objections raised, that the French Jewish experience wholly diverged from that of all other victims. A close analysis of public statements from all the Jewish organizations reveals that— whatever their other disagreements—they concurred on one central issue: Jewish child war victims functioned as compelling symbols to commemorate the genocide and underline its Jewish specificity. The positions put forth by the Communist UJRE, the Zionist FSJF, and individuals associated with the two competing weeks indicate a more nuanced picture than Wieviorka presents. The sometimes warring French Jewish organizations actually did agree on the past, but not on the past's implication for present policies.

The French Jewish agencies behind the Week of the Martyred Jewish Child repeatedly rejected any notion of commensurability between French Jewish and non-Jewish suffering. On October 27, Rabbi Jacob Kaplan took to the airwaves to argue that Jewish children alone had "been killed by persecution and fated for extermination."[90] The Jewish youth journal *Le Réveil des Jeunes* similarly stressed the "horrible suffering" of Jewish youth compared to the violence that touched all Europeans: "In this martyrology, the Jews have taken, alas, a prominent place. Six million of ours are dead . . . in the extermination camps. And among these Jews, children have notably suffered horribly."[91] Equally assured of the singularity of the Jewish experience, the FSJF's journal *Notre Parole* distinguished between French suffering and Jewish extermination: "More than the others, Jewish children have suffered during this war. Not only have they endured the restrictions placed upon the entire population, but they have been targeted for extermination by the Nazis."[92]

French non-Jews, in this emerging landscape of memory, could at once be receptive to narratives that stressed Jewish specificity and at the same time instrumentalized them to pursue other ends. For instance, the day before Rabbi Kaplan's broadcast sermon, the bishop of Nice, Monsignor Paul Remond, took to the airwaves to explore the horrific and specific fate of "Jewish martyred children." Focusing exclusively on Jewish children, the bishop's broadcast chronicled the exterminatory plans of the Nazis and highlighted the singularity of the Jewish experience. But Remond left a certain amount of ambiguity in his parting words, revealing how his position on Jewish martyrdom stood in stark contrast to republican Jewish and non-Jewish interpretations. After explaining how young Jews had met their deaths in the gas chambers, Remond concluded his broadcast by appealing to Christian language and morality: "No place in the world must ever see the return of the bestial crimes committed against Jewish martyred children, or against any other children." In a postwar world recovering from the violence of racism, France's new civilizing mission entailed "sending new apostles . . . that will preach to these pagans justice, kindness, respect for human beings . . . [and] faith in God."[93] Despite his participation in the Week of the Martyred Jewish Child and his recognition of the tragic wartime fates of Jewish children, he ultimately rendered Christian and universal the meaning of Jewish "martyrdom."

French Jews failed to arrive at the same conclusion. Statements by French Jews, in contrast, highlighted the unique experience of Jewish youth and the need to assist them in their postwar recovery. Even the UJRE, so vehemently opposed to the sectarian politics animating the Jewish week, also remained convinced of the unique experience of Jewish youth. Several days after the Week of the Martyred Jewish Child was launched, *Droit et Liberté*—the journal of the Communist UJRE—

rationalized its refusal to participate in an event that seemingly benefited one of its main missions, Jewish child welfare. Its contributor, S. Aronson, grieved for the tragic loss of young life and innocence that war had brought to France, indeed to all of Europe's youth. Yet he singled out one group: "Among all these unhappy children, there is nonetheless a particularly targeted category: Jewish children. They were not only exposed to deprivation like all the other countries' children, but they were marked first of all by the yellow star, then targeted for extermination. The tragedy of Jewish children was immense." Nonetheless, the UJRE appealed to *all* French citizens in helping Jewish youth recover from their traumatic experiences. Despite the uniqueness of the war against Jewish children, their ability to rebound from tragedy depended on the kind of equality that only French democracy delivered. "Nothing" argued Aronson, "would be more destructive to the cause of Jewish children, the Jewish community, and democracy than raising artificial barriers between children of different faiths." Thus, while he sympathized with Jewish children's attachment to the communities "where they belong and from which they confuse their suffering with their first memories," it was universalism that would ensure a future "spirit of concord and fraternity." The UJRE viewed Nazi racism as imposing particularism, whereas French universalism—offering both material aid and a national identity—provided the foundation for equality for all French youth. Among the many messages urging French Jewry to ensure the future of its destitute children, the UJRE's most squarely placed the onus, the "sacred work," on the French nation as a whole.[94]

The Week of the Martyred Jewish Child and its French doppelgänger, the Week of the Child Victim of War and Nazism, emerged as flash points for underlying conflicts among French Jews and between French Jews and non-Jews over the memory of the persecutions. Agreeing on the past, the Jewish child welfare organizations envisioned different paths toward the future. For the Zionist FSJF, its conviction in the unique experience of French Jewish children served to cement communal solidarity. In this spirit, Rabbi Kaplan entreated the "brothers and sisters of Israel" to come to the aid of their less fortunate brethren. Unlike its competitors, the Jewish Communist UJRE, as discussed above, appealed to the French nation as a whole to recognize the specificity of the Jewish past and ensure French Jewish children's equality in the present. In fact, in another planned article the UJRE outlined the high stakes: "*Mommies and Daddies of France will think of the children of the shot and deported. Among these children, they will think particularly of little Jewish children whose martyrdom is unique and without precedent in the history of humanity. In aligning their fate with the children of the entire country and according them this place with all unhappy children, the forces of life and progress will have once again been victorious against the forces of destruction and death.*"[95] The Catholic representative, Monsignor Remond, made some concessions to the singular wartime fate of Jews, but his narrative of Jewish children's suffering brought into focus the violent repercussions of rejecting Christianity and humanity. The French state, as exemplified by Billoux and the Comité national, maintained that the very concept undergirding the Week of the Martyred Jewish Child was anathema to French republicanism. All French citizens were united in their shared suffering and grief.

The debates around the Week of the Martyred Jewish Child illustrate the ease with which Holocaust memory was universalized and the difficulty of articulating its specificity. This cacophony of memories at the Liberation arose from a number of barriers to a unified Holocaust memory. The symbolic ambiguity of the Jewish child war victim only multiplied the interpretive possibilities. In postwar France, ideas about children's suffering proved highly elastic and contested: they could assert the importance of Jewish memory after the Holocaust, French republicanism after Vichy, and Catholicism in the resurrected postwar society. For Jewish agencies in postwar France, the Week of the Martyred Jewish Child promoted the first two goals because its supporters recognized the genocidal nature of Jewish persecution under the Nazis and embraced French national identity under the Fourth Republic. In various public programs, exhibits, and newspaper articles during these years, Jewish children's suffering served as a synecdoche for Nazi genocide, the reassertion of republicanism, and French Jewish communal survival.

France's national mood further inhibited the articulation of a coherent Holocaust memory. The volatile and diverse range of emotions that characterized French society after Vichy hampered acceptance of a wartime memory that implicitly raised questions about France's failure to take responsibility for all of its citizens. In fact, guilt over collaboration and the lingering presence of anti-Semitism could have very well intensified, among segments of the population, a growing resistance to recognizing the Holocaust. Yet, even those well-intentioned toward French Jews displayed deafness to alternative memories of the war. Eager to restore republicanism, many bureaucrats and ordinary French citizens refused to countenance the kinds of racial distinctions they considered antithetical to universalism. They saw the murder of French Jewish children as a cause for mourning, and their rescue as a source of national pride. Anxious to promote French nationalism and republicanism, French public rhetoric instrumentalized the symbol of the suffering Jewish child to foster national pride and loyalty. Paradoxically, the fact that in this atmosphere of inclusion Jews continued to uphold a particularist memory of the war may have heightened opposition among non-Jews to acknowledge the notion of "martyrdom for Judaism."

These clashing interpretations were only fueled by French Jewry's dogged insistence that the murder of innocent Jewish children testified to the unique brutality and extremity of the racial deportations, and reclaiming those Jewish children who were still alive functioned as an alternative, not to mention pragmatic, means of invoking loss. For French Jews, the image of orphaned Jewish children enticed or forced into Christianity and the persecution of their babies by the Nazis offered a forceful metaphor for the Nazi program to eliminate the Jewish people. Retrieving and representing "our children" provided an emotional, if not always effective, strategy to memorialize "our martyrs."

NOTES

1. Heidi Fehrenbach, "War Orphans and Post-Fascist Families: Kinship and Belonging after 1945," in *Histories of the Aftermath: The Legacies of World War II in Comparative European Perspective*, ed. Frank Beiss and Robert G. Moeller (New York: Berghahn Books, 2009), 175–95. For photographic and narrative descriptions of European children's wartime experiences, see Thérèse Bonney, *Europe's Children, 1939 to 1943* (N.p.: Privately published, 1943); Robert Collis, *The Lost and the Found: The Story of Eva and László, Two Children of War-Torn Europe* (New York: Women's Press, 1953); John P. Carroll-Abbing, *A Chance to Live: The Story of the Lost Children of the War* (New York: Longmans, Green, 1952); Witold Majewski, *Polish Children Suffer* (London: F. P. Agency, 1944).

2. On the role of suffering in postwar Europe, see Nicholas Stargardt, *Witnesses of War: Children's Lives under the Nazis* (New York: Knopf, 2005), 335–47, 373–74; Robert Moeller, *War Stories: The Search for a Usable Past in the Federal Republic of*

Germany (Berkeley: University of California Press, 2001); Frank Beiss, "Survivors of Totalitarianism: Returning POWs and the Reconstruction of Masculine Citizenship in West Germany, 1945–1955," in *The Miracle Years: A Cultural History of West Germany, 1949–1968*, ed. Hanna Schissler (Princeton, NJ: Princeton University Press, 2001), 57–82, esp. 58; Atina Grossmann, *Jews, Germans, and Allies: Close Encounters in Occupied Germany* (Princeton, NJ: Princeton University Press, 2007), 30, 37, 48–68; Michael Kelly, "Death at the Liberation: The Cultural Articulation of Death and Suffering in France, 1944–47," *French Cultural Studies* 5 (1994): 227–40. On gender and martyrdom, see Kelly Ricciardi, "Engendering Frenchness: Gender and French Identity during the Long Liberation" (PhD diss., Brown University, 2008); Megan Koreman, *The Expectation of Justice: France, 1944–1946* (Durham: Duke University Press, 1999), 65, 73–91, 200–212.

3. Henry Rousso, *The Vichy Syndrome: History and Memory in France since 1944*, trans. Arthur Goldhammer (Cambridge, MA: Harvard University Press, 1991); Pieter Lagrou, *The Legacy of Nazi Occupation: Patriotic Memory and National Recovery in Western Europe, 1945–1965* (New York: Cambridge University Press, 2000); Sarah Farmer, *Martyred Village: Commemorating the 1944 Massacre at Oradour-sur-Glane* (Berkeley: University of California Press, 1999).

4. Maud Mandel, *In the Aftermath of Genocide: Armenians and Jews in Twentieth-Century France* (Durham, NC: Duke University Press, 2003); Leora Auslander, "Coming Home? Jews in Postwar Paris," *Journal of Contemporary History* 40 (2005): 237–59; Annette Wieviorka, *Déportation et génocide: Entre la mémoire et l'oubli* (Paris: Plon, 1992).

5. Koreman, *Expectation of Justice*, 3.

6. Annette Wieviorka, *The Era of the Witness*, trans. Jared Stark (Ithaca, NY: Cornell University Press, 2006); Lagrou, *Legacy of Nazi Occupation*, 260; Samuel Moyn, *A Holocaust Controversy: The Treblinka Affair in Postwar France* (Waltham, MA: Brandeis University Press, 2005), 82; Joan Wolf, *Harnessing the Holocaust* (Palo Alto, CA: Stanford University Press, 2004), 29; Annette Wieviorka and Françoise Rosset, "Jewish Identity in the First Accounts by Extermination Camp Survivors from France," *Yale French Studies*, no. 85 (1994): 135–51; Bruno Bettelheim, postface to Claudine Vegh, *I Didn't Say Goodbye*, trans. Ross Schwartz (New York: Dutton, 1984); Pierre Vidal Naquet, "The Holocaust's Challenge to History," in *Auschwitz and After*, ed. Lawrence Kritzman (New York: Routledge, 1995), 25–34; Karen Adler, *Jews and Gender in Liberation France* (New York: Cambridge University Press, 2003), 27; Mandel, *Aftermath*; David Weinberg, "The Reconstruction of the French Jewish Community after World War II," in *She'erit Hapletah, 1944–1948: Rehabilitation and Political Struggle; Proceedings of the Sixth Yad Vashem International Historical Conference, Jerusalem, 1985* (Jerusalem: Yad Vashem, 1990), 168–86.

7. Wieviorka, *Déportation et génocide*, 185.

8. Mark M. Anderson, "The Child Victim as Witness to the Holocaust: An American Story?," *Jewish Social Studies* 14 (2007): 3.

9. On Hitler's reticence on making the evacuation of German children compulsory, see Stargardt, *Witnesses*, 52; on the improvement in food distributions in the wake of the first Continental victories, see Stargardt, *Witnesses*, 47; on the Lebensborn program, see ibid., 353; Tara Zahra, *Kidnapped Souls* (Ithaca, NY: Cornell University Press, 2008), 197–98; Tara Zahra, *The Lost Children: Reconstructing Europe's Families after World War II* (Cambridge, MA: Harvard University Press, 2011), 126; Isabel Heinemann, "Until the Last Drop of Good Blood: The Kidnapping of 'Racially Valuable' Children in Occupied Eastern Europe," in *Genocide and Settler Society: Frontier Violence and Stolen Indigenous Children in Australian History*, ed. A. Dirk Moses (New York: Berghahn Books, 2004), 252–55.

10. On the murder of the handicapped, see Stargardt, *Witnesses*, 81–102; Henry Friedlander, *The Origins of Nazi Genocide: From Euthanasia to the Final Solution* (Chapel Hill: University of North Carolina Press, 1997), 39–61.

11. The efforts to save children in France during World War II are fairly well documented. See Debórah Dwork's chapter on "hiding" in Dwork, *Children with a Star: Jewish Youth in Nazi Europe* (New Haven, CT: Yale University Press, 2001), 31–66; Katy Hazan, *Les orphelins de la Shoah: Les maisons de l'espoir, 1944–1960* (Paris: Les Belles Lettres, 2000), 33–62; Renée Poznanski, *Jews in France during the Second World War* (Waltham, MA: Brandeis University Press, 2002), 137–43; Lucien Lazare, *Rescue as Resistance: How Jewish Organizations Fought the Holocaust in France*, trans. Jeffrey M. Greene (New York: Columbia University Press, 1996), 126–40, 172–215; Jean-Marie Pouplain, *Les enfants cachés de la Résistance* (Geste: La Creche, 1996); Phillip P. Hallie, *Lest Innocent Blood Be Shed: The Story of Le Chambon and How Goodness Happened There* (New York: Harper and Row, 1979); Sabine Zeitoun, *L'Oeuvre de secours aux enfants (O.S.E.) sous l'occupation en France: Du légalisme à la Résistance, 1940–1944* (Paris: L'Harmattan, 1990). For firsthand accounts, see Vivette Samuel, *Sauver les enfants* (Paris: L. Levi, 1995); Ernst Papenek, *Out of the Fire* (New York: William Morrow, 1975).

12. For some recent studies on postwar youth in Europe, see Stargardt *Witnesses*; Zahra, *Lost Children*; Fehrenbach "War Orphans."

13. Zahra *Lost Children*; Zahra, "Lost Children: Displacement, Family, and Nation in Postwar Europe," *Journal of Modern History* 81 (2009): 45–86; Fehrenbach, "War Orphans."

14. Michael Marrus, "The Vatican and the Custody of Jewish Child Survivors after the Holocaust," *Holocaust and Genocide Studies* 21, no. 3 (Winter 2007): 378–403; Katy Hazan, "Récupérer les enfants cachés: Un impératif des oeuvres juives dans l'après guerre," *Archives juives* 37 (2004): 16–31.

15. Congrès juif mondial, "Report on the Situation of the Jewish Children in France and on the Activities of the Children's Service of the Congress," July 11, 1946, File 13, Childcare and Adoption, 1946–1947, Box 87, Roll 37, Stephen Wise Papers, American Jewish Historical Society (hereafter AJHS), Center for Jewish History (hereafter CJH). Also see Samuel, *Rescuing the Children*, 133; Témoignage du George

Garel, 31, Fonds Anny Latour, DLXI, *Centre de documentation juive contemporaine* (hereafter CDJC).

16. Les jours de l'OSE journal de bord du Centre médico-social de Nice, June 1945, p. 36, 2.4.3.3 Fonds Abadi, CDJC.

17. The 30,000 figure (as cited by Marrus, "The Vatican," 385) comes from "Ellen Hilb, Report: December 1945–October 1946, Part I, Activities in Europe," United States Holocuast Memorial Museum (hereafter USHMM): WJC London Office, reel 191, File 1929.

18. Catherine Poujol, *Les enfants cachés: L'affaire Finaly (1945–1953)* (Paris: Berg, 2006), 29; "Congrès: Juif Mondial, juillet 11, 1946: Report on the Situation of the Jewish Children in France and on the Activities of the Children's Service of the Congress," Box 87, File 13, Childcare and Adoption, 1946–1947, Stephen Wise Papers, AJHS, CJH. On Israeli estimates, see letter addressed to Youth Aliyah Jerusalem (Aliyah Ha'noah Jerushalim) dated June 26, 1946, S75/1900, Central Zionist Archive (hereafter CZA).

19. Richard Owen, "Pope Pius XII—Sinner or (Almost) Saint," *Timesonline*, February 5, 2005, as cited by Marrus, "The Vatican," 396; Wieviorka, *Déportation et génocide*, 390.

20. Hazan, *Les orphelins*, 85–88.

21. PV de la séance du CRIF, 16.12.46, Fonds CRIF, MDI 3, CDJC.

22. Wieviorka, *Déportation et génocide*, 388; Hazan, *Les orphelins*, 81; Hazan, "Récupérer les enfants cachés," 16–31.

23. "Un peu de bonheur," *Droit et Liberté*, June 30, 1945. For similar fears about living conditions, see OSE extrait du Rapport Général d'activité, AJ-43/1252, Archives Nationales (hereafter AN).

24. "300 Jewish Orphans Kept as Slaves in France," *Der Tog*, February 10, 1950.

25. Also see Max Loiret, "Sans famille, 1948," *Droit et Liberté*, October 1, 1948, November 1, 1948, November 15, 1948; "Que devons nous dire à nos enfants," *Journal des Communautés*, August 25, 1950; E. Minkowski's statements at the FSJF Conference of March 1945, available in "Conférence nationale de la Fédération des sociétés juives de France," *Quand Même!*, nos. 10/11 (March 1945); "Marc Jarblum, rendez-nous nos enfants," *Notre Parole*, October 20, 1945; FSJF, "La vie de nos enfants abandonnés," CVXVII-13; CDJC, "Cri d'alarme," *La Terre retrouvée*, May 1, 1946.

26. Max Loiret, "Sans famille, 1948," *Droit et Liberté*, November 15, 1948; also see "L'autre danger," *Quand Même!*, nos. 10/11 (March 1945).

27. Paul Giniewski, "L'église n'a pas encore rendu tous les enfants," *La Terre retrouvée*, March 15, 1949.

28. OSE, February 8, 1945, File 294, AR 45/54, AJDC.

29. David I. Kertzer, *The Kidnapping of Edgardo Mortara* (New York: Knopf, 1997).

30. Caroline Ford, *Divided Houses: Religion and Gender in Modern France* (Ithaca, NY: Cornell University Press, 2005), 12; Lita Linzer Schwartz and Natalie Isser, "Some Involuntary Conversion Techniques," *Jewish Social Studies* 43 (1981): 1–10.

31. Ford, *Divided Houses.*

32. Rapport d'activités du Centres médico-social, September 1944–April 1945, 2.4.1.2, Fonds Abadi, CMXCIV, CDJC.

33. Les jours de l'OSE, Journal de Bord du Centre médico-social de Nice, June 1945, p. 81, 2.4.3.3, Fonds Abadi, CMXCIV, CDJC.

34. Letter from Arthur Greenleigh, May 24, 1945, File 4336, AR 45/54, AJDC.

35. Bintel Brief section, commemorative edition, *The Forward at 100,* April 6, 2007.

36. Témoignage de George Garel, p. 31, Fonds Anny Latour, DLXI, CDJC. Samuel René Kapel, a postwar rabbi and child welfare advocate, also recollected that social workers raised similar considerations when they attempted to persuade children that they must "in memory of [their] parents, come back to [their] Jewish people."

37. "Rapport moral de l'activité de la FSJF, 1945–1946," *Quand Même!*, March 25, 1946; "Enquête sur les enfants," *Bulletin de Service centrale déportés israélites*, June 1945. For similar links of children to vengeance, see "Paul Ginewski, l'école Pougatch: Un reportage," *Notre Parole*, July 24, 1946; and, in the displaced persons camps, see Grossmann, *Jews, Germans, and Allies*, 196–200.

38. Sermon given at the rue de la victoire synagogue on Yom Kippur by Rabbi Jacob Kaplan, October 2, 1949. File Sermons et Discours, Box 22, Fonds Kaplan, CDJC. For other Kaplan speeches in which he raises the issues of memory, children—both orphaned and not—and Jewish education, see his speech at the commemoration at Vel' d'Hiv (where mainly women and children were arrested and deported in 1942), in Kaplan, *Réponse aux convertisseurs* (Paris: Fondation Sefer, 1948); also reproduced in *L'affaire Finaly* (Paris: Cerf), 61–68. Also see his August 8, 1951, speech given at the opening of Mulhouse's Jewish Community Center, File Discours et Sermons, Box 23, Fonds Kaplan, CDJC.

39. Letter to RK from Anna Costa, Paris, File Correspondance Finaly, February 1953, Box KAP-FI 1, Fonds Kaplan, CDJC.

40. "Le Consistoire israélite du Haut-Rhin, File Correspondance Finaly," June 1953, Box KAP-FI 1, Fonds Kaplan, CDJC.

41. "Note d'information n 10, l'affaire Finaly, June 23, 1953. 23 juin 1953," File Publications, KAP-FI 4, Fonds Kaplan, CDJC.

42. Emphasis in the original. 1947 calendar, Commission centrale de l'enfance auprès de l'UJRE, File Commission centrale de l'enfance calendars, Box 56, David Diamant Collection, Musée National de la Résistance, Champigny (hereafter MNR/Champigny).

43. "Émission La Voix d'Israël, 27 octobre 1945," in *N'oublie pas* (Paris: Stock, 2011), 46. This speech was given on the radio program *The Voice of Israel* for the Week of the Martyred Jewish Child, which will be explored in more depth later in this chapter.

44. "Le discours du Grand Rabbin Kaplan, Congrés national de la Fédération des sociétés juives de France," *Quand Même!*, March 25, 1946.

45. "Le sponsorship des enfants juifs," *Notre Parole*, December 14, 1946, 6.

46. The SERE becomes the OPEJ, File 41–67, Fonds Lublin, CMXXI, CDJC.

47. "Honorez le souvenir de vos chers disparus dans la déportation," *La Colonie scolaire*, no. 4 (June 1946), YIVO Library, CJH.

48. "Le parrainage des enfants juifs," *Notre Parole*, December 14, 1946.

49. CRIF Bulletin d'intérieur d'information, File CRIF Bulletin d'intérieur d'information, 26 AS/6, AN.

50. "Adoptez les orphelins," *Notre Parole*, November 27, 1946; "Leurs petits? Nos petits! Poème par S. Hofman, Janvier 1947," File Comité général de défense des juifs de France, Box 27, UJRE/David Diamant Collection, MNR/Champigny.

51. As stated by the article for the women's section of the UJRE, "La vie de la femme: Les buts et les tâches de notre Union des femmes," *Droit et Liberté*, February 7, 1945.

52. For some of the many examples, see *Droit et Liberté* throughout the years 1944–1947. Also see *Quand Même!*, August 21, 1946, and September 30, 1946, for lists of donations for orphaned and destitute Jewish youth to attend summer camp; also see the donations published in the Colonie scolaire's newsletter, *La Colonie scolaire*, no. 3 (May 15, 1946), YIVO Library; *La Colonie scolaire*, no. 4 (June 1946), YIVO Library, CJH.

53. *Droit et Liberté* published a list of such donations in each edition between the years 1944 and 1947.

54. *Droit et Liberté*, January 21, 1947.

55. Ibid., May 15, 1946.

56. Ibid., January 21, 1947.

57. "Imitez-les," *La Colonie scolaire*, no. 4 (June 1946), YIVO Library, CJH.

58. Emphasis in the original. *Bulletin du Service central des déportés israélites*, May 15, 1945. Also cited in Adler, *Jews and Gender*, 27.

59. Jaqueline Mesnil Amar, "Le guerre aux enfants," *Bulletin de Service centrale des déportés israélites*, commemorative issue, no. 12 (1947); for other examples in which authors clearly distinguish the experience of Jewish children from that of other children, see "Enfance juives, à la recherché d'un climat sentimantale," *La Terre retrouvée*, May 1, 1946, 4; M. Lichinsky, "Bilan d'extermination," *Le Monde juif*, March 19, 1947; F. Shneersohn, "La martyrologie de l'enfance juive," *Le Monde juif*, January 1949; "Oeuvre de protection des enfants juifs," S32/1899, CZA.

60. Letter from Myriam Jurovics to Kaplan, November 7, 1946, File Correspondance 46, Box 53, Fonds Kaplan, Consistoire centrale Archives.

61. "À l'exposition de la Commission centrale de l'enfance," *Droit et Liberté*, May 15, 1946; "La maison entre le ciel et la terre," *La Terre retrouvée*, May 1, 1949: 3; "L'exposition de dessins de travaux des enfants de nos foyers, *Aide à l'enfance, Bulletin d'information*, CCE Collection, Box 9, CDJC; "Henri Wallon, les enfants de la guerre et leurs dessins," *Droit et Liberté*, January 13–19, 1950; there is also a series of catalogues—including reproductions of the children's drawings—for the 1949, 1950, 1952, and 1954 exhibits in Box 17, CCE Collection, CDJC.

62. Stargardt, *Witnesses*, 363.

63. Ruth Klüger, *Still Alive* (New York: Feminist Press, 2001), 155.

64. "L'exposition de dessins de travaux des enfants de nos foyers," *Aide à l'enfance: Bulletin d'information*, Box 9, CCE Collection, CDJC.

65. For a description of the 1950 conference, see "À l'exposition de la Commission centrale de l'enfance," *Droit et Liberté*, May 15, 1946; and for the 5,000 figure, see *Aide à l'enfance: Bulletin d'information*, March 1950, Box 9, CCE Collection, CDJC.

66. *Nous Continuons/Mir Lebn Do*, UJRE Production, 1946. While the title in French translates to "We Continue," the Yiddish title translates to "We Live Here."

67. For more examples of reporting of Jewish youth in the postwar French press, see "Il n'y a pas d'enfants qui reviennent . . . ," *Le Populaire*, May 5, 1945; "Quant les petits ne rentrent pas," *Ce Soir*, May 8, 1945; "Une enquête de Daniel Provence sur l'enfance juive martyre: La recherche des enfants perdus," *Nice Matin*, March 27–30, 1947, E3, I3, Box 22, OSE, USHMM; "Une enquête de Daniel Provence sur l'enfance juive martyre: À la recherche des enfants perdus; Une armée d'orphelins de toutes nationalités, est prise en charge par l'Oeuvre de secours aux enfants," *Nice Matin*, March 31, 1947, Fonds Abadi, 2.4.1.2, and available in Box 22, OSE, USHMM ; "Les chasseurs des enfants," *Carrefour*, December 1, 1944, and November 16, 1945, Fonds Abadi, 2.2.7, CDJC.

68. For an analogous example in the German context, see Bill Niven, *The Buchenwald Child: Truth, Fiction, and Propaganda* (Rochester, NY: Camden House, 2007).

69. Letter from M. Kamerman to M. Maget, July 15, 1945, Box 20, E2, OSE Collection, USHMM.

70. "Le martyre des enfants déportés: Quand les petits ne rentrent pas," *Ce Soir*, May 8, 1945, Box 22, E2, OSE Collection, USHMM.

71. Ibid. See Daniel Provence, "À la recherche des enfants perdus: Le plus jeune déporté de France est arrivé à Buchenwald cousu dans un sac," *Nice Matin*, March 27, 1947, Fonds Abadi 2.4.1.4, CDJC ; "L'humanité," "Rescapés des bagnes nazis . . . Mille petits à sauver," Box 20, Folder 2, OSE, USHMM; "Sortis de l'enfer de Buchenwald," *Libération*, June 2, 1945.

72. "Quant les petits ne rentrent pas," *Ce Soir*, May 8, 1945; "Il n y a pas d'enfants qui reviennent . . . ," *Le Populaire*, May 5, 1945.

73. Serge Knabel, "1945: La libération d'un adolescent," *Le Monde juif: Revue d'Histoire de la Shoah* (September–December 1995): 40.

74. Hasia Diner, *We Remember with Reverence and Love: American Jews and the Myth of Silence after the Holocaust, 1945–1962* (New York: New York University Press, 2009), 31.

75. Renée Poznanski, "French Apprehensions, Jewish Expectations: From a Social Imaginary to a Political Practice," in *The Jews Are Coming Back*, ed. David Bankiers (New York: Berghahn Books, 2005), 57.

76. "Semaine de l'enfance juive martyre," S75/1899, CZA.

77. The Comité national de l'enfance originally encompassed thirteen organizations, including Comité des oeuvres sociales des organisations de la résistance (hereafter COSOR), Secours populaire, the Entreaide française, and the Union des femmes françaises.

78. Annette Wieviorka, *Entre déportation et génocide: entre la mémoire et l'oubli* (Paris: Plon), 386.

79. Comité national pour le soutien de l'enfance victime de la guerre et du nazisme, File Comité national pour le soutien de l'enfance, Box 129, David Diamant Collection, MNR/Champigny.

80. Comité national pour le soutien de l'enfance victime de la guerre et du nazisme, Compte rendu de la réunion du comité du 8/10/45, File Comité national pour le soutien de l'enfance, Box 129, David Diamant Collection, MNR/Champigny.

81. Press statement, Bureau de la FSJF not dated, MDIII-14, Fonds Kelman, CDJC.

82. Minutes of plenary assembly meeting, Comité national de la semaine de l'enfance juive martyre, August 27, 1945, File Semaine de l'enfance juive martyre, Box 125, David Diamant Collection, MNR/Champigny.

83. Letter to Mr. Jefroykin (of the FSJF and the Comité de l'enfance juive martyre) from the secretary of the Comité national de l'enfance, Monsieur Mudry, October 2, 1945. File Semaine de l'enfance juive martyre, Box 16, David Diamant Collection, MNR/Champigny.

84. The minister of health retracted his support for the Week of the Martyred Jewish Child in the beginning of October. However, since the posters had already been printed, his name remained attached to public advertisements for the event; Compte rendu de la réunion du lundi 8 Octobre, 1945, File 2, Box 16, MNR/Champigny; Minutes of plenary assemble meeting, Comité national de la semaine de l'enfance juive martyre, August 27, 1945, File Semaine de l'enfance juive martyre, David Diamant Collection, Box 126, MNR/Champigny; Semaine de l'enfance juive martyre, S75/1899, CZA.

85. For a brochure and schedule of the gala, see Palais de Chaillot, Grand gala de la Semaine de l'enfance juive martyre, L58/446, CZA.

86. Letter from M. Brandis of Lille to the Consistoire centrale, File Lille 1945, Box Communauté 1945–1948, Consistoire centrale Archives.

87. Wieviorka, *Entre Déportation*, 387.

88. On the clash between Jewish and French expectations and apprehensions about Jewish claims to special privileges, see Renée Poznanski, "French Apprehensions," 25–57.

89. "Semaine de l'enfance juive martyre," S75/1899, CZA.

90. "L'enfance juive martyre, émission du voix d'Israël, 27 octobre 1945," Jacob Kaplan, *N'oublie pas*, 43.

91. "L'enfance juive martyre," *Le Réveil des Jeunes*, October 15, 1954.

92. "Une initiative de notre parole," *Notre Parole*, July 1, 1945.

93. "L'enfance juive martyre," radio broadcast by Msgr. Paul Remond, bishop of Nice, October 26, 1945, CDXCIV-II, Fonds Abadi 2.3, CDJC.

94. "S. Aronson, "La Semaine de l'enfance victime du nazisme," *Droit et Liberté*, November 7, 1945. For similar arguments maintaining that Jewish children suffered differently but that their successful futures depend on equality, see "Le drame de l'enfant meurtri," *Droit et Liberté*, April 1, 1948. Also see the children's play *La fée solidarité* (Paris: E. Ravel). For the OSE's position, see "À propos d'une affiche," *Bulletin OSE*, November 15, 1945.

95. Emphasis in the original. "Projet d'article," File 2, Box 16, UJRE/David Diamant Collection, MNR/Champigny.

6

Orphans of the Shoah and Jewish Identity in Post-Holocaust France

From the Individual to the Collective

SUSAN RUBIN SULEIMAN

At the end of World War II, more than 10,000 Jewish children in France found themselves without one or both of their parents. By "children," I refer to boys and girls who were between infancy and adolescence (up to age fifteen or sixteen) when they first experienced the sudden, violent separation from a parent. Most of these orphaned or semi-orphaned children had been born in France to impoverished immigrants from eastern Europe who had arrived there in the 1920s and 1930s; some came from more well-to-do immigrant families, and a few were from families of established "israélites" (as the euphemism went), who had lived in France for generations but had still not escaped persecution. In addition, a number of adolescent concentration camp survivors from other countries had been transported to France by Jewish rescue organizations after liberation and placed in children's homes. This was the case with Elie Wiesel, no doubt the best known of these orphans internationally.

In the years following the war, some of these children left for Israel, especially those among the camp survivors who had no relatives in France; some who had family members in the United States immigrated to America; the large majority remained in France; and an impressive number grew up to become distinguished—even world-renowned—writers, intellectuals, and public figures, a number of whom have published autobiographical books and essays.[1] In one sense such successful individuals are not "typical," but insofar as their wartime experiences were shared by thousands of others, they can be said to represent many who lived more anonymous lives. In fact, the latter have also become more visible in the past two decades; the founding of the French Association des enfants cachés (Association of Hidden Children) in 1992, in the wake of similar associations that were started around the same time in the United States and elsewhere, produced a large number of oral testimonies and published memoirs by child survivors who had remained silent until then, unacknowledged as a specific category by themselves as well as by others.[2]

The psychological literature in France about "hidden children"—that is, children who survived the war without being deported—has also grown exponentially in recent years. While I will focus on a few highly visible members of this generation of survivors (which I have elsewhere called the 1.5 generation), the works I have read by and about the more anonymous majority confirm both the enormous variety of individual lives and the similarities in the wartime experiences and psychological profiles of child survivors.[3] They also confirm the similarities in the issues they faced after the war, including the one that is my main concern here: their relation to Jewishness and Jewish identity.

Orphans

By and large, Jewish children survived the war in France in some form of hiding, separated for at least a time from their parents, most often under false names and having to pretend that they were Christians, or at least not Jewish; a number were baptized during that time. What this kind of masquerade did to their sense of self varied from individual to individual and circumstance to circumstance: it could lead, later in life, to an excessive sense of power and invulnerability ("Nothing can harm me"), or to its opposite ("I deserve to die"), and often to the paradoxical coexistence of the two. Boris Cyrulnik, a neuropsychiatrist and a specialist in theories of resilience, himself a child survivor who became an orphan at age five, has analyzed the combination of a sense of invulnerability and a sense of melancholic culpability in "resilient" children who survived situations of extreme danger.[4]

Age at the time of separation also made a significant difference in the way children reacted: a child of five or six who suddenly found himself or herself alone or with a parent missing, forced to pretend to be somebody else, lived through that experience differently, and recalled it differently later, from one who was ten years older. In my previous work on the 1.5 generation, I proposed three categories according to age: those too young to remember the war (infancy to around three years old), those old enough to remember but too young to understand (age four through ten), and those old enough to understand but too young to be responsible (age eleven through fourteen or a little older).[5] Obviously, these are approximate categories, useful for establishing differences. But similarities are just as important—first of all, the fact that these were all children, not adults, even if many were prematurely forced into an adult role, having to fend for themselves in a hostile environment. They were youngsters who in normal life could rely on at least some degree of security and stability provided by the presence of parents, and who suddenly found their lives turned upside down by the disappearance of one or both of them. Not all children forced into hiding and masquerade lost a parent in the process, and some were lucky enough to survive with both parents. But very few lived through the war without any separation at all; most ended up living with strangers at least temporarily.

In the psychological literature on hidden children, one does not find a strong distinction made between children who were orphaned and those who were reunited with their parents after the war. In one sense, all hidden children underwent similar experiences of dislocation and trauma, especially if they spent an extended period separated from their family. Children whose parents returned to claim them after a long separation often experienced a second trauma upon being separated from adoptive families who had sheltered them during the war, and the younger ones may even have had trouble recognizing their biological parents. Many parents had been transformed both physically and emotionally by their own suffering; some who returned from concentration camps were unable to give their children security and love. Because of such negative factors, the psychologist Marion Feldman suggests that all hidden children experienced psychological disturbances in their relation to their personal past and to their family after the war; she calls these disturbances "troubles de filiation," in distinction to broader problems relating to group identity ("troubles d'affiliation").[6] But I believe that no matter how troubled the relation to a parent is, the difference for a child is enormous between having one and not having one, or between losing a parent for a while and losing one, or both, forever. Émile Copfermann

(1931–99), who became a journalist and novelist after doing odd jobs for a number of years, was eleven when his parents were arrested in September 1942 and deported to Auschwitz. An aunt managed to send him and his two brothers to a family of farmers in the southwest, where they spent the rest of the war. Afterward, when it was clear that their parents were not coming back and the aunt could not take care of them, the boys were sent to a Jewish children's home where they spent several years. In a memoir he published when he was in his late sixties, two years before he died, Copfermann wrote:

> A normal childhood and adolescence unfolds under the influence of one's parents, so that later it becomes impossible to tell which of your memories you remember as something you lived through, and which were only told to you later, over and over. Our life as children was not only reduced to very little, but the memory of the years we spent with our parents was not revived by anyone. As an adult, no matter how hard I tried to assemble the pieces of the past, they didn't stick together: people were missing, places had become erased, even the years ran together. To reconstitute the puzzle, we would have had to question our elders, verify the facts with them. . . . Impossible, [for] most of our close relatives had also disappeared.[7]

Copfermann's experience was a common one: his family were poor immigrants from Romania, and they did not keep archives. The novelists Georges Perec (1936–82), Raymond Federman (1928–2009), and Berthe Burko-Falcman (b. 1935), the playwright and novelist Jean-Claude Grumberg (b. 1939), the philosopher Sarah Kofman (1934–94), and the neuropsychiatrist Boris Cyrulnik (b. 1937) are among those with similar backgrounds. Some children of immigrants, like the historian Saul Friedlander (b. 1932) and the writer and editor Elisabeth Gille (1937–96), belonged to middle-class families of acculturated, urban eastern European Jews—but the autobiographical works of all these writers insist on the missing pieces in their lives, the impossibility of assembling the pieces of their past after the destruction of their families.[8] Gille stands out as the child of a famous mother, Irène Némirovsky, who was a well-known novelist in France in the 1930s; Némirovsky's celebrity did not prevent her from being deported as a "foreign Jew" in July 1942, followed a few months later by her husband, Michel Epstein, and most of the Epstein family. The Némirovskys and the Epsteins had immigrated to France soon after the Russian Revolution but had never obtained French citizenship.

Pierre Vidal-Naquet (1930–2006) was somewhat luckier in the realm of family ties, although he too lost his parents to deportation. They were arrested in Marseille in May 1944, when Pierre was fourteen, and were deported to Auschwitz a few weeks later on the last transport to leave the camp of Drancy. Pierre and his younger siblings, who spent the remaining months of the war in hiding with family members, were taken care of after the war by close relatives, part of a large extended family of lawyers, civil servants, and businessmen who proudly traced their roots in France back to the seventeenth century. His mother and father were part of the elite of French "israélites," loyal citizens and defenders of the Republic. Pierre grew up to be a world-renowned classicist and historian, as well as one of France's best-known public intellectuals: he was among the first to protest against torture by the French Army in Algeria in the 1950s, and among the first to attack the wave of Holocaust negationism that hit France in the late 1970s in the work of Robert Faurisson. Vidal-Naquet carefully documents his family's history in his two-volume autobiography, published when he was in his sixties.[9]

Despite their different backgrounds, however, Copfermann and other children of immigrants had a number of things in common with more privileged orphans like Vidal-Naquet. First and most importantly, they all hoped and expected to see their parents return after the war. Those old enough joined the lines waiting at the train stations and at the Hotel Lutetia, where an office was set up to receive returning deportees. It took months, sometimes years, for them to truly accept the fact that their parents were not coming back. Vidal-Naquet writes that he finally had to face that fact in October 1945, but that even years later he could not comprehend the senseless murder of his mother. His father was in the Resistance, so he could rationalize his death as a political reprisal inflicted by the enemy, even though Lucien Vidal-Naquet was deported not as a *résistant* but as a Jew; but the murder of his mother, and the millions like her who were killed deliberately and individually, even if as part of an anonymous mass, he finds literally incomprehensible.[10] Raymond Federman, whose parents and two sisters were rounded up in the Vél d'Hiv in July 1942 when he was fourteen, immigrated to the United States five years later. Starting in 1971, he published more than a dozen innovative autobiographical novels, in French and English; in all these works, he signaled the incomprehensible loss of his family with the symbol of four Xs in a row (X*X*X*X), representing both the lost family and the impossibility of saying anything about their disappearance.[11]

Another thing that orphans of the Shoah shared is that after the war, they almost never spoke with other children about their wartime experiences, not even with those who had suffered similar losses. In the children's homes and summer camps where many spent time, the rule was not to dwell on the past but to look forward. Berthe Burko-Falcman's father, Aron Falcman, a poor Polish tailor, served in the French Army in 1940 but was arrested in 1941 as a "foreign Jew" and sent to the camp at Pithiviers, from where he was deported to Auschwitz on June 25, 1942. (Elisabeth Gille's mother, Irène Némirovsky, was deported from the same camp a few weeks later, on July 17.) In the spring of 1942, when Berthe was seven years old, her mother arranged for her to live with a farm family in Normandy; nine months later, Berthe joined her mother in a village in the southwest, where they survived the war. Berthe married, became a teacher, and published three novels in the 1980s and 1990s based on her wartime and postwar experiences; but her memoir of childhood, *Un prénom républicain*, appeared only in 2007, when she was seventy-two. She recalls that in the Yiddish-speaking summer camps where she and other Jewish children who had lost parents were sent after the war, none of the children talked about what they had gone through: "Maybe we didn't know that what had happened to us was unusual. With a few variations, we all had the same story. There was therefore nothing to say, and we didn't speak about it."[12] It was only many years later, she adds, when some were already grandparents, that they finally told each other the stories of their survival.

Similarly, Jean-Claude Grumberg was already a famous playwright and in his mid-sixties when he published a book about his father, who had arrived in France from Romania as a child and became a tailor like his own father. Little Jean-Claude was three years old when the French police knocked on the door of his family's apartment early one morning in February 1943 and, getting no answer, broke the door down. Grumberg has no personal memory of that incident, which he nevertheless considers as the determining event of his life. He writes that it was through the broken door that he was "born into the world . . . torn from a protected childhood and thrown into this world where violence, injustice and madness reign."[13] For a long time, he adds, he thought that the men who broke the door down were Germans—later, he "learned that one had to say French police, but who to say it to? We never even spoke about it among ourselves" (91). Grumberg writes at length about his own wartime and postwar experience in his 2010 book *Pleurnichard*, where he refers to himself most often in the third person, by his nickname: Crybaby. Grumberg recounts that after the father's arrest, "Pleurnichard" and his older brother were taken in charge by the Jewish aid agency Oeuvres de secours aux enfants (OSE), which worked clandestinely to protect Jewish children during the war; the two boys were sent to children's homes in the southwest, while their mother stayed alone in Paris. After the war, when Jean-Claude first saw her again, he did not recognize "the lady with the Parisian accent who assured him that she was his mommy."[14]

The long silence of Holocaust survivors, whether children or adults, is one of the permanent themes treated in the psychological literature; the most frequent explanation for it is that in order to move ahead with their lives, survivors felt compelled to follow the dictum: "Put the past behind you." In the case of children, there was the added factor that many were too young to give coherent accounts of what had happened to them. But historians have pointed out another important factor: in the postwar years, after a first brief flurry of fascination as the full horror of the Nazi concentration camps became known, the public lost interest in hearing survivors' stories. Like the survivors themselves, those who might have listened to them felt the necessity to "forget" and move on.[15] Boris Cyrulnik explains, in his slender book of reflections about how he survived the war after the deportation of his parents, that the compulsion to "always keep going forward" (*aller toujours de l'avant*) became his "strategy of survival" for many years, a defense mechanism against depression and helplessness.[16] This ability to bracket off the most painful aspects of the past is an important component of what Cyrulnik and other theorists of childhood trauma call resilience; it may account for his and many other orphans' professional success.

With a few notable exceptions, most of the memoirs and testimonies by French child survivors of the Holocaust date from the 1990s or later. During the decade after the war, these children were not only too young to give coherent accounts of their experiences, but—as Burko-Falcman and Grumberg make clear—they were unable to talk about them even with other children who had undergone similar ones.[17] This temporal delay in recalling the painful past, while particularly poignant in the case of children who had suffered the traumatic loss of a parent, corresponds to a collective historical phenomenon of forgetting and remembrance, which I will discuss later.

Conflicted Jewishness

Being Jewish in Europe has never been simple. Starting in the late eighteenth century, Jews emerged in increasing numbers from the isolation of the ghetto and could begin to aspire to full citizenship in their countries of residence. This gave rise to the "Jewish question," which is often defined as an anti-Semitic slur: "What shall we do with the Jews, who don't really belong?" However, Jews too faced a "Jewish question"— indeed, more than one. Throughout the nineteenth century and later, "emancipated" Jews were confronted with often painful issues of affiliation and group loyalty: What was their relation to Judaism as a religious practice and to Jewishness as an identity, in comparison to their status as citizens of the nation? Could one ever cease being Jewish?[18] These questions continue to be asked and debated by individual Jews today, in France and elsewhere. They became tragic during the Holocaust for many Jews, who discovered that their own existential choices had no weight or meaning in the eyes of their persecutors: to the Nazis, all Jews were the same, even those who no longer considered themselves Jews.

While vexing questions about identity present themselves to all Jews in modern times (perhaps with the exception of those who are unquestioningly orthodox in their practice), the wartime experiences of Jewish children stand out for the conflicts they engendered. All children who were in hiding, whether alone or with family, were in the position of having to deny their Jewishness—a feat all the more remarkable in the case of children from assimilated or left-wing families (most Jews in France were one or the other), who had little sense of Jewish identity to begin with. Serge Klarsfeld, the famed activist lawyer and historian who with his wife Beate has devoted his life to documenting the persecution of Jews in France and bringing perpetrators to justice, lost his father at age eight, when Arno Klarsfeld was arrested by the Gestapo in Nice while the rest of the family hid in a closet. The Klarsfelds were Romanian and middle-class—Arno Klarsfeld was a businessman from cosmopolitan Bucharest, not a left-winger or a Yiddish speaker. The family identified themselves as Jewish, and after the war Serge went to a Jewish day school and got some religious instruction. Yet, looking back on his childhood many years later, Klarsfeld explained that while he felt like a foreigner during the war (born in Bucharest, he carried a Romanian passport), he did not know what it meant to feel Jewish: "I was aware of being hunted not as a Romanian but as a Jew. But what did it mean, to be a Jew? It must have been what I was, what we were. My parents' friends in Nice were also Central European Jews, people who spoke foreign languages. I didn't have the feeling of being guilty of anything whatsoever."[19]

It made sense to the eight-year-old that in order to be hunted, one had to be guilty of something: Were Jews guilty by definition? Klarsfeld adds that he considers himself lucky to have had to confront only the Gestapo, rather than French police the way Jewish children did in the rest of the country—since the Germans were clearly the enemy, it made things "less ambiguous and less complex" (24). However, the association of guilt with Jewishness, even if in the form of a later disavowal ("I didn't feel guilty"), is a heavy burden for an eight-year-old boy. After his father's arrest, when Serge and his sister were hiding in a village with their mother, he was registered in school as Greek Orthodox and was slated for conversion to Catholicism. In fact, his one period of genuine religious feeling, he recalls, occurred that year, when he frequented the village church—it was "marvelous, with an unforgettable smell of incense" (24). But he was waiting for his father to return, and when he did not return, it was over between Serge and God: "I didn't have a crisis. But I recall that I never again had the feeling of the presence of God" (25).

Berthe Burko-Falcman's family, unlike Klarsfeld's, was working-class, Yiddish-speaking, Communist, and atheist, similar to many other Polish

Jewish immigrant families at the time—but she too had a moment of religiosity, linked to Catholicism. During the months she was living with the farming family in Normandy, she went to church with them and learned all the prayers. She was going to be baptized on her eighth birthday, in February 1943, had it not been for the sudden arrival of a messenger from her mother: he came to pick her up and take her south to join her mother the week before her birthday. But, she notes, "despite the missed baptism, for several years I felt Catholic in my own way." Then one day, after the war, she came across a pamphlet full of horrifying photographs of dead bodies in piles, and she was filled with "retrospective terror." She notes: "If I had been baptized, it would have been a betrayal. Of whom? I had no answer for that, in words or in thought. But it would have been a betrayal."[20] She later married Jacques Burko, from a middle-class Jewish family in Warsaw who had survived the war in the Soviet Union and immigrated to France after the war. Jacques's family did not speak Yiddish and looked down on Yiddish speakers. This was yet another kind of conflict in Jewish identity, revolving around class difference. But the betrayal that Berthe worried about almost having committed referred to religion.

It is extraordinary how often, and how consistently, one comes across the theme of self-division or inner conflict linked to religious identity in the memoirs of orphaned Jewish children. Emile Copfermann writes that his aunt had him and his brothers baptized "as an extra measure" before sending them to the farm, which resulted in their going to church every Sunday. Ironically, the farmers they were living with had stopped going to church years earlier, but started going again because of the boys! Copfermann adds that he can still recite "Our Father" and "Hail Mary," but has no knowledge whatever of the Torah or the Mishna. And while he knows perfectly how to make the sign of the cross, it was only when he was over sixty years old that he learned how and why to light Hanukkah candles.[21]

Georges Perec, who was not only a Jewish orphan but one of France's great twentieth-century writers, made inner division the structural principle as well as a major theme in his groundbreaking 1975 book *W ou le souvenir d'enfance*, which alternates autobiographical chapters about the fragments of memory that he retains of his childhood with chapters of a science-fiction novel that is itself broken in two. And Sarah Kofman, who lost her father when she was seven years old, recounts with shattering precision, in the last book she wrote before committing suicide, *Rue Ordener, rue Labat*, the struggle over her soul that went on between her Polish Jewish mother and the French Catholic woman who saved her during the war.

As for Pierre Vidal-Naquet, the conflict he emphasizes occurred not only between religions or between social classes, but between that eminently French pair: Enlightenment universalism and Jewish particularism. He writes that his family was proud of their history as French "israélites" and observed endogamy through his parents' generation, but "in the matter of religion, my parents and most of my family worshipped only culture and the fatherland, which were closely intertwined" (*Mémoires, I*, 45). Zionism was totally foreign to them, as was any form of religious practice. He notes with some irony that the first Passover seder he ever attended was in 1975 in Israel—his own family had dinner together at Passover, but it was definitely not a seder (*Mémoires, I*, 43). In the early 1940s, when he wanted to join a boy scout troop, his mother put him in a Protestant troop, rejecting both the Jewish scouts ("In my family we feared above all anything resembling a ghetto")[22] and the secular Republican scouts, the Éclaireurs de France. His ignorance of Judaism was so profound in his adolescence that during a discussion in his scout troop, he insisted that Jews did not reject Jesus Christ as the Messiah—whereupon his leader remarked, "You really must be very special Jews" (Vous devez vraiment être des Juifs très particuliers).[23]

In fact, Vidal-Naquet came to Judaism through his work as a historian, both of the Hellenistic period (where he discovered the work of the second-century Jewish historian Flavius Joseph) and of modern Jewish history starting with the Dreyfus affair. He notes quite touchingly in the preface to his first book of essays on Jewish themes, *Les juifs, la mémoire et le présent* (which consists of articles he published between 1967 and 1980), that "it is not so much because I'm Jewish that I wrote these pages, but rather the opposite: it was in writing this book, and a few other works, that I became a Jew, a voluntary Jew one might say, or a Jew through reflection."[24] His biggest inspiration on his way to Jewishness, he explains, was the Dreyfus affair, which he first studied in detail in 1965, when he

published his first book review in *Le Monde*. The defense of universalist ideas of truth and justice, which he found in the Dreyfus affair,
made perfect sense for a Jew who considered himself, as Vidal-Naquet
did, a follower of the Enlightenment and a "Jewish Frenchman" rather
than a "French Jew." However, it placed him at odds, on occasion, with
Jews in France who, after the 1967 war, became more and more unconditional in their support for Israel. Vidal-Naquet, espousing general
principles of human rights and the rights of peoples, considered himself both pro-Israeli and pro-Palestinian, a divided position that earned
him, he notes wryly, accusations of being a "Jewish anti-Semite" from
some people and threats as a "dirty Jew" from others (*Mémoires, II,*
266). Indeed, he sees inner division, *dédoublement*, as his characteristic
way of being in the world, in every aspect of his life: "What do I mean
by that? Essentially, that I never ask myself a question with a single
voice" (*Mémoires, II,* 341).

Vidal-Naquet did not continue the tradition of endogamy still
observed by his parents' generation. The woman he married belonged
to a Catholic family, and although she was not a believer, they were
married in a church to please her parents. Vidal-Naquet notes that of the
fourteen cousins in his own generation, only three married Jews
(*Mémoires, I,* 41). If *dédoublement* is his characteristic way of being in the
world, it is also, he recognizes, "the way I live my Jewishness" (*Mémoires,
I,* 164).

The Historical View: The Emergence of "Jewish Memory"

After these glimpses into individual lives, I want to take a step back and
look at the larger historical picture. As I stated earlier, the individual need
to "forget and move on" had its collective, national counterpart. Henry
Rousso, in his classic work *Le syndrome de Vichy*, published in 1987,
adopted a psychoanalytic model for tracing the evolution of French memories of the occupation years: the period of "incomplete mourning" and
"repression" during the first twenty-five years after the war was followed
by the "return of the repressed" and by what Rousso saw as a veritable
obsession with Vichy, especially with Vichy's role in the persecution
of Jews, starting around 1970. Although Rousso has been criticized on

various grounds for his application of the psychoanalytic model to history, I think it is useful to see individual preoccupations as part of larger historical trends. Even though exact parallels between individual psychology and national history are hard to draw, a contextualizing of the existential within the historical seems fruitful and necessary.

In historical terms, the question concerns the emergence of a specifically "Jewish memory" within the larger French context. As we saw, the silence of Jewish children about their wartime trauma can be explained as a psychological defense mechanism; one observes a similar phenomenon on the level of the larger Jewish community, corresponding to the incomplete mourning and repression that Rousso discusses in the country as a whole. Just as the broader French discourse during those years was silent about the role of Vichy in the persecution of Jews and put all the blame on "the Germans," so Jews who had been adults during the war and had precise memories of official Vichy anti-Semitism nevertheless found ways to elide them. Serge Klarsfeld recalls, with indignation, that in his youth during the 1950s, he heard many Jewish leaders talk about the persecution of Jews in France "by the Nazis," as if Vichy had had nothing to do with it.[25] It would probably be more exact to say, however, that Jews—including religious leaders like Rabbi Jacob Kaplan, who became chief rabbi of France in the 1950s—adopted a position similar to that of de Gaulle and the postwar French government: Vichy did not represent "true France," the France of the Declaration of Human Rights which had been the first country in Europe to grant Jews full citizenship. The historian Annette Wieviorka writes that "for Jacob Kaplan, as in fact for the immense majority of Jews, whatever their place of origin, who wished to live in France, Vichy was not France."[26] The status of France in relation to Vichy continues to be a fraught issue, even though Jacques Chirac's famous apology, in July 1995, for the crimes of the "French State" (Vichy) against Jews did much to allay it.

The conflicted religious identity of Jewish children after the war also had a collective historical counterpart. Many Jews in France asked themselves whether to remain Jewish after what they had gone through. One indication of such doubts is the large number of Jews who changed their names to sound "less Jewish" in comparison to earlier periods: of all those Jews in France who changed their names between 1803 and 1957, 85 percent did so after 1945.[27] Conversions to Christianity also increased, in a country where that had been relatively rare. Many who came of age after the war married non-Jews, which was another way of leaving Jewishness behind.[28] In underlining the fact that his family's tradition of endogamy ended with his parents' generation, Pierre Vidal-Naquet attributed that change to "the distance [from Jewishness] that was suddenly created after the war" (*Mémoires, I*, 41).

Why, then, did Vidal-Naquet, like a number of other "français juifs," start to get deeply interested in Jewish history in the mid-1960s? As we saw earlier, he dates his interest in this subject to around 1965, when he first engaged in a detailed study of the Dreyfus affair. By that time he was a well-known public intellectual, having fought against French policies in Algeria along with other friends on the left (many of whom were "Jewish Frenchmen" like himself). He had also made a name for himself as a specialist of ancient Greek history, and in 1966 was invited to join the influential group of classical scholars, led by Jean-Pierre Vernant, who were revolutionizing the field through their work at the prestigious École des hautes études. As a professor at the École, where he remained until his retirement in 1997, Vidal-Naquet was at the pinnacle of French intellectual life, and was also at the center of exciting new developments in what the French call "the sciences of man"—psychoanalysis, anthropology, linguistics, literary studies. Happily married, a father of three sons, and approaching his midlife, Vidal-Naquet was in a good position to start reflecting on his Jewish heritage. But it must be emphasized that his turn to Jewish history and to questions of Jewish identity corresponded to that of many other Jewish intellectuals in France at around the same time.

What were some of the historical factors to account for this turn? First, there was the influx of North African Jews into France, which had started in the 1950s when Gamal Abdel Nasser came to power in Egypt, and which accelerated greatly after the end of the Algerian war in 1962. The Jewish population in France increased dramatically as a result, especially in the Paris region and the cities of the south and southwest.[29] The North African Jews, who had not been directly victimized by the Holocaust, were more outspoken in affirming their Jewish identity than the prewar Ashkenazi immigrants whose families had been decimated— not to mention the "Jewish Frenchmen" or "israélites," who had been traumatized by their own losses during the war. Possibly, the latter group also suffered from a certain disillusionment with France's promise of equality, despite what they proclaimed in public.

A second historical factor was the increasing public awareness, in France and elsewhere, of the Holocaust as the defining event of the twentieth century—and in particular, of the centrality of Jewish suffering. The early 1960s, following the Eichmann trial of 1961, saw the beginning of "the era of the witness"—an era that is probably now moving toward its end with the imminent death of those who were alive during the war, but that has given rise to thousands of written and oral testimonies in the past several decades. In France, the realization that the Holocaust was first of all a *Jewish* tragedy did not take hold until around 1966, when Jean-François Steiner, a twenty-eight-year-old writer whose father had died in Auschwitz, published his "nonfiction novel" *Treblinka*, which became a best seller and unleashed a brief but fiery controversy. The controversy concerned Steiner's representation of the uprising of August 1943 at the Treblinka extermination camp, which was organized by Jewish worker-prisoners. Some former (non-Jewish) members of the Resistance accused Steiner of "Jewish racism," since he emphasized the specifically Jewish character of the uprising. Many Jews were critical of the book as well, for various reasons (including the fact that it was not well written). Samuel Moyn, in his excellent study of the so-called Treblinka affair, shows how many and complex were the issues of Jewish identity involved in the debate.[30] His main argument is that this affair brought to the fore, for the first time in France, the specificity of Jewish deportations by the Nazis. Until then, surprising as it may appear today, mainstream French discourse about deportation had never really distinguished between those deported as *résistants* and the 80,000 men, women, and children who had been deported as Jews. All deportees had "died for France," proclaimed an inscription on the wall of the Mémorial de la déportation behind Notre-Dame Cathedral, inaugurated by Charles de Gaulle in 1962 during the height of the "period of repression" regarding Vichy's role in Jewish persecution (the inscription is still there). Whatever its shortcomings, Steiner's book brought the Jews' suffering into the center of public discourse—and Pierre Vidal-Naquet was among its defenders in an article he published in *Le Monde*. Identifying himself as "a Jew, atheist, Marxist, and French," Vidal-Naquet came down on the

positive side concerning Jewish specificity: he viewed the Treblinka uprising not as part of "the anti-Nazi struggle," as some *résistants* had claimed,
but rather as a *Jewish* revolt against the inhuman conditions of the
extermination camp.[31]

The third historical factor was, of course, the 1967 war, whose consequences the world is still struggling with today. To many Jews in France,
even those who did not consider themselves Zionists, the Six-Day War
appeared as Israel's attempt to ward off a threat against its very existence.
Richard Marienstras (1928–2011), a professor of Elizabethan literature at
the Sorbonne who had immigrated to France from Poland, explained at
a roundtable discussion, "Jews in France, Today," published by the journal *Esprit* in April 1968, that he and his friends perceived the 1967 war
not just as a political threat to Israel but as an "ontological" one that could
not fail to arouse strong emotion among Jews in France.[32] The *Esprit*
roundtable consisted of an intense discussion among four Jewish
intellectuals—Marienstras, Vidal-Naquet, Wladimir Rabinovitch (who
wrote under the pseudonym Rabi), and Alex Derczansky—and two
Christian editors of *Esprit*—Jean-Marie Domenach and Paul Thibaud.
Although the Jewish speakers expressed various views about Jewishness
(Marienstras and Vidal-Naquet both defined themselves as non-Zionists,
albeit with different attitudes to the idea of a Jewish people or nation—
Marienstras affirming it, Vidal-Naquet demurring), they were unanimous
in affirming their support for the existence of Israel. The two non-Jewish
speakers also affirmed their support for the existence of the Jewish state,
but revived an old French debate by voicing concern about the possible
"double allegiance" of French Jews who supported Israel—a notion
strongly and variously refuted by Marienstras and the others. This led to
the longest and most interesting development in the discussion, concerning the ambiguities of Jewish identity, as well as of other national or
ethnic identities, in the modern world. In the summer of 1967, Marienstras, along with a few others, had founded the Cercle Gaston Crémieux,
whose self-definition still appears on its website: "un cercle de réflexion
juif, laïque, diasporiste, engagé à gauche" (a Jewish, secular, diasporist
discussion group committed to the left).[33]

The "emotion" among French Jews, which according to the *Esprit*
roundtable signaled a new turn in Jewish self-awareness in France,

became positively fiery after the famous press conference given by General de Gaulle in November 1967, where he referred to the Jews as a "peuple d'élite, sûr de lui-même et dominateur" (an elite people, sure of itself and dominating)—a phrase that was interpreted by many as deeply anti-Semitic, with echoes of the *Protocols of the Elders of Zion* and its paranoid theories of Jewish world domination. By all accounts, de Gaulle's remark—which he tried to explain away later as a compliment to Jews—played an immense role in the affirmation of Jewish identity and group solidarity in France.[34] But this affirmation was actually part of a much broader trend toward identity politics, on the part not only of Jews but of other minorities, which gained momentum in France in the 1970s and 1980s and is still an issue of debate and questioning. Most liberals in France reject "le communautarisme," which they see as endangering French egalitarianism and republicanism; but this rejection is itself challenged by the continuing existence of group affiliations among many Muslims and Jews, and by the increasingly multicultural reality of French society.

A full enumeration of historical factors in the emergence of Jewish memory in France would have to include the revision of the historiography of Vichy in the 1970s and 1980s, inaugurated by the work of the American historian Robert Paxton; the responses to the rising wave of Holocaust negationism beginning in the early 1980s; the importance of the trial of Klaus Barbie in 1987 and of the string of trials of Vichy officials that culminated in the trial of Maurice Papon in 1997; the enormous role of Serge Klarsfeld's massive documentary projects, starting with the *Mémorial de la déportation des Juifs de France* in 1978; and the similarly important role of Claude Lanzmann's 1985 film *Shoah*, as well as of Steven Spielberg's Shoah Foundation testimony project.[35] All of these contributed to the increasingly open self-affirmation of Jews in France, as well as to their ongoing questioning of their relation to the French Republic. That relation is a topic of enormous complexity, whose detailed treatment is obviously beyond the scope of this discussion. I hope to have shown, however, that Jewish children in France who experienced the loss of a parent, and often of their whole family, with the knowledge that the reason for their otherwise incomprehensible loss was their Jewishness, embody in an extreme form some of the dilemmas of identity that French Jews have been struggling with for more than two centuries.

NOTES

1. A partial listing includes the writers Georges Perec, Raymond Federman, Jean-Claude Grumberg, Berthe Burko-Falcman, Emile Copfermann; the philosopher Sara Kofman; the writer and editor Elisabeth Gille; the historians Pierre Vidal-Naquet and Saul Friedlander; the lawyer, historian, and activist Serge Klarsfeld; and the neuropsychiatrist Boris Cyrulnik, among others.

2. The Association des enfants cachés was dissolved in 2007 due to lack of funds, unlike similar associations in other countries which continue to function. A number of hidden children from France currently live in Israel and are members of Aloumim, an association whose members were hidden children in France. Nathalie Zajde's recent study, *Les enfants cachés en France* (Paris: Odile Jacob, 2012), is based primarily on interviews with members of Aloumim. This skews her results somewhat, since her subjects no longer live in France and many express disappointment with the country.

3. For a good overview of the psychological literature on hidden children, in France and elsewhere, see Marion Feldman, *Entre trauma et protection: Quel devenir pour les enfants juifs cachés en France (1940–1944)?* (Toulouse: Éditions Érès, 2009), 81–112. Feldman, a psychologist, interviewed thirty-five child survivors and published detailed accounts of ten, seven of whom lost one or both parents to deportation. Other recent studies by psychologists in France include Marcel Frydman, *Le traumatisme de l'enfant caché: Répercussions psychologiques à court et à long termes* (Paris: L'Harmattan, 2002); Danielle Bailly, ed., *Enfants cachés, analyses et débats* (Paris: L'Harmattan, 2006); Yoram Mouchenik, *Ce n'est qu'un nom sur une liste, mais c'est mon cimetière: Traumas, deuils et transmission chez les enfants juifs cachés en France pendant l'occupation* (Grenoble: La Pensée sauvage, 2006); and Nathalie Zajde, *Les enfants cachés en France* (Paris: Odile Jacob, 2012). These studies follow on the heels of published testimonies by hidden children, including a number of collective volumes; the first of these was the pioneering work by Claudine Vegh, a psychologist and hidden child who lost her father in the war and who in the 1970s interviewed twenty-eight other hidden children who had never spoken about their experiences until then; Vegh, *Je ne lui ai pas dit au revoir: Des enfants de déportés parlent* (Paris: Gallimard, 1979). Some recent collections of testimonies include D. Bailly, ed., *Traqués, cachés, vivants: Des enfants juifs en France 1940–1944* (Paris: L'Harmattan, 2004), and Alain Vincenot, ed., *Je veux revoir maman* (Paris: Editions des Syrtes, 2005). For the concept of the 1.5 generation, see Susan Rubin Suleiman, "The 1.5 Generation: Thinking about Child Survivors and the Holocaust," *American Imago* 59, no. 3 (2002): 277–95, and *Crises of Memory and the Second World War* (Cambridge, MA: Harvard University Press, 2006), chap. 8: "The Edge of Memory: Experimental Writing and the 1.5 Generation (Perec/Federman)."

4. Cyrulnik, *Un merveilleux malheur* (Paris: Odile Jacob poche, 2002), 47–51.

5. Suleiman, "The 1.5 Generation," 280–84.

6. Feldman, *Entre trauma et protection*, 233–70.

7. Émile Copfermann, *Dès les premiers jours de l'automne* (Paris: Gallimard, 1997), 95. Here and throughout, translations from the French are my own.

8. Georges Perec, *W ou le souvenir d'enfance* (Paris: Denoël, 1975), and *Je suis né* (Paris: Seuil, 1990); Raymond Federman, *Double or Nothing* (Chicago: Swallow Press, 1971), and *The Voice in the Closet* (Buffalo, NY: Starcherone, 2001); Berthe Burko-Falcman, *Un prénom républicain* (Paris: Seuil, 2007); Sarah Kofman, *Rue Ordener, rue Labat* (Paris: Galilée, 1994); Jean-Claude Grumberg, *Mon père: Inventaire* (Paris: Seuil, 2003), and *Pleurnichard* (Paris: Seuil, 2010); Boris Cyrulnik, *Je me souviens* (Paris: Odile Jacob, 2010); Saul Friedlander, *Quand vient le souvenir* (Paris: Seuil, 1978); Elisabeth Gille, *Un paysage de cendres* (Paris: Seuil, 1996).

9. Pierre Vidal-Naquet, *Mémoires, I: La brisure et l'attente (1930–1955)* (Paris: Seuil/La Découverte, 1995); *Mémoires, II: Le trouble et la lumière (1955–1998)* (Paris: Seuil/La Découverte, 1998); page references in the text to these works are to the 2007 Seuil paperback edition. Vidal-Naquet's first book protesting torture in Algeria appeared in 1958—*L'affaire Audin* (Paris: Editions de Minuit)—and was followed by several others. The book on negationism first appeared in 1987; see Vidal-Naquet, *Les assassins de la mémoire: "Un Eichmann de papier" et autres essais sur le révisionnisme* (Paris: La Découverte, 1987).

10. Vidal-Naquet, *Mémoires I*, 177–78.

11. The first page of *Double or Nothing* (1971), for example, which consists of a single very long sentence, includes the lines "his parents (both his father and mother) and his two sisters (one older and the other younger than he) had been deported (they were Jewish) to a German concentration camp (Auschwitz probably) and never returned, no doubt having been exterminated deliberately (X*X*X*X)." I analyze this work in detail in *Crises of Memory and the Second World War*, chap. 8.

12. Burko-Falcman, *Un prénom républicain*, 92. Burko-Falcman's earlier works are novels, loosely based on her wartime experiences: *La dernière vie de madame K.* (1982), *Chronique de la source rouge* (1984), and *L'enfant caché* (1997).

13. Grumberg, *Mon père*, 90.

14. Grumberg, *Pleurnichard*, 135–40.

15. Annette Wieviorka, in her important book *Déportation et génocide: Entre la mémoire et l'oubli* (Paris: Plon, 1992), documents the large number of testimonies by camp survivors that appeared right after the war, but also notes that the public tired of them very quickly (167–76). In her subsequent book, *L'ère du témoin* (Paris: Plon, 1998), she concurs with other historians that the change in public attitudes occurred after the 1961 trial of Adolf Eichmann.

16. Cyrulnik, *Je me souviens*, 49. In 2012, Cyrulnik published a full-length memoir about his childhood and youth, in which he juxtaposes his personal story with general observations about the psychology of trauma and survival: Cyrulnik, *Sauve-toi, la vie t'appelle* (Paris: Odile Jacob, 2012).

17. This is also a major theme in Saul Friedlander's moving memoir, *Quand vient le souvenir* (*When Memory Comes*), which along with Perec's *W ou le souvenir d'enfance*

(*W, or, the Memory of Childhood*) is one of the rare such memoirs published in the 1970s. Since both works have often been discussed, I do not dwell on them here. I wrote about Friedlander in my book *Risking Who One Is: Encounters with Contemporary Art and Literature*, chap. 11, and about Perec in *Crises of Memory and the Second World War*, chap. 8.

18. For a fuller discussion, see my article "Irène Némirovsky and the 'Jewish Question' in Interwar France," *Yale French Studies*, no. 121 (2012): 8–33.

19. Claude Bochurberg, *Entretiens avec Serge Klarsfeld* (Paris: Stock, 1997), 23. Page references in the subsequent paragraph are to this work.

20. Burko-Falcman, *Un prénom républicain*, 203.

21. Copfermann, *Dès les premiers jours de l'automne*, 99.

22. Vidal-Naquet, "Protestants et juifs pendant la Seconde Guerre mondiale en France," in *Les juifs, la mémoire et le présent, II* (Paris: La Découverte, 1991), 185.

23. Ibid., 189.

24. Ibid., 12.

25. Bochurberg, *Entretiens avec Serge Klarsfeld*, 151.

26. Wieviorka, *Déportation et génocide*, 349.

27. See the essay by Anne Grynberg, "Après la tourmente," in *Les juifs de France de la Révolution à nos jours*, ed. Jean-Jacques Becker and Annette Wieviorka (Paris: Liana Levi, 1998), especially 262–68; see also Wieviorka, *Déportation et génocide*, 365–67.

28. Catherine Grandsard, a psychologist who has studied children of mixed marriages between Jews and Christians, cites statistics that show an enormous rise in such marriages after the war, and continuing into the 1970s. See Grandsard, *Juifs d'un côté: Portraits de descendants de mariages entre juifs et chrétiens* (Paris: Les Empêcheurs de Penser en Rond, 2005), 21.

29. For a detailed table comparing the number of Jews in French cities before and after 1963, see Becker and Wieviorka, *Les juifs de France de la Révolution à nos jours*, 308–9. In the Paris region, the Jewish population increased from 50,000 to 80,000; in Marseille, from 4,000 to 20,000; in Lyon, Toulouse, and Nice, the Jewish population tripled or quadrupled.

30. Samuel Moyn, *A Holocaust Controversy: The Treblinka Affair in Postwar France* (Waltham, MA: Brandeis University Press, 2005).

31. Vidal-Naquet, "Treblinka et l'honneur des juifs," *Le Monde*, May 2, 1966, 17. In his later memoirs, Vidal-Naquet called the novel "very bad" ("fort mauvais"), and blamed himself for "taking it seriously" at the time—but his views on the Polish Jewish resisters had not changed, he added (*Mémoires, II*, 196, 244–46).

32. "Les juifs de France ont-ils changé?," *Esprit*, April 1968, 581–82. The full text of the roundtable is on 581–608.

33. For a number of years, the Cercle published a journal, *Diasporiques*, which ceased publication in 2007 but is partially available on its website (www.cercle-gaston-cremieux.org). Vidal-Naquet discusses his own early participation in the group in his *Mémoires, II*, 261–22.

34. Among de Gaulle's most eloquent critics on this occasion was Raymond Aron, who had been with the general in London during the war; Marienstras and Vidal-Naquet also condemned the statement as anti-Semitic (see "Les juifs de France ont-ils changé?," 582).

35. I discuss several of these subjects in my book *Crises of Memory and the Second World War*. See especially chapters 2 and 4.

7

Jewish Children's Homes in Post-Holocaust France

Personal Témoignages

LUCILLE CAIRNS

This chapter will examine the experience of young Jewish girls who, having survived the Shoah as hidden children (*enfants cachés*) sheltered by French opponents of the collaborationist Vichy regime, found themselves orphaned at Liberation and placed in Jewish children's homes. Their particular vulnerability, and correspondingly the special duty of care toward them expected of state and community assistance organs, betoken a much bigger ethical picture than their apparently very spatially singular and temporally limited situation might at first suggest. It is an ethical picture that, albeit in inflected form, globally permeates various different geopolitical configurations today.

My methodology consists in analysis of a selection of personal testimonies or *témoignages*, supplemented by reference to a number of secondary texts that document the infrastructure of (largely) Jewish welfare aid in France in the immediate postwar years. In order to set the historical context for these testimonies, a few key facts and figures will first be adduced. These will be drawn from the very sparse secondary literature on the subject of postwar Jewish children's homes in France *specifically* (as opposed to postwar Jewish children's homes more generally). This literature, emanating from the social sciences, comprises three monographs, by Denise Baumann (1988),[1] Jacques Ladsous (1993),[2] and Katy Hazan (2000),[3] one journal article by Jean Laloum (1992),[4] and one chapter by Annette Wieviorka (1993).[5]

Baumann avers that it is impossible to determine the precise number of Jewish children in France who had lost either one or both parents during the war, but estimates their number as being between 12,000 and 16,000 (21). The impossibility of numerical precision is borne out by the fact that fourteen years later, Serge Klarsfeld asserted as a given the much higher figure of 20,000.[6] Baumann states that of these children, 6,000 to 8,000 were placed in children's homes (21); Hazan gives the figure of more than 4,500 for the Oeuvre de secours aux enfants (OSE) alone (106). A sizable proportion of these children were not, it should be noted, "full" orphans. By far the biggest network of Jewish children's homes came under the aegis of the OSE, and Hazan notes that 40 percent of children in the OSE homes had one surviving parent (316). However, very often the remaining parent (usually the mother) was materially unable to support his or her child or children; thus, the latter ended up in a children's home. And while most of these children still had some surviving family members, frequently those relatives were either unable or unwilling to take the child into their own home (Hazan, 287). Hazan foregrounds certain mitigating circumstances: "Economic poverty, particularly the lack of housing, but equally psychological distress, explain why semi-orphans were kept in the homes (39%): many single parents were unable to take on their children. Conversely, second marriages or cohabitations often made relationships between parents and children even more complicated" (108).

The French state did take some responsibility. It officially recognized these orphans of Jewish deportees as war orphans (*pupilles de la Nation*), and provided a small allowance until their majority or until their entrance into the workforce.[7] But what was the role of the French *Jewish* community in these children's care? Some would argue that Judaism places on all Jews a particular duty of care for orphans. Baumann points out:

> According to the Old Testament, helping orphans, who along with widowed women and foreigners living in the country are the most vulnerable of people, is an act of piety prescribed by law, a sign of justice that can distinguish sincere religion.
>
> And we find this protection of orphans in different books of the Torah, which is all the more necessary after times of war when many families have suffered heavy losses and now comprise only widowed women and orphans lacking any financial support.
>
> If the family is too poor or absent, the Talmud holds the community responsible for the upbringing and well-being of orphans, for setting them

up in life, for their marriage; the community must ensure that it provides the orphans what they would have received from their parents. (139–40)

Certainly, the vast majority of welfare organizations responsible for Jewish children's homes at the Liberation were run largely by Jews. But many were secular Jews, and thus not motivated by the specific religious teachings of Judaism. Baumann effectively conveys the spiritual and cultural diversity of the various Jewish homes, some observant, others not, and the efforts made to respect the family background of the individual Jewish child.[8] Indeed, the homes were many and varied in their institutional and ideological bases, as the following list from Laloum demonstrates: "the OSE, the OPEJ, the EIFs, the UJRE, the MNCR, the FOJ, the WIZO, the Colonie scolaire and many other organizations" (247).[9]

Two points need to be made here. First, these homes were funded less by the French Jewish community than by the American Jewish Joint Distribution Committee. Second, a striking perception among a significant number of the orphans was that the Franco-Jewish community had abdicated responsibility for them. Baumann's study is based on one hundred respondents in the demographic concerned. What she says of one of them, Henri, has a representative value that justifies the length of the following quotation.

We only mentioned his last grievance because it was common in numerous cases and posed a seemingly unanswered question (has that question even been heard?). While Henri does not believe society owes him anything (he was a war orphan), he judges harshly the attitude of the Jewish community, which, as a whole, should have felt responsible for the children of deportees. These children felt rejected by the very people who should have been there for them. It was as if guilt about being alive was intensified in the presence of orphans of the disaster, the children of the "others," those who had died; as if the creation of hostels and children's homes "relieved" the community of this cumbersome legacy as it did for close or distant families who had survived. And the latter adopted the attitude of the former, with the highest authorities setting the example. "We represented shame, the dead person's child." (43)

What is implicit in this quotation, although not identified in these terms, is the survivor's guilt syndrome which psychologically blocked out care for the sources of this guilt, namely, the orphans of Jewish deportees. This point is reinforced later on in Baumann's study (152).[10] Again, the wider occurrence of what some might reduce to just two boys' personal grievances is underscored in Baumann's musings toward the end of her study (and here I understand "hostel" [*foyer*] to be distinct from "children's home" [*maison d'enfants*]): "And what about Jewish charities? The Community? I was astonished to note that while some of my interlocutors recognized help that had been given, either by the communities that had raised them (and one day for a child in a hostel costs a lot!), or by the social services that gave out loans with no guarantee of repayment and various forms of aid, a similar number expressed their sense of having received limited or no help from the Community charities, or even bitterly reproached them for their indifference" (195). Yet Hazan's later counterpoint about fund-raising for Jewish orphans should also be acknowledged: "'The working-class masses' were constantly asked to give, particularly by Jewish communists, and they responded generously. This contrasts markedly with the sense of indifference and lack of solidarity that the children felt, at the time, within a community whose boundaries were poorly defined" (223).

There is insufficient space in this chapter to adequately assess the validity of claims about the broader Jewish community's defalcation of duty. What this chapter will attempt to do, inter alia, is to assess, on the basis of four primary texts, how and how well the staff of the various Jewish children's homes discharged their *delegated* duty. There is a conspicuous contrast between the first text, Patricia Finaly's *Le gai ghetto*, published in 1970,[11] and the subsequent three, all published in the first decade of the twenty-first century: Marianne Rubinstein's *Tout le monde n'a pas la chance d'être orphelin* (2002),[12] Annette Zaidman's *Mémoire d'une enfance volée (1938–1948)* (2002),[13] and Francine August-Franck's *Les feux follets de Bourg d'Iré: Espoir et survie d'une âme d'enfant* (2006).[14] In my monograph *Post-War Jewish Women's Writing in French* (2011), I observed that among the many objects of Finaly's censure in *Le gai ghetto* is "the entire infrastructure of Jewish welfare aid in France. She conveys a sense of having been treated as a mere object both during the war by the Union Générale des Israélites de France and after the war by the organization to which it passed her on."[15] That organization is named by Finaly as the Société protectrice des enfants (SPE), which is a fictionalized representation of the OSE. As I also observed in my monograph:

Both are Jewish organizations, but both are presented as dehumanizing: "j'étais devenue une valise à qui on demande pas son avis" [I'd become a suitcase whose opinion isn't wanted]. The official image of the OSE was of tolerance, as Jean Laloum has observed: "L'OSE . . . résolut de respecter toutes les sensibilités de la vie juive en organisant côte à côte des maisons de stricte observance et d'autres dans lesquelles régnait l'esprit le plus libéral" [The OSE . . . resolved to respect all sensibilities in Jewish life by organizing side by side some devout homes and others which were entirely liberal]. A rather more damning perspective is furnished by Finaly. The ideological dogmatisms of the post-war Jewish community are suggested by the comic scene of interrogation to which the child is subjected by the OSE in 1945: "–Es-tu pour l'assimilation du peuple juif selon la théorie de Karl Marx ou pour le regroupement du people hébraïque selon les principes de Chaïm Weizmann?" [Are you for the assimilation of the Jewish people according to Karl Marx's theory, or for the reunification of the Hebrew people according to Chaïm Weizmann's principles?]. Her blackly humorous response, pragmatic given historic Jewish experiences, is "– Je suis pour celui qui n'est pas juif!" [I'm for whoever isn't Jewish!]. (118–19)[16]

This sense of having been shunted from one place to another with no regard for her own feelings is shored up by the high number of OSE children's homes through which she passes: five in fewer than five years. Hazan's study suggests the representativity of Finaly's experience: "Consultation of the OSE's lists shows a significant to-ing and fro-ing and demonstrates emergency management. Names are continually crossed out, children go from one home to another without understanding why, according to personal backgrounds and needs" (109).[17]

In Le gai ghetto, Finaly satirizes the ethos of those Jewish children's homes which aspired to nonhierarchical relationships between children and staff and to a child-centered, child-participative pedagogy. Such progressive ideals certainly characterized many of the homes in reality, as Baumann's and Hazan's studies attest. Nonetheless, under Finaly's writerly scalpel, there is an ironic hiatus between ideal and reality. At the Château de Corbeville par Orsay, she is told upon arrival that the teachers (*éducateurs*) are not her supervisors (*surveillants*), but rather her friends. Paradoxically, though, informality is officialized: "You can call them by their first name: Guy and Alain. You must also be informal when you address them as we apply a modern educational method here, the Montessori method" (Finaly, 98–99). Finaly's depiction of Guy strongly suggests that he was hardly a model exponent of the Montessori method, hating teaching and even falling asleep in the middle of it (100). More perturbing than Guy's narcoleptic neglect of pedagogical duties is his recourse to physical violence: "Guy rushed towards my pupil to land her a clout" (Finaly, 103; cf. 113). Corporal punishment is also casually meted out at the third children's home to which she is sent, Le Vésinet (Finaly, 117).

Yet in Finaly's studiedly nonchalant narrative, such physical violence is of little consequence, and certainly no more objectionable than her other numerous targets. One of these targets again relates to the earnest principles of the OSE, this time in its ideal of physical health and community spirit, which she dryly ridicules (105). At least here she does not question the sincerity of the ideal. With reference to religious education, however, she very plainly posits cynical venality on the part of the non-Orthodox children's home: "Among the many S.P.E. homes, some were *very* pious and their piety was *considerably* boosted by the dollars handed over by the American rabbis. Others—like Le Vésinet—had a management that was entitled 'liberal,' but which forced us to make a little show of faith so that no portion of the cake should crumble away. In the month of October, for the first time, I heard talk of a Feast of Tabernacles" (Finaly, 128). Tempering this slightly is her allusion to the reparative mission of the home's directors, which is corroborated by Baumann's and Hazan's later quantitative findings: "In 1945 the directors were people who wanted at all costs to rebuild the world after 'the horrible storm that had beaten down upon the chosen people'" (Finaly, 151). Even in the late 1940s, the new directors of Le Plongeoir sincerely wanted, Finaly concedes, to transform their charges: "They wanted at whatever cost to make *somebody* of me." But even here she hints at less noble motives, suggesting that one of the two directors, because he felt intellectually threatened by her, condescendingly suggested she was destined to become merely a short-hand typist (152).

Finaly also caustically discredits the ZOWI, which is a fictional representation of the WIZO (Women's International Zionist Organization): "According to my information, the ZOWI was regarded as an organization of stinking rich Zionists who with the help of their cash were sending poor unarmed schmucks to the war in Israel" (156).[18] In Finaly's relentlessly damning account, that encouragement is degraded into compulsory army training: "Before leaving for Israel, the volunteers will have to do military training in an S.P.E. home in Versailles" (163).[19]

Thirty-two years after Finaly's *Le gai ghetto*, Marianne Rubinstein published *Tout le monde n'a pas la chance d'être orphelin* (2002). Significantly, it bears a laudatory preface from Serge Klarsfeld, who in 1979 created the Association des fils et filles des déportés juifs de France (FFDJF). Rubinstein's work is a hybrid, blending first-person narrative of the author's own, third-generation reflections with third-person narrative of her father's loss of his parents in the Shoah, and, in addition, first-person testimonies from some fifteen other Jewish children orphaned during World War II. One of the salient points emerging from these numerous testimonies is the preeminence of the children's home Le Renouveau (at Montmorency) and the singularity of its director, Madame François. Of Rubinstein's father, we learn that Le Renouveau had enabled him to pursue his education well beyond what appeared to be his limited options, to the point where he obtained the *baccalauréat* and embarked on successful medical studies, later becoming a cardiologist (Rubinstein, 27–28).

I would like at this point briefly to intercalate one reference to another testimony, this time solely of the author's own experiences: Francine August-Franck's *Les feux follets de Bourg d'Iré: Espoir et survie d'une âme d'enfant* (2006). Here the reader has an example of a child who had one surviving parent, her father, but who was nonetheless placed in a children's home, and this the most famous of them all—Le Renouveau. August-Franck's description of Le Renouveau's director, Madame François, concords remarkably with descriptions found in the secondary literature: "A dark-haired little woman with a piercing stare and a loud voice, Madame François exuded authority. She could be curt, but that didn't stop her being a good listener for every boarder. As a known specialist in psycho-pedagogy, her educational plan was to restore a taste for life to this group of broken children, who had been disorientated by the Shoah. She would try to uncover each child's personality in order to better guide him or her. She had a preference for sturdy characters, indeed for rebels, and there were certainly some of those at Le Renouveau" (167).

Rubinstein's account of Madame François is less critical than August-Franck's, perhaps because it is a mediated account, based less on the personal, often very ambivalent experience of those orphans placed under Madame François's dominion. Nevertheless, Rubinstein's greater distance affords her account a counterbalancing function, as she quotes directly from Madame François herself. What Madame François said about her young charges is persuasive, and may go some way to explaining the often conflictual nature of her relationships with them: "They were demanding and hard, very, very hard. They had something against me and I constantly asked 'What do they have against me?' I read books on psychology. But they didn't help me. No children whose parents had been gassed and had died in the ovens had previously been studied by psychologists.... They were special cases, and hatred had built up in their hearts. They were child victims, but ashamed of being victims, and they had something against everyone because of this situation" (Rubinstein, 51).[20] A particularly disturbing memory from Madame François suggests a form of acting-out on the part of these children, an unconscious mimeticism via which they perpetuate a destruction, albeit of a very different sort, previously wrought on them:

> For example, they didn't know how to play. But one fine day, from my window, I saw that they had lined up in the playground, a dozen of them. I said to myself: Good! We can't make them play, but *they* have the right to invent games to prove to us that they can play if they want to.
>
> I watched. I didn't go down and, suddenly, I heard a noise: a broken window pane! But what were they doing? Well, just imagine the first game invented by them. They lined up. They filled their jackets with chestnuts, sweet chestnuts, and they aimed at all the window panes. And the one who broke the most was entitled to a prize. This game is the first thing they invented: the game of destruction. (Ladsous, 38–39)

Madame François and Le Renouveau will be revisited in the final section of this chapter. Before that, my last case study is a personal testimony that presents two other Jewish children's homes, both administrated by the Communist-oriented CCE, which itself depended on the Communist UJRE. These two homes are Le Manoir de Denouval, in Andrésy, and the Villa Massilia at Sainte-Maxime. Andrésy is where the young Annette Zaidman, author of *Mémoire d'une enfance volée (1938–1948)* (2002), is placed after a long and distressing succession of short-term stays in various settings (Zaidman, 135–36). All was not, of course, perfect at Andrésy; Zaidman recalls, for example, the inadequate training of the teachers, which sometimes led to well-intentioned but psychologically disastrous interventions:

> The teachers rarely had any qualifications and, besides their good will, their commitment, and their devotion, they had no specific training. So it was not uncommon for clumsy words "of encouragement" to cause an orphan to break off all dialogue with "the world of adults." For example, at the end of the war, without any malice but also without pulling any punches, the adults would say to the war orphans: "Be happy to be alive!" As if the child could be happy about having survived when his or her parents had died, when fathers and mothers had been shot or deported and gone up in smoke! (140)

But offsetting this emphasis on lack of psychological empathy, there is also emphasis on the genuine compassion and humanity of the staff. On the whole, Zaidman's memories of the personnel are imbued with affection and respect.[21] And it is not merely the devotion of the staff to their orphaned charges that Zaidman stresses. She also points to their efforts to inculcate in the children an awareness of their Jewish origins: "Beyond activities linked to school and games, our education, although essentially secular, was also marked by Jewish culture. Thus our 'progressive' little home would celebrate traditional Jewish holidays, such as Purim, as well as national holidays. We were also taught the Hebrew alphabet" (144). It is noteworthy that this concern of the Andrésy home, managed by the Communist-oriented CCE, to transmit a Jewish heritage that would otherwise have been lost to the orphans is also ascribed by the historian

Wievieorka to the non-Communist OSE homes (177). This commonality suggests at least one goal transcending the partisan divisions between the different homes. What is more particular to the CCE homes is, not surprisingly, their efforts to raise the children's consciousness of their parents' sterling contributions to the Resistance (which, recall, owed much in France to the Communists). But just as important as these more overtly ideological considerations is Zaidman's accent on efforts by the CCE staff to inspire in the orphans a pride in their parents as Jews who had not, *pace* the infamous myth, been passively complicit in their own destruction (Zaidman, 144). As Laloum states in his detailed case study of the CCE homes: "These children were the heirs to the history of their elders, Jewish and communist heroes killed in the course of the Second World War. They were brought up in the cult of their memory" (254). All of these efforts bear ample fruit in the young Annette, who begins to recover the capacity for positive childhood sensations such as curiosity, joy, and optimism:

> Through these elders I discovered words I had not known, words which spoke of a "brighter future." And among other songs, be they revolutionary or not, they taught me those in Hebrew and in Yiddish, and so I retained a link with the roots I had lost in Auschwitz and Warsaw. And also the Hora, that dance of the Israeli pioneers, where everyone can enter into joyous ring-dancing.
>
> All of that made a difference to the little girl I was. Such a difference that, straightaway, I confidently followed my new family so that, together, we could all "go to meet life" and "build a new world." (Zaidman, 145)

Even more constructive is her experience at the second CCE children's home to which she is sent, Sainte-Maxime, considered more suitable than Andrésy for children whose health was fragile, as hers certainly still was. "At Sainte-Maxime, there were barely forty of we children, in a heavenly place where the prevailing atmosphere was more intimate and family-like than at Andrésy. This was no doubt due to the fact that there were not many of us, and also to the great affection with which we were treated by Maurice and Myra Honel, the home's directors, as well as by their small team" (Zaidman, 151). In fact, her physical and psychological flourishing during the two years in these two CCE children's homes is so rich that "real" family life comes as a painful shock when she is removed from the children's home and taken in by an uncle, her official guardian. "When I went back to my uncle's, I felt like a stranger there, an unwelcome intruder. What to begin with was only an impression proved to be a sad reality. So, after more than two years in Children's Homes, where I had been more or less put back on my feet, there I was again losing my bearings. . . . Far from the community life with my companions at the Children's Homes, I was shrinking back into my shell" (Zaidman, 157–58).

How might we explain the marked discrepancy between Finaly's jaundiced representation of the Jewish children's homes and the other three texts' far more generous stance? One approach may be to consider the publication dates of these texts within the life cycles of their authors. Finaly published her text in 1970, when she would have been in her early thirties, whereas the other three books were published in the first decade of the twenty-first century, when their authors would have been in their sixties at least. Does greater age bring greater maturity and awareness of the constraints under which the directors and teachers of the homes labored? And might the possibility open to the older women of belonging to an organization such as the Association des fils et des filles des déportés juifs de France have militated against Finaly's tendency to systematic vitriol? This association was only founded in 1979, and seems to have had a therapeutic effect for many of the authors surveyed in the wider corpus.

The final part of this chapter will draw out some headline points from a slightly extended corpus of textual material. One headline point is the immeasurable psychological damage inflicted on these children by their parents' murder, summed up poignantly by August-Franck: "What we'll never be able to assess is how much we had been despoiled, emotionally and psychologically shaken, by that brutal wrench, without reason or explanation" (181). This may elucidate at least to some extent the corrosive diatribes launched by Finaly against virtually every aspect of the children's homes. Finaly's mordant critique of the OSE homes in particular includes many charges, including bias against working-class Jewish orphans and objectification of all Jewish orphans as ideological raw material to be shaped into pawns for political causes such as Communism or Zionism.

In fact, if Hazan is to be believed—and there seems no reason not to believe this professional historian's carefully researched work—Finaly's bile was not as exceptional as it might seem, even though it finds little, if any, echo in the published testimonies of those orphans grown into adults: "All the teachers who wrote educational reports mention nervous, unruly, aggressive children, some borderline delinquent. . . . But all the teachers questioned talked rather of withdrawn, secret, inscrutable children. . . . The teachers noted a lack of initiative, a lack of will, a fear of making a sustained effort, often going hand in hand with rudeness, instability or superficial resourcefulness" (Hazan, 230–31). That said, it would be too extreme to suggest that all or even a majority of the children reacted as negatively as Finaly to their "éducateurs." And it is vital to recall Zaidman's point that these "éducateurs" had often received no proper training (140). What does appear to be a constant across all the accounts, in both the secondary and the primary literature, is the ideal cherished by the staff of these homes to ensure the renaissance of Jewry. From the perspective of the secondary literature, an article published as early as March 1945 in the *Bulletin OSE* conveys this ideal unequivocally:

> Finally, as a replacement for parents and as a Jewish charity, we have a duty to ensure that our children are brought up in a way that, above all, reasserts in their minds the value of their connection to Judaism. Since our children come not only from different social backgrounds but also backgrounds that were more or less assimilated and in which religious tradition had endured to varying extents, we consider it essential to create a Jewish atmosphere in each of our homes that is nuanced according to how we would have practiced among our children in normal circumstances.[22]

But this was not the only ambition of the children's homes. In addition, they sought to provide the orphans with cultural riches: "In all the children's homes, music is considered a permanent educational tool. Each home has at the very least its choir, more or less famous, more or less prestigious. . . . All the children of all the homes acknowledge having been immersed in an exceptional cultural atmosphere" (Hazan, 345). Le Renouveau is singled out for its additional emphasis on liberatory self-expression through the written word: Hazan observes that "recourse to the written text was the rule at Le Renouveau. When they arrived, the children were invited to talk about their experience of the war, which, as at Brunoy, triggers the beginning of a liberatory process" (Hazan, 344).

Indeed, one salient topos running throughout the literature, both primary and secondary, is the uniqueness of Le Renouveau. One of its distinctive features was provision of considerable educational opportunities (as we saw earlier in the case of Rubinstein's father): "Certain children's homes built their educational system on this compensatory aspect of studies and job choices, using them as a lever to 'oblige' their children to be successful and to restore in them a confidence destroyed by their past as 'war victims.' Le Renouveau at Montmorency was the finest example of this" (Baumann, 170). Most notable of all in all evocations of Le Renouveau is the controversial personality of its director, Madame François. This is her nom de guerre; in fact, she was a Polish Jew named Frania Propper, born in 1905, whose husband had died in Auschwitz in 1942. She was a recognized educational psychologist with, claims August-Franck, a humanitarian approach. However, what emerges from other accounts is a harsher, more domineering side to Madame François: "Many confirm it, she loved rebels, those who wanted to fight, those who asserted their character. You had to oppose her to be recognized by her. In a way, she took up the challenge of the Shoah. Through their upbringing, these broken, mistreated beings had to be able to face life, to hold their head up high. But take heed those who did not succeed in their studies, who did not enter into her plan" (Hazan, 144). Rather disquietingly, there appears to have been a pronounced gendered dimension to her authoritarianism. She certainly seems to have accorded preferential treatment to boys, even going so far as to bully girls.[23] Yet Hazan's final verdict on Madame François is nonetheless valorizing: "All were divided between admiration and resentment, love and hate. But, at the end of the day, it was respect and admiration that prevailed, for Le Renouveau wanted to be a real family, with the tensions inherent in any family, and Madame Françoise was its soul" (145–46).

Armelle Bonis adopts a similarly dimorphic and ultimately familial paradigm in reference to the orphans in Madame François's charge: "Their ambivalent memories reflect the inextricable mixture of love and hate that they felt for her. Authoritarian and manipulative, she made them cast off their victim status and neglected to console their undying sorrow. . . . Her victory, however, is perhaps to have allowed her wards to grow up against her, to make unfailing friendships, and to recompose, through her, the family of which they had been deprived."[24] In fact, with respect not just to Madame François but to the Jewish children's homes more generally, and with the egregious exception of Finaly, that pattern of critique followed by ultimate tribute characterizes all of the texts I have been able to access. This applies to both the secondary and the primary texts, and in the case of the primary texts it is irrespective of the specific children's homes focused on.

I would like to end this chapter by citing one instance of both. For the secondary texts, a pithy comment from Baumann puts the case simply: "The criticisms appear fewer than the good memories" (159). And from the primary texts—here in the broadest of senses—are foregrounded the words of Sylvia, one of the respondents of Baumann's survey who had spent three years of her adolescence (from fifteen to eighteen years old) in one of the OSE homes: "For me the children's home has been, at various points in my life, a lifeline. There I found the best coeducational and fraternal school. Given the great devotion of the people who selflessly gave themselves to us, I wouldn't dare criticize their clumsiness; they had not received any training in education and their enthusiasm was only equaled by their kindhearted nature. I was unable to thank them at the time, but whenever I can help someone, I try to act thinking about them and how they themselves would have gone about it" (Baumann, 145). In her last sentence here, Sylvia's words suggest the ethical exemplarity of the OSE workers, despite, or possibly all the more so because of, their eminently human clumsiness in the altruistic execution of their humanitarian mission. That execution is one from which twenty-first-century aid and public assistance workers globally, and in a constructively critical perspective, might draw valuable lessons.

NOTES

1. Denise Baumann, *La mémoire des oubliés: Grandir après Auschwitz* (Paris: A. Michel, 1988).

2. Jacques Ladsous, *Madame François: Aventurière de l'éducation nouvelle* (Toulouse: Éditions Érès, 1993), 38–39.

3. Katy Hazan, *Les orphelins de la Shoah* (Paris: Éditions Les Belles Lettres, 2000).

4. Jean Laloum, "La création des maisons d'enfants: L'exemple de la Commission centrale de l'enfance auprès de l'UJRE," *Pardès* 16 (1992): 247–70.

5. Annette Wieviorka, "Éléments pour servir à l'histoire des maisons d'enfants de l'OSE dans l'après-guerre," in *Au secours des enfants du siècle: Regards croisés sur l'OSE*, ed. Martine Lemalet (Paris: NIL Éditions, 1993), 159–83.

6. Serge Klarsfeld, preface to Marianne Rubinstein, *Tout le monde n'a pas la chance d'être orphelin* (Paris: Éditions Verticales/Le Seuil, 2002), 7.

7. However, this allowance was paid to the adults whose charges they became, either other family members or organizations like the OSE. This, argues Baumann, is why "the children placed in communities felt they had been given no personal help" (*La mémoire des oubliés*, 194).

8. "The religious orientation of each home depended on its executives and on the body funding it. Only the OSE had a sufficient number of establishments for the majority of politico-religious tendencies to be able to express themselves. More or less orthodox, 'kosher' or not, right-wing Zionists or left-wing Zionists, Bundists, communists: the homes took children in according to what was known of their parents' opinions and traditions. The essential point was that teachers should combine tolerance with the sincerity of their beliefs" (ibid., 142-43).

9. CCE: Commission centrale de l'enfance; EIF: Éclaireurs israélites de France; FOJ designates a left-wing Zionist movement; Poale Zion, meaning "Workers of Zion"; MNCR: Mouvement national contre le racisme; OPEJ: Oeuvre de protection des enfants juifs; OSE: Oeuvre de secours aux enfants; UJRE: Union des juifs pour la résistance et l'entraide; WIZO: Women's International Zionist Organization.

10. "Henri will concur with Joseph in his criticism of the community and of families: 'Nothing positive came from the families; putting us into hostels relieved everyone of a burden: the Jewish community's conscience and kinship. The leaders of the community did not set an example and families followed suit: uncles, aunts and cousins looked after themselves. We were a living reproach, shame, the child of the dead uncle or cousin . . . whereas *they* were there'" (Baumann, *La mémoire des oubliés*, 152).

11. Patricia Finaly, *Le gai ghetto* (Paris: Gallimard, 1970). For further information, see the INA video clip at http://www.ina.fr/video/CPF11000061/patricia-finaly.fr.html.

12. Marianne Rubinstein, *Tout le monde n'a pas la chance d'être orphelin* (Paris: Éditions Verticales/Le Seuil, 2002).

13. Annette Zaidman, *Mémoire d'une enfance volée (1938–1948)* (Paris: Ramsay, 2002).

14. Francine August-Franck, *Les feux follets de Bourg d'Iré: Espoir et survie d'une âme d'enfant* (Paris: L'Harmattan, 2006).

15. Lucille Cairns, *Post-War Jewish Women's Writing in French* (Oxford: Legenda, 2011), 118.

16. The citation is from Laloum, "La création des maisons d'enfants," 256.

17. The first home to which Finaly is sent is nicknamed "Le Plongeoir," at Saint-Genis-Laval (Rhône) (*Le gai ghetto*, 97)—very probably a pseudonym for Le Tremplin (see Hazan, *Les orphelins*, 397); the second is Château de Corbeville par Orsay (Seine-et-Oise) (Finaly, *Le gai ghetto*, 98); the third is Vésinet (and may have been based on the Villa Concordia in Le Vésinet (Hazan, *Les orphelins*, 398); the fourth is in Fontenay-aux-Roses (Finaly, *Le gai ghetto*,148), which may have been based on Boucicaut at Fontenay-aux-Roses (Hazan, *Les orphelins*, 398); and finally, she comes full circle, arriving back at Le Plongeoir (Finaly, *Le gai ghetto*, 150).

18. As Wieviorka explains, "The OSE was not a Zionist organization, in the sense that it did not prepare for Aliyah the children in its care. However, it showed active sympathies for the Jewish Homeland and, later on, for the new Hebrew State, and encouraged those of its children who were so inclined to emigrate there" ("Éléments pour servir," 168–69).

19. Interestingly, Hazan's historical and sociological study contains comment on the literary work of Finaly, and it is well worth citing as a conclusion to this section on *Le gai ghetto*: "Patricia Finaly was one of the first to discuss in writing in 1970 what she calls 'her real war,' her experience in an OSE children's home. She had become, she says, 'a suitcase whose opinion isn't wanted.' Constantly rebelling against everything and everyone, she settles her scores in a deliberately provocative and vulgar style, in the manner of *Zazie dans le métro*. Some of her criticisms are obviously not without foundation, the 'brown-nosing,' the road to hell paved with good intentions seen in some of the teachers, the compulsory shows to thank the charity ladies, the absurdity of certain punishments" (Hazan, *Les orphelins*, 286).

20. Rubinstein here quotes from Ladsous, *Madame François*, 38–39.

21. "The directors of the UJRE, like our teachers, were for the most part former Jewish resisters in the FTP, close to the communist party. The devotion of these men and women, who had taken into their care the distraught and traumatized children we were, knew no bounds. After the turmoil we had all just been through, we had become family-less, and our elders, those idealists, had the ambition of recreating with us a big family. In this undertaking, all those around us . . . all gave us their affection and—through the example of their attitude towards us—they passed on to us their sense of humanism" (Zaidman, *Mémoire d'une enfance volée*, 140–41).

22. Robert Job, "Nos maisons renaissent à la vie. Quelle est notre doctrine?," *Bulletin "OSE,"* no. 2 (March 15, 1945): 1–3 (quotation from 2).

23. "But some still spoke about teacher's pets, 'the head's intimates,' basically about boys who went into her bedroom, particularly in the second home at Beauséjour, to watch TV or quite simply to chat with adults and improve their minds! . . . 'It was the head, she shouted all the time, I was terrified; she was unfair, she sought to humiliate us in front of the others,' say many girls who suffered from her harshness. . . . Undeniably, she preferred those who got stuck into their studies and she pushed them as much as she could. Some girls bear a grudge against her for having given up on them, in a word for having invested nothing in them. . . . They were withdrawn,

shy, with a mental block, the complete opposite of what this woman expected of them: in short, they didn't get on" (Hazan, *Les orphelins*, 144–45). Also: "Those who were unable to establish an emotional relationship with an adult obviously lacked emotional bearings or, more seriously, foundations. You find children like them in all homes. It's no doubt what happened to certain girls at Le Renouveau who didn't interest Madame François, who, in her turn, didn't give them a reassuring image of women. 'She stood for authority, she frightened us, we weren't allowed to sit on the beds, we jumped when we heard her'" (ibid., 290).

24. Armelle Bonis, "'Attention aux enfants!': Sur un film de José Ainouz," *L'Arche*, March 2011, 134–35 (quotation from 135).

8

Post-Holocaust French Writing

Reflecting on Evil in 1947

BRUNO CHAOUAT

Beginnings

Two years after the war, in 1947, a significant number of literary, testimonial, and philosophical works appeared in France and in other European countries. This chapter examines how these works, offering different responses to the war, share one feature: each, in its own genre and style, engages, directly or obliquely, explicitly or not, with the question of evil.

Unsurprisingly, a period of latency, albeit a relatively short one, was needed before these works could appear.[1] Before turning to this corpus of texts published two years after the war, therefore, it is relevant to recall that in the early to mid-1940s, diaries, fictional works, and testimonies from survivors, *résistants*, or French Jews in hiding were published by prominent or minor presses. In 1944, for example, the Albin Michel publishing house brought out *Le camp de la mort lente*, a memoir written in 1943 by the playwright Jean-Jacques Bernard. Bernard was detained in Compiègne for several months from 1941 to 1942 along with other French Jewish intellectuals, including René Blum, brother of the Popular Front leader Léon Blum. This book was a poignant account of the first time he had ever been discriminated against, or practically even noticed, as a Jew. Bernard's memoir reflects the kind of Jewish self-effacement demanded by the French Third Republic in the name of universalism—a demand that could easily segue into strident anti-Judaism, if not anti-Semitism. To be sure, the author at the time did not know the fate of those sent east from Vichy internment camps; perhaps otherwise he would have shown more compassion toward his coreligionists.

We can also cite the example of the former pacifist Jean Bruller, son of a Jewish father, who joined the Resistance under the assumed name Vercors, and cofounded the underground publishing house Les Éditions de Minuit. In 1943, the same year Bernard penned his account, Vercors wrote and published both the short story *La marche à l'étoile*[2] and the book that would become a best seller, *Le silence de la mer*.[3] The latter is a robust defense, *pace* Jacques Derrida, of unconditional *in*hospitality as *résistance*.[4] Indeed, the main message of the novella, arguably a classic of Résistance propaganda, was that it was wrong to host even the most civilized enemy, that under German occupation there should be no exception to the laws of *in*hospitality.

The year 1945 saw the appearance of Guy Kohen's *Retour d'Auschwitz*,[5] a straightforward testimony by a twenty-year-old survivor who had been deported to Auschwitz via Drancy. In the following year, 1946, Grasset published a lengthy diary by Léon Werth, to whom Saint-Exupéry had dedicated his 1943 *Le Petit Prince*.[6] Werth scrupulously records everyday life in hiding between 1940 and 1944. His response to Vichy's anti-Jewish legislation was radically opposed to that shown by Jean-Jacques Bernard. While the latter deemed that accepting the forced identification of certain French citizens as Jews played into the hands of the enemy, Werth considered that reclaiming one's belonging to a "Jewish nation" was a matter of honor and dignity. As Hannah Arendt put it: "If one is attacked as a Jew, one must defend oneself as a Jew. Not as a German, not as a world-citizen, not as an upholder of the Rights of Man."[7] Likewise, Werth wrote: "Thus they tried to impose upon me another nationality, another identity. How cowardly it would be to quibble as to whether or not I feel Jewish. If you insult me because I can be called a Jew, then I am a Jew, wildly Jewish, Jewish from the tips of my fingers down to the deepest recesses of my guts. Once that's over, then one may ask oneself how Jewish one really is."[8] For Bernard, the rejection of Judaism as a collective ethnic identity (though not necessarily as an individual religious choice) was the only honorable response to legal anti-Semitism. In Werth's eyes, proudly acknowledging one's identity as a Jew was the sole tolerable reaction to anti-Semitic stigmatization.

In the same year, 1946, Suzanne Birnbaum, a humble Jewish tradeswoman, published *Une française juive est revenue*.[9] We can note that in conformity with French Republican assimilationism, "Jewish" is here employed as an adjective rather than as a noun: *A Jewish Frenchwoman Has Returned*, rather than *A French Jewess Has Returned*. The year 1946 also saw the publication of Jean-Paul Sartre's *Réflexions sur la question juive* and David Rousset's *L'univers concentrationnaire*,[10] the latter representing one of the most famous dissections of Nazi terror. It is also in 1946 that Vercors published *Les armes de la nuit*,[11] a harrowing account of Nazi dehumanization. *Les armes de la nuit* tells the story of a French *résistant* who claims to have lost his "human quality" in the camps. The reader, along with the narrator, learns that this loss of "human quality" is due to the survivor Pierre Canges's having served in a Sonderkommando where he was forced to fling a fellow worker alive—as well as numerous other anonymous inmates, both dead and alive—into a crematorium. The last section of the novella is entitled "Orphée." The myth of Orpheus, the poet who descends to the underworld, gazes back toward his beloved, and kills her anew, functions here as an allegory for the loss of humanity. It also uncannily heralds Maurice Blanchot's use, less than a decade later, of Orpheus to characterize the "fruitless" exercise of writing, and his topos of "the other night."[12]

Then came diaries and memoirs of those who did not survive the war, some of which would be published long after their authors' deaths. One example is Raymond-Raoul Lambert's *Carnets d'un témoin 1940–43*, published by Fayard in 1985. Lambert, who served as the director of the Union générale des israélites de France, was deported to Drancy and murdered along with his wife and four children in Auschwitz in 1943. Likewise, we shall have to wait until 2008, sixty-four years after her death at Bergen-Belsen, for Hélène Berr's *Journal 42–44* to be published, with a moving foreword by the novelist Patrick Modiano.[13] Many of these accounts bear witness to the existential conflict of French Jews, some of them veterans of World War I, who felt cruelly betrayed by their homeland.

1947

Coming in the wake of these earlier texts, 1947 proved to be an eventful year for literary, testimonial, and philosophical engagement with the question of evil. I shall first propose a brief survey of works published that year in France and beyond. There can be no doubt that their authors drew inspiration from recently published diaries, memoirs, written or oral testimonies, and fiction that had circulated clandestinely during the occupation. The vast literary, testimonial, and philosophical production is precisely what leads me to focus my contribution on 1947.

Just one year after his *Univers concentrationnaire*, Rousset published *Les jours de notre mort*,[14] a book that combines several literary genres—memoir, testimony, and novel. The same year, Georges Bataille wrote an intriguing commentary of Rousset's book in his journal *Critique*.[15] There, Bataille harnessed Rousset's book to a mode of thinking that would a decade later underlie his major theoretical work on the relationship among literature, excess, and evil, namely, *La littérature et le mal*.[16] More significantly, Bataille, in his original essay, quoted the conclusion of Rousset's book: "Victim and perpetrator alike were ignoble; the lesson to be learned from the camps is that of brotherhood in abjection." With this move, Bataille, besides displaying a certain perverse enjoyment of abjection and injecting a hearty dose of Sade into his reading of Nazi evil, launches the motif of the interchangeability between victim and perpetrator—a tendentious motif that will know a long posterity and that arguably pertains to the de-judaization of the Holocaust. The year 1947 also saw the publication of Robert Antelme's *L'espèce humaine* by Éditions de la Cité Universelle, a press founded in 1945 by Marguerite Duras and Antelme himself. Antelme's testimony, in contradistinction to Bataille's gloss on Rousset, can be read as an attempt to restore the ethical boundaries between victims and perpetrators and to rebuild humanism on the basis of a solid line between good and evil, resistance and collaboration. I shall not dwell on the novel published by Gallimard, Jean Genet's *Pompes funèbres*. Eric Marty has written on Genet's "anxiety of the Good," his metaphysical anti-Semitism, and the fascination exerted on the playwright by the figure of Hitler from the 1940s up to his enamorment with terrorists in works that deal with the Arab-Israeli conflict in the 1970s and 1980s.[17] It was also in 1947 that the same house, Gallimard, published Albert Camus's *La peste*, arguably an allegory of the war, wherein the epidemic suggests an analogy between the "cataclysm of the war and the concentration camps."[18]

Let us now consider Vladimir Jankélévitch, known for the literary tenor of his philosophical writings and his postwar rejection of German philosophy in favor of the ancient Greeks, the Church Fathers, Leibniz, and Pascal. His book *Le mal*, which also came out in 1947,[19] is a somewhat abstract and at times casuistic speculation on evil. Examined closely, it reveals the author's experience in the Résistance. The book is not devoid of references to recent history, though they are necessarily scarce in such a theoretical work. While Jankélévitch's *Le mal* cannot be reduced to a philosophical allegory of the war that had just torn France as well as the world apart, it is nonetheless deeply influenced by a past all too fresh. Consider direct references to the sacrifice of the *résistants*, to the "défaite" and to the "capitulards" or "defeatists," to the "surhomme" or Nietzschean superman, the "fascist toad" (*crapaud fasciste*), and, last but not least, to the "blond dolichocephal."[20] Jankélévitch's lexical imagination knew no limits. Note, far more troublingly, the omission of any explicit reference to the persecution of the Jews.

It is significant now to mention four major works published in the same year, but outside France. The first is Theodor Adorno and Max Horkheimer's *Dialectic of the Enlightenment*, whose core argument may be that the "dialectic of reason" is the condition of possibility of fascism. The second is Thomas Mann's *Doctor Faustus*. The third is Hans Falla-da's *Every Man Dies Alone*, a novel on German anti-Nazi resistance that illustrates what George Orwell once called "common decency," a rather extraordinary quality in times of totalitarian terror. Last but not least, there is the first publication of Primo Levi's *If This Be a Man*, whose first translation into French would appear in 1961.

The Corpses' Beech Tree

I shall now turn to a less-known literary work, published that very same year, by a writer who had long been associated with literary regionalism, although he arguably belongs to the great Western canon. Jean Giono, because of the association of his writing with the Vichy government's campaign for a return to the land, was imprisoned for five months, black-listed by the Comité national des écrivains, and unable to publish until 1947. Giono was a staunch pacifist. His unconditional rejection of war in the wake of the trauma of World War I, rather than anti-Semitic or fascist leanings, led him to embrace the Vichy regime. Giono, to be sure, was less a "crapaud fasciste" than a "capitulard." His first postwar novel was enti-tled *Un roi sans divertissement*, after Pascal's aphorism, "A king without diversion is a man full of miseries." The novel was first published by La Table Ronde, then banned due to the author's blacklisting, and republished one year later by Gallimard after charges of collaboration had been dismissed. The novel also inaugurates what Giono's critics have called his "seconde manière," to be sure a significant turning point in his poetics.

As Baudelaire had it, "ennui," this "delicate monster," can be seen as the motor of evil and cosmic destruction: "[Ennui] would willingly make of the earth a shambles/And, in a yawn, swallow the world."[21] Writing on Giono, Monica Kelley has argued that *Un roi sans divertissement* was an oblique response to the war and to the rapid and not always fair purging of collaborators thereafter. Giono's perspective on evil echoes Bataille's gloss on Rousset, as attested to by a letter to André Cayatte in which Giono wrote, "We are all murderers," soon to become the title of a film by Cayatte. And again, in a 1948 entry in his diary, referring to the "French atrocities" that followed the Libération and were perpetrated by ordinary neighbors: "Hitlerian or not, this is not the question. What we gained [from the war] is to have seen the bottom of our turpitude. I no longer have faith in the hairdresser, in the electrician, in the bartender. . . . I don't even have faith in myself. (Hence: Un Roi sans divertissement)."[22] It is not by chance that Giono set his plot in the first half of the 1840s, as if to confirm that one is reading an allegory of World War II. The novel opens with a mysterious serial killer, referred to by the initials M.V., who hides his victims in a large beech tree. The gendarmerie captain, Langlois, inquires about the murders, and ends up killing M.V. after a manhunt in the snow. Months later, Langlois, having let himself be distracted (*diverti*) and fascinated by the arabesques drawn by the blood of a freshly killed wild goose on the snow, smokes, instead of a cigar, a stick of dynamite and "assumes the dimensions of the universe."

This metaphysical thriller presents at least one original trait: its main protagonist happens to be a beech tree (hêtre) in which the serial killer, M.V., diligently hides his corpses. At this juncture and for the sake of my argument, it is necessary to understand that the beech, *le hêtre*, is both a fascinating, hypnotic presence and a metonymy of beauty as well as murder, a trope of the fatefulness of pagan beauty. "Pagan" must be heard here in its original sense of "pagus": landscape. The beech, *le hêtre*, is endowed with a sacred life and marked as the site of human sacrifices. The beech tree is less a tree than a "king," a pantheistic deity or a Shiva, that Giono refers to as the "Apollon citharède des hêtres": " "It was not quite a tree . . . ; it sizzled like embers; it danced as only supernatural beings can, multiplying its body around its inertia. . . . Such virtuosity of beauty was hypnotic as the eye of the snake or the blood of wild geese on the snow."[23] The beech tree embodies the sacred as such, *le hêtre* or its near homonym, *l'Être*, Being, as sacred. And the beauty of *le hêtre*, or of *l'Être*, triggers a deadly fascination, the fascination for evil and cruelty. Thus, in his prewar, neopagan period, Giono arguably sang a siren's song adumbrating Vichy propaganda, advocating a return to the land. Then, in the postwar period, this dreamlike cult of the household deities turned into a nightmare.

From (H)être to "Il Y A"

I have yet to find any evidence that Emmanuel Levinas read *Un roi sans divertissement* or anything else by Giono. However, we know that Heidegger read and admired Giono enough to visit him in Manosque in 1957 on the occasion of an Aix-en-Provence lecture, and dedicated to him a copy of the French translation of *The Essence of Truth*. Jill Robbins, in her book on Levinas and literature,[24] does not mention Giono. But then again, she also leaves out Céline, although Levinas had read and praised him, be it allusively, in the early 1930s shortly after the publication of *Voyage au bout de la nuit*.

Levinas spent most of the war in several camps in France and Germany. Thanks to Rodolphe Calin and Catherine Chalier, we now have access to the diary that the philosopher kept in captivity.[25] That Levinas had to work as a lumberjack during his detention may not be so trivial a fact, given the centrality of the figure of the tree in his philosophy.[26] Remember this line, from a famous 1961 lecture: "Man, after all, is not a tree."[27] Levinas contrasted the tree with the astronaut Yuri Gagarin. Gagarin was most definitely not rooted like a tree; he was man uprooted, the human who had the audacity to leave his humus, his home or Heimat. He was the patriarch Abraham for the age of space travels. As we have just seen with Giono, trees—with the exception, perhaps, of Abraham's tamarind tree, to which I shall return—have ties with the sacred.

Levinas wrote *De l'existence à l'existant*, his first major work to appear after the war, in detention, in complete intellectual and social isolation:

"The camp is mentioned here neither as a guarantee of depth, nor as an excuse, but merely to explain the lack of engagement with the philosophical works published, with such splendor, between 1940 and 1945."[28] In the foreword to the 1977 edition of *De l'existence*, Levinas noted, "The notion of the 'il y a' developed in this thirty-year-old book appears to be its pièce de résistance."[29] I suggest that the notion of the "il y a," that terrifying white noise from which a singular being, *un existant*, must surface, can be seen as an allegory of the war. There is, in other words, a relation between the notion of "il y a," as philosophically abstract as it may sound, and the very concrete evil of that historical era—the defeat of France, Nazi atrocities, and the camp experience.

Indeed, in two essays written shortly after Heidegger had joined the Nazi Party, in 1934 and 1935,[30] Levinas, revealing his disillusionment with Heidegger, had already indicated the moral bankruptcy of existential ontology, a morally blind philosophy privileging Being over the Good. The Levinassian scholar is familiar with the hierarchy between ontology and ethics, between Logos as truth or *aletheia* and the good: "That which stands above the question of Being is not a truth, it is the Good" (*EE*, 28).

In the prewar period and immediately after Hitler's rise to power, Levinas defined evil, and not just any evil, but the evil of what he called the "philosophy of Hitlerism," as the "being-riveted" to existence. He described the escape from the irremissibility of Being as a movement of "excendance" or "évasion." As a result of "évasion," *l'existant* is hypostasized and can ultimately face the other, that is, enter into an ethical relation. This relation is predicated upon the entry of a particular being into subjectivity and diachronicity. Such is the meaning of the hypostasis, or the emergence of a singular, nameable being against the anonymous background of the "il y a": "on the backdrop of the 'il y a' rises a being" (*EE*, 141).

The phenomenological speculation on the notion of "il y a," I would argue, stands as an allegory of the situation of being deprived of one's basic freedom and detained in several camps. The notion of "il y a" thus appears more and more as an allegory of Levinas's war, a philosophical and intimate war that began in the early 1930s with his struggle with Heidegger's political commitment.

"Il y a" is the notion whose outlines Levinas traced in detention and sharpened in 1947 to convey the terror of night, night as anonymous terror: "Night is the very experience of the 'il y a.'" We find such association between night and "il y a" in *De l'existence*, as well as in the *Carnets de captivité*. Being, instead of suggesting an opening—Heidegger's "clearing of Being"—pertains here to the experience of fear of the dark. In the preface to the second edition, Levinas will write: "The notion of the 'il y a,' that I described while I was detained and that I presented in this book published shortly after the Libération, must be traced to one of those strange childhood obsessions that resurface in insomnia, when silence resonates and emptiness remains full." Levinas stands Heidegger's "What Is Metaphysics?" (1929) on its head: "The 'il y a' does not amount to the pure nothing of Heidegger's anxiety. Horror of being as opposed to anxiety triggered by nothingness; fear of being and not fear for being" (*EE*, 102). While for Heidegger, anxiety was provoked by the possibility that there could be nothing rather than beings, Levinas's dread is provoked by the *il y a*, by the very fact of existence underlying any particular being, in other words, Being without beings (*EE*, 93). The opening of the chapter aptly entitled "Existence sans existant" echoes Heidegger's "What Is Metaphysics?": "Let us imagine a return of all beings, things and people alike, to nothingness. It is impossible to imagine this return without an event. But what of this nothingness itself? Something occurs, be it the night and the silence of nothingness" (*EE*, 93). In this noisy silence of nothingness that I have called, in a tribute to Don DeLillo, "white noise," the self is submerged by night and depersonalized (*EE*, 95). There is no longer a *this* or a *that*: there is the pure "there is." The subject becomes an exposed, vulnerable *on*; the singular being returns to the horrifying anonymity of Being: "It is impossible, when confronted with this obscure invasion, to recoil in oneself or to recede into one's shell. ONE is exposed. . . . Instead of giving us access to existence, night hands us over to Being" (*EE*, 96). A voracious reader of modern French literature, Levinas mentions, among a plethora of poets and novelists, Huysmans, Zola, and Maupassant. Those authors, he writes, "present things through a kind of night, as though a monotonous presence were suffocating us in insomnia" (*EE*, 97). While it is difficult to identify works by Zola or Huysmans that would evoke Levinas's "il y a," how not to think of Maupassant's *Horla*?

It is worth noting that the word *nightmare* comes from "mare," an evil female spirit that afflicts sleepers with a feeling of suffocation. This feeling of suffocation can be found in Levinas's image of a fateful embrace: "One is subjected to the embrace of Being as if to the grip of night" (*EE*, 28).

The night of the "il y a" pertains to what Levinas calls "the broken world," a recurring phrase in the writings of this period. Indeed, the time of war and captivity triggered in Levinas the recurrent image of a "broken world" or a "world upside down," notions that echo the theme of *tikkun olam*, mending or restoring the world, in Jewish mysticism (*EE*, 25–26): "When one must eat, drink and warm oneself to cheat death, when food becomes mere fuel as it does in hard physical labor, the world seems to near its end, it appears to be upside down, absurd, in need of repair" (*EE*, 68). The image of the "broken world" that ought to be mended was associated, earlier, in the *Carnets*, with the defeat of France, a defeat that was itself considered the end of everything "official," the collapse of the "drapery" of the official, the official as drapery, as witness this strange and laconic note from *Carnets de captivité*: "The drapery falls. The world appears in its naked outlines. The world is always adorned with the official. Such is the fatherland: the fall of the drapery—the defeat."[31]

A world—cosmos or mundus—requires an official drapery, a "drapeau" or flag, what one could call the symbolic. To be sure, Levinas's "patrie" should not be confused with the neopagan Heimat. Indeed, it reveals more affinities with the "patrie" of Charles Péguy, Bernard-Lazare, or Jean Améry than with that of Maurice Barrès or Charles Maurras. Levinas's patriotism was perfectly attuned with that of Raymond-Raoul Lambert and of the French Jews whom Pierre Birnbaum called the "Jews of the Republic": it privileged the "pays légal" over Maurras's "pays réel."

The war and the defeat of the homeland will have unveiled an upside-down world, a world as impersonal as the anonymous *il y a*, an antiworld, "immonde." This anomic and asymbolic world resembles that of Baudelaire's "Le squelette laboureur," a poem mentioned in Levinas's *De l'existence* (*EE*, 49). One should read this poem as an allegory of the absolute exposure of the camp inmate to the elements. Baudelaire's poem is henceforth uncannily close, through Levinas's evocation in 1947, to Primo Levi's famous opening poem in *Se questo è un uomo*, published that same year:

> Do you wish (clear, frightful symbol
> Of too cruel a destiny!)

> To show that even in the grave
> None is sure of the promised sleep;
> That Annihilation betrays us;
> That all, even Death, lies to us.[32]

To conclude, I want to suggest in this chapter that what Levinas saw as having led the world to a universe skinned alive was the return of the pagan sacred to Europe, that is, Nazism as a return of an idolatry long repressed by the West. This idolatry manifests itself through a numbing of consciousness and individual subjectivity, a form of contagion or "participation": "The horror is . . . a movement that will strip consciousness of its own subjectivity . . . by precipitating it into a form of impersonal vigilance, into a participation, in the sense that Levy-Bruhl gave to this word" (*EE*, 98). *Il y a* is thus another phrase for impersonal, mystic participation, the sacred as pure presence of Being that we have encountered in Giono's beech tree. This pure presence of Being is construed by Levinas as the evil of a time "before the light of Revelation." Further, I suggest that Levinas sees this as the Nazi perversion of the monotheistic tradition and of the eradication of the Jews as bearers of, and heirs to, the Name: "While for Durkheim the impersonality of the sacred in primitive religions is still the impersonal God whence will emerge the God of developed religions, for us it signifies, instead, a world in which nothing heralds the coming of a God" (*EE*, 99). This notion of "participation," borrowed from Lucien Levy-Bruhl's anthropology of "primitive mentality,"[33] stands, I argue, as an allegory of the Nazi *Mit-sein*. Instead of preserving the "drapery of the official" as a principle of separation, the Nazi *Mit-sein* establishes the fusion of stage and audience. Nazism denies the world as representation, and replaces it with the nonworld as participation. Ethics, for Levinas, is indeed a departure from a "participation" that pertains to esthetic existence. In a penetrating essay published in 1991, Jean-Luc Nancy and Philippe Lacoue-Labarthe used Levy-Bruhl's concept of participation to define the "Nazi myth," "fusion or mystical participation . . . *methexis*, of which the best example is the Dionysian experience, as described by Nietzsche."[34]

One should not be misled by the fact that Giono called his beech tree "Apollon citharède." To be sure, Giono's tree was a figure, if not of fascism, then of the Dionysian experience and of the fascination for evil that is part of the esthetic experience. This esthetic experience numbs moral consciousness and results in sacrifice.

Finally, to the experience of God's absence conveyed by the notion of the "il y a" as the horror of pure Being and of the sacred, Levinas's ethics, inspired by his conversation with Talmudic tradition, will respond with the holy and messianic figure of Eliyahu, the fierce enemy of the worshipers of Baal, "Ilya" in its Slavic avatar.

I will end on a lyrical excerpt from the 1961 lecture on Heidegger and Gagarin, which one can read as an echo of Giono's *Un roi sans divertissement*, and as Levinas's ultimate warning against Heidegger's sacrifice of beings to Being, of humans to the Heimat: "Oh! Tamarind planted by Abraham in Beersheba! One of the only 'individual' trees of the Bible that rises . . . to enchant the imagination of so many wanderings amid so many deserts. But beware! The Talmud fears lest lulled by southern breezes we be seduced by the tree's song and that we seek within it the meaning of Being. . . . Tamarind is an acronym; the three letters required to write its name in Hebrew are the initials of Food, Drink and Shelter, three things necessary to man and that man offers to man."[35]

NOTES

1. Special thanks to Alan Astro for his suggestions and for his feedback on original translations.

2. Paris: Éditions de Minuit, 1943.

3. Paris: Éditions de Minuit, 1942.

4. See Jacques Derrida, *De l'hospitalité* (Paris: Calmann-Levy, 1997).

5. Paris: G. Kohen, 1945.

6. Léon Werth, *Déposition* (Paris: Grasset, 1946). I am using a more recent edition: *Déposition: Journal 1940–44* (Paris: Points, 2007).

7. Hannah Arendt, *Essays in Understanding, 1930–1954* (New York: Schocken Books, 1994), 12.

8. Werth, *Déposition*, 130.

9. Paris: Éditions du Livre français, 1946.

10. Paris: Éditions du Pavois, 1946.

11. Paris: Éditions de Minuit, 1946.

12. See Maurice Blanchot, *L'espace littéraire* (Paris: Gallimard, 1955).

13. Paris: Tallandier, 2008.

14. Paris: Éditions du Pavois, 1947.

15. See Georges Bataille, "Réflexions sur le bourreau et la victime," *Critique* 17 (October 1947): 337–42.

16. Paris: Gallimard, 1957.

17. See Eric Marty, *Bref séjour à Jérusalem* (Paris: Gallimard, 2003).

18. See Monica Kelley, "Borrowed Voices: Diversions of Writing and Responsibility in Jean Giono" (PhD diss., Emory University, 1998), 92.

19. Grenoble: B. Arthaud.

20. Jankélévitch, *Le mal*, 57, 59, 151.

21. Charles Baudelaire, *The Flowers of Evil*, trans. William Aggeler (Fresno, CA: Academy Library Guild, 1954). For the original French version, *Les fleurs du mal*, see http://fleursdumal.org/poem/099.

22. Jean Giono, *Oeuvres romanesques completes, six volumes* (Paris: Gallimard, 1971–83), 1300.

23. Ibid., 1306.

24. Jill Robbins, *Altered Readings: Levinas and Literature* (Chicago: University of Chicago Press, 1999).

25. Emmanuel Levinas, *Carnets de captivité* (Paris: Grasset, 2009).

26. Pierre Bouretz, *Témoins du futur: Philosophie et messianisme* (Paris: Gallimard, 2003), 869.

27. Emmanuel Levinas, *Difficile liberté: Essais sur le judaïsme* (Paris: A. Michel, 1976), 41. See also 144, 195, and 325.

28. Emmanual Levinas, *De l'existence à l'existant* (Paris: Vrin, 1978) (hereafter cited in text as *EE*). This quote is from the foreword.

29. Ibid.

30. See Emmanuel Levinas, *De l'évasion* (Paris: Fata Morgana, 1982), and *Quelques réflexions sur la philosophie de l'hitlérisme* (Paris: Rivages, 1997).

31. Levinas, *Carnets de captivité*, 112.

32. Baudelaire, *Flowers of Evil*.

33. Lucien Levy-Bruhl, *La mentalité primitive* (Paris: Librairie Felix Alcan, 1922).

34. Jean-Luc Nancy and Philippe Lacoue-Labarthe, *Le mythe nazi* (La Tour d'Aigues: Éditions de l'Aube, 1991). I use the translation published in *Critical Inquiry* 16, no. 2 (Winter 1990): 291–312.

35. Levinas, *Difficile liberté*, 326.

9

Léon Poliakov, the Origins of Holocaust Studies, and Theories of Anti-Semitism

Rereading Bréviaire de la haine

JONATHAN JUDAKEN

Introduction

Léon Poliakov was one of the great historians of the twentieth century. He remains the doyen of critical scholarship on the history of anti-Semitism, a founding father of Holocaust and genocide studies, and a forerunner in the history of racism, stereotyping, persecution, and demonization. Yet the importance of his contributions is not well known to many scholars, let alone a wider public.[1] This chapter focuses on Poliakov's often unacknowledged contributions to the establishment of Holocaust studies and explores how he understood a key engine in the machinery of the destruction of European Jewry: anti-Semitism.

Poliakov's breakthrough book, *Bréviaire de la haine: Le IIIe Reich et les juifs* (translated as *Harvest of Hate*) was published in 1951 with the help of Raymond Aron.[2] It was the first general history of the Holocaust. In rereading *Bréviaire de la haine* there are three aspects that I want to emphasize. First is the prescience of the volume: as a foundational survey of the Holocaust—widely disseminated, wide-ranging, and with penetrating insights—Poliakov's work became a palimpsest that sketched key aspects of the Shoah that were developed and treated by others, but rarely with full credit to their origins in his work. Second, Poliakov's interpretation of Nazi anti-Semitism was profoundly perceptive and merits consideration in its own right. Third, I also want to problematize some of Poliakov's own conclusions in *Bréviaire de la haine* about the causes of anti-Semitism derived from the insights of Sigmund Freud,

Maurice Samuel, and Jacques Maritain. At the same time, I want to show from reading Poliakov intertextually with these other authors the beginnings of a Jewish-Christian dialogue on the significance of anti-Semitism in the wake of the Holocaust. Let us begin this rereading of Poliakov by reviewing his biography.

Poliakov's Intellectual Demarche

While in fact Poliakov's oeuvre was extremely wide-ranging, covering Holocaust and genocide studies, Jewish social, cultural, and intellectual history, the history of sexuality, and Russian history, in addition to the history of anti-Semitism, his great works are certainly focused on Jew hatred. "If it is true that all one does is to write the same book over and over again," Poliakov averred in his autobiography, *L'auberge des musiciens*, "then my case is a blatant one."[3] How did he come to the problem of anti-Semitism? In Poliakov's case, as Georges Elia Sarfati put it, "it was a response to the personal question, 'why do they want to kill me?'"[4] It was a question Poliakov must have asked from an early age.

Poliakov's childhood was affected by three linguistic, cultural, and political influences: Russian, German, and French. Named for Léon Tolstoy, who had died on the eve of Poliakov's birth, he was born in Saint Petersburg in 1910. He was the eldest son of Vladimir Poliakov, who already had five daughters with his first wife and an older daughter with Léon's mother. He grew up with no religious or intellectual affiliation for Judaism. Indeed, his father used to cite a Romany proverb: "Only God knows the truth, and He only knows a small part of it!" (*ED*, 25). Vladimir was a Crimean Jew with no formal education who had made his wealth publishing leftist newspapers, but who supported the Whites in the civil war. As a result, the family fled to Paris in 1920, where Léon was enrolled in lycée Janson, a school where he felt strongly "isolated." His father initially had difficulty establishing a business in France, and so they left for Berlin, where at eleven, Léon became an "enthusiastic German patriot" (*ED*, 19). The Poliakovs returned to France in 1924 when his father got a position as the head of a publicity firm. In 1934, at Léon's urging, Vladimir returned to his vocation and created a daily newspaper, *Pariser Tageblatt*, catering to the influx of primarily Jewish immigrants arriving from Germany and eastern Europe.[5] Beginning his career writing for the paper, Léon simultaneously completed his studies in law, a degree that he never directly used.

The chief editor of the newspaper was a dodgy character, Georg Bernhard, and the paper was thoroughly underfinanced, with the result that he was rarely paid on time. In 1936 a scandal broke when Bernhard indicated on the front page of *Pariser Tageblatt* that the owner, Vladimir Poliakov, was a traitor in the pay of the Nazis. This was a huge shock for the readers of the paper, since its orientation was explicitly antifascist. After a long defamation trial, the Poliakovs were victorious, but his father was ruined. Léon's first published book was on the *Pariser Tageblatt* affair in order to restore his father's reputation. Interest in Léon's book came from the many famous individuals who were wrapped up in this affair, such as Vladimir Jabotinsky, who was a contributor to the newspaper. Jabotinsky thought enough of Léon's book to encourage him to become a writer. While in retrospect Léon considered himself a little "anti-Semitic" at the time, this was tempered with his first injection of "a certain Zionist enthusiasm," which came when in 1937 he visited his sister, who had married a settler in Palestine (*ED*, 24).

The death of his father in May 1939 closely coincided with the outbreak of World War II, and his mother died the following spring. This, Poliakov later thought, was a good thing, since two Russian Jews who spoke French with difficulty would probably not have survived the occupation of France by the Nazis.[6] With the beginning of war, despite having never been naturalized, Poliakov was called up for duty, since there was a law that stateless persons from Russia, Poland, and Armenia could be mobilized. Along with 1.8 million other French soldiers, he was promptly captured and interned in a camp called Domart.[7] Here his German gave him a distinct advantage, since he could help procure things for his captors. When he accompanied the camp commander on a trip to Paris, he escaped. Poliakov spent the rest of the war as a stateless Jew in hiding using false papers, doing odd jobs, and moving among Paris, Marseille, Nice, Grenoble, Saint-Étienne, La Ricamarie, and Tence near Le Chambon-sur-Lignon. He sometimes fabricated papers for others also resisting the Nazi occupation.

His father's death had led to an important contact, Rabbi Zalman Schneerson, who came from the illustrious Lubavitch line of Chassids. Despite his secular upbringing, Poliakov wanted to bury his father in a religious ceremony. So he visited Rabbi Schneerson in his office near the Place de la République in the appropriately named rue Dieu. Still in shock, he asked the rabbi, "What does one do to have faith in God?" In a quintessential rabbinic response, Schneerson replied, "Come to my house for thirty days and say *Kaddish*, as the tradition requires. Then, we'll speak about it seriously" (*ED*, 33). So as not to appear frivolous, Poliakov trekked across Paris each day. Although they never had that conversation about faith, the contact was made, and it proved important when Poliakov moved to Marseille hoping to avoid the roundups that had begun in the occupied zone in the summer of 1941. There he once more encountered Rabbi Schneerson, who offered him a job as his secretary despite the fact that Poliakov was a nonbeliever. In this way, he came to live among the rabbi's entourage, known as the Association israélites pratiquants (AIP).

In Marseille, he would also often meet his friend the philosopher Alexandre Kojevnikov, who gallicized his name, shortening it to Kojève. Kojève would gain fame as a renowned commentator on Hegel, with his famous seminar in the 1930s serving as one of the key crucibles of twentieth-century French thought.[8] It was Kojève who would introduce Poliakov to philosophy. Later in the war, when living near Le Chambon-sur-Lignon, he met Jacob Gordin and his wife and children. Gordin was an erudite Jewish thinker who dramatically expanded Poliakov's horizons through his initiation into Jewish thought, facilitating his "intellectual conversion to Judaism" (*ED*, 50).[9]

In the immediate aftermath of the war, Poliakov reconnected with another Schneerson, Isaac, a wealthy industrialist and an important personality in the Union général des israélites de France (UGIF), the representative body for Jews in France under the occupation.[10] Poliakov first met Isaac Schneerson in 1943 in the Italian occupation zone. At that time, Schneerson had already created the Centre de documentation in Grenoble. Meeting for the first time on April 28, 1943, in Schneerson's apartment, forty activists from across the Jewish community convened to figure out how to document the persecution of the Jews in order to bear witness and in the hope of demanding justice at the end of the war. The group began by creating a list of all "Aryanized" Jewish businesses with notations taken from the *Journal officiel* (the official daily of the French state that documents all legislative actions).

This list constituted the origins of the first archive in the world dedicated to documenting the genocide of European Jewry, the Centre de documentation juive contemporaine (CDJC), which would later also produce the first journal on the topic, *Le Monde juif,* and today is the site of the major Holocaust memorial in Paris, the Mémorial de la Shoah. After the war, Schneerson proposed that Poliakov become the general secretary of the group, and shortly thereafter made him head of research.

Poliakov was instrumental in establishing the cache of archival materials at the CDJC. How he did so was a good example of the contingency of history. As Poliakov recounts the story in his memoirs, he was at the Sûreté nationale (French National Police headquarters) poking around for what he could find. The permission to do so was granted as a result of a letter from the honorary president of the CDJC, Justin Godard, a former senator. He was shown a box that had just arrived from Poland; it happened to contain the archives of the Gestapo and the SS in France. It turned out that neither Commissaire Berger nor the personnel in his office read German. Thus Poliakov became the expert translator of these documents and the organizer of the archive. This became the basis of the holdings at the CDJC.

With the beginning of the Nuremburg trials, the French delegation, headed by François de Menthon and many other lawyers, was in the awkward position of not really having many sources with which to indict the Nazi criminals in the dock, especially compared to the Americans and the Soviets. So Poliakov was called upon as a result of his "expertise" to accompany them to Nuremberg. There he spent most of his time immersing himself in the huge trove of documents that the chief prosecutors made the basis of the trial.

Poliakov's copies of these sources would become the archive of the *Bréviaire de la haine* and the foundation of the collection at the CDJC. *Bréviaire de la haine* would catapult Poliakov into a career as a historian of great import, if only limited renown. With the success of the book, in 1952 he was appointed a research fellow at the Centre national de la recherche scientifique. In 1954, he joined the prestigious École pratique des hautes études, then directed by the eminent historian Fernand Braudel, the kingpin of the *Annales* school's domination of the historical discipline in the aftermath of the war.[11] Identified with the journal

Annales d'histoire économique et social, this constellation of historians introduced new methods for studying social and cultural history over the long term, becoming the preeminent academic historians in France in the postwar period. While always marginal within the *Annales* school, let alone the French academy, Poliakov nonetheless imbibed the ethos of the Annales school's multidisciplinary approach to history and wide-ranging use of source material. Never having been trained as a historian—his first published works with the CDJC were collections of documents—some of his later success was a result of the fact that he always quoted extensively from the sources in his books. His legal training and experience at Nuremberg are also evident in his historical works, since Poliakov often writes like a prosecuting attorney, indicting criminals with the evidence from what they said themselves about their own crimes. With the *Annales* school, he shared a broad vision and panoramic scope, writing not only "total history" but the *histoire des mentalités* over the *longue durée*. Poliakov's magnum opus, his monumental five-volume *L'histoire de l'antisémitisme*, would emerge out of the problem of Jew hatred first posed in *Bréviaire de la haine*.

Bréviaire de la Haine and Nazi Anti-Semitism

Bréviaire de la haine was the first all-encompassing survey of the genocide of European Jewry in any language. As such, it was a groundbreaking work in the field of Holocaust studies, effectively establishing the terms of many of the debates that have defined the field. Today Poliakov's book is seldom acknowledged for the pioneering part it played. When it first appeared in 1951, however, it was hailed for what it was at the time. Across the board in the major French dailies (*Le Monde, L'Aurore, Le Parisien libéré*) and weeklies (*L'Observateur, Les Nouvelles litttéraires*), it was heralded as a trailblazing work of scholarship. P. Grappin in *Politique étrangère* termed it a "magisterial study . . . a historic work of the first rank" that blazed a new trail. A. Latreille in *Le Monde* proclaimed, "M. Poliakov has painted a tableau more impressive by his objectivity than any literary reconstruction." Pierre Naville, writing under the pseudonym J. Gallois in *L'Observateur*, called it "a book . . . of exceptional force and truth, that must not only be read and studied but studied in the universities, especially in Germany."[12] It was soon translated into English and Spanish (in 1954), Italian (in 1955), Czech (in 1965), and Portuguese (in 1988).

When it came out in America, Jacques Maritain lauded the English translation in *Social Research*: "M. Poliakov's book traces, with inexorable and infallible objectivity, the stages of the business of extermination. In the face of such horror, one need not raise one's voice; it suffices to *say* it. One can barely perceive, here or there, a restrained shudder, and occasionally, concerning the hangman, something like a terrible humor, which grips the heart. This is precisely the Jewish humor, but in extreme tension of anguish and pierced by tears of blood." Perhaps most clearly it was R. H. S. Crossman in the *New Statesman* who signaled the massive contribution Poliakov had made to the early work on the Holocaust by setting his contribution against the other key work in the formative period of Holocaust studies: "I had always assumed that Mr. Reitlinger had written the last word about Hitler's extermination camps. Now Mr. Poliakov has proved me wrong. [Reitlinger's] *The Final Solution* [published in 1953] was a masterpiece of cold clinical research. *Harvest of Hate* is a bigger book with a wider sweep."[13]

Bréviaire was published the same year as Hannah Arendt's monumental *Origins of Totalitarianism*, and no one more than Arendt recognized Poliakov's signal achievement. She itemized his many contributions in her review of the French text in *Commentary*.[14] She highlighted Poliakov's elucidation of the Taylorist approach of the "death factory technicians" (303); his recognition that "the only country on the Nazi side of the lines that resolutely and effectively shielded the Jews was Germany's one important European ally, Italy" (303);[15] his delicate balance in discussing "the terrible dilemma of the *Jüdenrate*, their despair as well as their confusion, their complicity and their sometimes pathetically ludicrous ambitions" (303);[16] and Poliakov's "deflation of the myth" about the role "the German officers' corps and the old pre-Hitler civil servants" had played in the destruction of European Jewry.[17] Most importantly, Arendt also trumpeted the landmark link that Poliakov established between the euthanasia program and the Final Solution.

Beyond what Arendt emphasized, more could be said about Poliakov's innovations. For example, Poliakov anticipated the debates about Jewish resistance, as well as the Nazi treatment of "inferior peoples" (that is, the assault on Slavs and the Sinti and Roma), devoting a separate chapter to each issue long before these topics were integrated in the historiography on the Holocaust.[18] In addition, he antedated Michael Marrus and Robert Paxton on Vichy's role in the Holocaust. "Vichy antisemitism," wrote Poliakov, "was the product of a cross between the xenophobia so characteristic of certain sections of the French middle class, and an old, traditionally reactionary, clerical antisemitic doctrine. . . . *The Germans forced nothing on Vichy*; they advised, they made suggestions. . . . The Vichy government went along willingly, and even with real zeal when German policy conformed to its own doctrine."[19]

Poliakov also made numerous suggestive comments that prefigured Arendt's and later Zygmunt Bauman's arguments about the role of bureaucratic efficiency and the "banality of evil" thesis in accounting for what Poliakov called "the psychology of the executioners."[20] Predating the divide between intentionalists and functionalists, Poliakov also managed to strike a balance between the positions taken most recently in Daniel Jonah Goldhagen's argument about the "eliminationist antisemitism" of Hitler's willing executioners and Christopher Browning's discussion of "ordinary Germans."[21] Part of the shock of Goldhagen's account was the harrowing detail about the bloodied hands of hundreds of thousands of German killers, which Poliakov discussed. At the same time, in detailing the formation and tasks of the Einsatzgruppen, Poliakov was clear that those who were selected were a result of a largely random bureaucratic function. "The personnel of the action groups," he wrote, "were not sadists lusting for blood, but an average and representative selection from the German police corps of 1941" (119).

When Poliakov died in 1997, the French press made evident that his contributions to Holocaust studies should be recognized. The first line of his obituary in *Le Figaro* said it all: "One of the pioneers of the historiography of the Holocaust died yesterday, aged eighty-seven." *Bréviaire de la haine, Le Figaro* went on to state plainly, was "the first global analysis of the processes of Nazi annihilation."[22] In *Le Monde*, Christian Delacampagne elaborated: "He was one of the pioneers of the French research on the Shoah and on anti-Semitism in a period when these subjects did not interest his contemporaries." Moreover, Delacampagne declaimed, *Bréviaire* should today be considered "a work of reference" as "the first serious work consecrated to the study of the Final Solution."[23] *L'Humanité*, for its part, mourned the "death of a great witness," and indicated that *Bréviaire* had a "large echo" that was well known among specialists.[24] The *New York Times* noted a macabre version of this "echo" when its obituary pointed out that "books by Mr. Poliakov were on the prison reading list of Adolf Eichmann as he awaited trial in Jerusalem in 1961 for arranging the transport of millions of Jews to Nazi death camps."[25]

It is no wonder that Eichmann sought a measure of self-objectification in Poliakov's oeuvre, since the explanatory and affective power of *Bréviaire de la haine* was the way that Poliakov juggled the rational and irrational aspects of the Nazi slaughter of Jews. Poliakov maintained that the bureaucratic, managed process of the machinery of destruction and the rapacious, carnivalesque unleashing of the worst in human beings combined in the Nazi genocide. Nazi anti-Semitism was therefore a deadly combination of irrational and mystical Jew hatred—"the tragic twilight of a Wagnerian night," as Poliakov put it, or what Saul Friedländer has called the "redemptive antisemitism" of the Bayreuth Circle[26]—and the rational, but no less brutal, anti-Semitism of many of the functionaries of the Final Solution, where Poliakov's example was Eichmann's boss, Heinrich Himmler. It was these two alternating currents of anti-Semitism, which Poliakov called "sacred" and "profane," that combined to create the cataclysmic destruction wrought by the Nazi executioners.

Elaborating on the sacred dimensions of Nazism, in a section called "The Basis and Meaning of Nazi Antisemitism," Poliakov contended that at its core "Nazism was primarily a religion." He argued that the sacral measures that were essential to Nazi anti-Semitism were what distinguished it from other forms of anti-Semitism (4). "The Nazi theodicy," Poliakov explained, "demanded the existence of an Enemy, that *Gegenreich* (Anti-Reich)," which meant, as Hermann Rauschning's aphorism put it, "If the Jew did not exist, we should have to invent him" (2). The representation of "the Jew" as the "plastic demon" of decadence, as Wagner famously put it, functioned to transform the abstractions of the racial soul, blood and soil, and the antitype of the German Volk into a concrete antipathy "because a devil was indispensable to the Nazi religion. The Jew, principle of impurity and evil, symbolized the devil. This Manichean duality was essential" (5). Norman Cohn, in *Warrant for Genocide*, a book that Poliakov translated into French, would later argue that the myth of the world Jewish conspiracy was "a modern adaptation of . . . [the] ancient demonological tradition,"[27] and this notion was key to the genocidal anti-Semitism of the Nazis, as Jeffrey Herf has recently demonstrated once more in *The Jewish Enemy*.[28]

Poliakov suggested that the demonization of Jews is what distinguished Nazi anti-Semitism from Nazi racism: "If the Jew occupied Satan's place in Nazi eschatology, the non-German or 'sub-human' lacking any sacred attribute was for the most part classified among the animals; at best, he was considered, according to a contemporary definition, as a 'transitional form between the animal and Nordic man'" (263). This was an early gloss on a theme that would long preoccupy Poliakov, who would later conclude, "Here we see another of the differences between anti-Semitism and racism: blacks [and Sinti and Roma and Slavs] were generally bestialized, whereas Jews were generally seen as diabolical."[29] In short, the road to Auschwitz was built by diabolical anti-Semitism—the sacred horror made abject in Nazi anti-Semitism—but it was paved by the profane anti-Semitism that aroused a general disrespect for Jews and Judaism.[30]

Poliakov's distinction between the sacred and the profane in Nazi racism not only facilitated an insightful differentiation within Nazi ideology, but also helped to account for the seemingly contradictory practices of the Nazi persecution of Jews, which wavered between "pillage and enslavement" (discussed in chapter 3 of *Bréviaire*), ghettoization (addressed in chapter 4), and deportation, concentration, and extermination (elaborated in chapters 5–8). It also enabled a useful opening toward the comparative framework of genocide pursued in the last chapters of the book (chapters 11–12).[31]

From its opening pages, Poliakov's account of Nazism as a religion plumbed the depths of the Western vilification of Jews and Judaism. Christianity was heavily implicated in this charge, as the French title of the book clearly indicates, since the breviary is the book of the daily Catholic liturgy.[32] Emphasizing the point, Poliakov proffers, "Does not the catechism teach tens of millions of modern children that the Jews were the murderers of Jesus and therefore condemned until the Last Judgment?" (299). While insisting upon the religious dimensions of Jew hatred as central to anti-Semitism, Poliakov knew this would ruffle the feathers of his mostly Christian readers.

This was, in fact, a major concern for Poliakov. From the start, he was particularly concerned about the Catholic response to the book, and he wanted a Catholic intellectual to write the preface. He explained to Aron in a letter on October 12, 1950, that it would be a good idea, since he had cited sensitive documents about the Vatican.[33] Maritain originally agreed to write the preface but then renounced his willingness upon actually reading the manuscript, insisting in a sharply worded letter to Poliakov, "I see that you have spoken of the position of the Vatican in inexact terms (there is not a shadow of anti-Semitism in the thought of the Pope)."[34] Ten days after Maritain's refusal, Poliakov secured the agreement of François Mauriac to introduce the book, despite pointing out to him the lines that had so disturbed Maritain.

Mauriac was willing to do so because he thought Poliakov's book helped to explain the "inexplicable crimes" with which "all Christianity finds itself indirectly associated." Nonetheless, Mauriac and Poliakov disagreed about the role of the Jews in anti-Semitism. Mauriac reproached Poliakov for not accounting at all for the comportment of Jews themselves in causing anti-Semitism, which he maintained in no way excuses anti-Semitism or the Nazi infamy, but insisted that it was a part of the problem. Poliakov countered that he had indirectly alluded to the role of Jewish behavior, pointing Mauriac to a set of pages where this was the case. But he asked Mauriac to consider whether this behavior was a cause or an effect of anti-Semitism. Poliakov also objected to Mauriac's use of the term "nature" when speaking about Jews, a point he indicated that he and Aron agreed about, since it smacked of the language of race and could easily be exploited by unsympathetic polemicists (with Poliakov naming Maurice Bardèche as his example). These matters remained unresolved between the two thinkers when the book was published with Mauriac's preface.[35]

The concluding notes of the *Bréviaire*, where Poliakov attempts to name the *mysterium tremendum* that underlies anti-Semitism, might well have assuaged his Christian readers, however. The passage bears citation at some length:

The measures that they advocated, ostracism or banishment, were only symbolic murders [i.e., profane]. But when moral barriers collapsed under the impact of Nazi preaching, and the genocidal passion was free to slake itself, the hatred of God slumbering in men's hearts awoke and stood revealed in the light of day; the same anti-Semitic movement that led to the slaughter of the Jews gave scope and license to an obscene revolt against God and the moral law. An open and implacable war was declared on the Christian tradition. Hitlerism's universal iconoclasm was only the logical consequence of Nazi anti-Semitism; by an atrocious demonstration *in vivo*, it tragically confirmed the penetrating insights of such great thinkers as Sigmund Freud and Jacques Maritain [and if you look at the footnote, the crystallization of this thesis by Maurice Samuel], who saw in original anti-Semitism a "revolt of the illbaptized" against the moral law, a frenzied and unavowed hatred of Christ and the Ten Commandments that in its furious search for satisfaction vented itself on the only object that was allowed to be fair and legal game, the baffling people of God. Here we have the *causa specifica* of antisemitism; and so by another route, we again find our way to the deep meaning of the Nazi explosion: Hitlerism attacked the Jews as the symbol of all established values, which it had marked down for destruction. Here one perceived the deep paradox of the Jews' Calvary: they were the first victims of the anti-Christ sacrificed, in the last analysis, for a cause that was hardly theirs. (300)

As Poliakov attempted to achieve closure on the questions his text had opened about anti-Semitism, he suggested that the *causa specifica* in Maurice Samuel's terse formulation was "Christophobia." Let us succinctly unpack this complex and troubling claim by briefly examining how Freud, Maritain, and Samuel understood anti-Semitism.

Freud, Maritain, and Samuel on "Christophobia"

Aside from some marginal comments in his earlier work, Freud wrote little on anti-Semitism until his last completed work, *Moses and Monotheism* (1939). He first speculated on the origins of anti-Semitism, suggesting that it was rooted in the fear of castration aroused by circumcision, in a footnote in "Analysis of a Phobia in a Five-Year Boy" (1909):

The castration complex is the deepest unconscious root [*Wurzel*] of antisemitism; for even in the nursery [*Kinderstube*] little boys hear that a

Jew has something cut off his penis—a piece of his penis, they think—and this gives them the right to despise Jews. And there is no stronger unconscious root for the sense of superiority over women. Weininger (the young philosopher who, highly gifted but sexually deranged, committed suicide after producing his remarkable book, *Geschlecht und Charakter* [1903]), in a chapter that attracted much attention, treated Jews and women with equal hostility and overwhelmed them with the same insults. Being a neurotic, Weininger was completely under the sway of his infantile complexes; and from that standpoint what is common to Jews and women is their relation to the castration complex.[36]

As Jay Geller points out, "The note condenses many of Freud's multiple identity and theory constructions by binding gender, sexuality, and ethnicity/religion/race to the workings of the unconscious, neurosis, and the castration complex."[37]

The footnote intimated a shift in Freud's oeuvre that took shape with *Totem and Taboo* in 1912, where he moves from a focus on individual psychology to mass psychology, generalizing to groups and civilizations his exploration of identity construction as a result of the sublimation of incestuous, parricidal, and murderous wishes. With the backdrop of World War I, he began to explore the relationship to death and narcissism at work in group psychology.[38] His writing on "The Uncanny" (1919), where Freud examined the stranger who is at the same time "secretly familiar" and who might therefore be constructed as the "internal enemy," proved central to his analysis of anti-Semitism in *Moses and Monotheism*.

These insights about anti-Semitism were all brought together in Freud's interpretation of *Moses and Monotheism*, which was certainly the source of Poliakov's closing comments. In the work, Freud discussed the oedipal relationship between the "religion of the father" (Judaism) and the "religion of the son" (Christianity). He connected the claim of Jewish "chosenness" and his analysis of circumcision as the foundation of anti-Semitism. And he evoked the notion of the "narcissism of minor differences," which leads to the rigidification of group boundaries and the domination of group identity in terms of the superego. Finally, in the specific passage invoked by Poliakov, Freud suggested that anti-Semitism was the product of a culture that was never fully Christianized:

We must not forget that all those peoples who excel today in their hatred of Jews became Christians only in late historic times, often driven to it by bloody coercion. It might be said that they are all "misbaptized." They have been left, under a thin veneer of Christianity, what their ancestors were, who worshipped a barbarous polytheism. They have not got over the grudge against the new religion which was imposed on them; but they have displaced the grudge on the source from which Christianity reached them. The fact that the Gospels tell a story which is set among Jews, and in fact deals only with Jews, has made this displacement easy for them. *Their hatred of Jews is at bottom a hatred of Christians*, and we need not be surprised that in the German National Socialist revolution this intimate relation between the two monotheistic religions finds such a clear expression in the hostile treatment of both of them.[39]

In a formula that was shared by Samuel and Maritain and many others at the time, Hitlerism was barbarism, a barely disguised paganism.[40] It marked a vicious revolt against the ethical ideals of monotheism, whose mandates impose a difficult set of constraints on human behavior, while at the same time they are generally recognized as ideal values. Christ was the incarnation of these values, and the wrath of the Nazis finds a convenient target in "the Jews" who were the source of Christianity; this helps to explain the unconscious motivations for the assault on the Jews in World War II.

No doubt, Freud's ruminations were partly the result of his inherently vexed situation as a central European Jew, an expression of the double binds of his own identity.[41] The list of epithets that have been applied to him make this evident: for Peter Gay he was a "godless Jew"; for Isaac Deutscher, "a non-Jewish Jew"; for Yerushalmi, "a psychological Jew," who in thus naming him derides those who have called him "an ambivalent Jew," which he was, especially as concerned the dominant Viennese Christian culture that had given birth to Hitler.[42] *Moses and Monotheism* was a working through of personal and political questions around the "Jewish question." As he did so, Freud hinted that Christianity constitutes a more complete development of the working through of the sublimation of civilizing instincts. I will not linger here to consider the ways in which Freud introjected an inferiority complex in relation to Christianity or even internalized the supercessionist logic at the heart of

Christian theology, or embodied the internal colonization of the norms of the Viennese culture that he shared so much with, as Daniel Boyarin suggests.[43] This is certainly only half the story of Freud's ambivalence and a limited reading of *Moses and Monotheism*, which has proved to be a seed for deeply fruitful understandings of anti-Semitism. I would like to emphasize, however, the ways in which Freud's position constitutes the exact obverse of the Christian claim that "the Jews" are a deicide people, since Freud maintained that the root of Nazism was the wish to terminate God's principles by railing against religion's ethical demands and targeting Jews as their original spokespeople. This is echoed in Poliakov's allusion to the work of Maritain and Samuel.

It is hard to avoid the intertextual resonances of Freud's analysis with Maurice Samuel's in his once influential account of anti-Semitism, *The Great Hatred* (1940).[44] Samuel is today a forgotten figure, but in the first half of the twentieth century he was, in Milton Hindus's words, "the most popular platform personality of American Jewry."[45] "A Zionist who thinks, a wit with ideas," as Louis Fisher put it,[46] Samuel was born in Macin, Romania, in 1895. He moved to Paris at age five and to Manchester a year later, finally settling in the United States in 1914. A student and later a secretary of Chaim Weitzmann's, Samuel was a prolific writer, translator, and lecturer, also appearing for almost twenty years on the radio program *The Eternal Light: The Words We Live By*. He published hundreds of essays and articles as well as six books of fiction, twenty of nonfiction, and twenty-two translations from French, German, Yiddish, and Hebrew. He wrote and spoke on issues of general cultural interest, but most of his work deals with Jewish topics: Jewish identity, Jewish values, Zionism, the Hebrew Bible, Yiddish, and anti-Semitism.[47]

The Great Hatred sought to explain "the susceptibility of the western world to the diabolisation of the Jew" (47). As had Freud, Samuel maintained that anti-Semitism is the unleashing of primitive instincts in a world devoid of the moral restraints of what he termed "Judaeo-Christianity." The hyphenated construct "Judaeo-Christian" that Samuel repeatedly deployed in its contemporary sense of the shared principles of Christianity and Judaism had only begun to be used in 1930s, replacing the then common "Christian civilization" as a result of Hitler's attacks on Jews.[48] Underlying these attacks, Samuel contended, was a seething rage and resentment that Christians were fettered by the precepts of ethical monotheism, embodied in the Jew-Christ.

In lecture after lecture that made up the book, Samuel hammered home his thesis that "Christophobia" was the underlying cause of anti-Semitism: "Jews are loathed as the Christ-givers, the creators or representatives of the non-force principle in human relations" (168). Samuel maintained that liberals, who tend to dislike religion as a whole, believed that anti-Semitism was like other forms of bigotry—amenable to economic, political, or social diagnoses—and consequently failed to apprehend that diabolical anti-Semitism was a totally different form of prejudice. The churches refused to acknowledge that the Christian patina was a thin skin over a repressed paganism. Christianity was in need of a "self-purgation . . . [of the] sympathetic, superstitious dread of Christ, lying concealed within the heart of Christianity itself."[49]

Christ the Jew was the incarnation of Judaeo-Christian values, which Samuel enumerated: "to do what is just and right" (Genesis 18:19). To achieve this end, "Thou shalt love thy neighbor as thyself" (100), which entailed the "passionate emphasis on God's . . . guardianship of the human individual and the person-to-person interpretation of moral relationships" (97). Moreover, he contended that Judaism was the revelation of a "permanent protest" and the "perpetual after-thought" (104) of human conscience, and that incarnate in Christ the Jew there stood a "recurrent outcry" of humanity's perpetual responsibility to work to establish peace, compromise, decency, justice, and goodness.

Nazi fascism on the other hand was, for Samuel, a purely mechanistic and biological worldview, a philosophy of nature, force, and materialism, an ethos purely guided by "survival of the fittest" and "might is right." As such, Samuel sounds at times like Emmanuel Levinas in "Reflections on the Philosophy of Hitlerism."[50] Indeed, Samuel maintained that Nazism's attraction was "not merely the worship of power, but the worship of the worship of power" (113). He spelled out the bifurcation of values between anti-Semitism and Judaeo-Christianity: "Deification of the body as opposed to the mind, of force as opposed to consideration, of statistical process as opposed to the sanctity of the individual" (111).

Nazi fascism had erupted with such vengeance when it did because modernity had enabled the "mechanical mastery over nature," engendering an unprecedented "challenge to the sense of social responsibility"

(191). Precisely at this moment of unparalleled possibility and challenge, moral conscience was overwhelmed, and Nazi fascism triumphed. Samuel's *The Great Hatred* was a prophetic and passionate plea to liberals to appreciate the differences between racial bigotry and anti-Semitism, and an injunction to Christians to fulfill the credo of their faith by educating their followers that it is sinful and anti-Christian to hate anyone.

It is no wonder that arguably the most important Catholic intellectual of the twentieth century, Jacques Maritain, embraced wholesale Samuel's thesis that anti-Semitism is Christophobia. Samuel's argument constituted the crystallization of a position in Maritain's work that he had been ambling toward throughout the interwar period, for it offered him a formula that he developed with theological profundity and eloquence.[51] "The most impressive Christian formulas concerning the spiritual essence of anti-Semitism," Maritain wrote in October 1941, "may be found in a book recently published by a Jewish writer, who seems himself strangely unaware of their profoundly Christian meaning."[52] Arguing that Samuel, Sholem Asch, Waldo Frank, and Marc Chagall were among a number of Jewish thinkers who were converging on the profound significance of the crucifixion of Christ to explain the suffering of Jews as a result of the Nazi assault, Maritain gave a distinctly Christian reading to the propositions of Samuel and Freud.

As they had, Maritain makes clear that anti-Jewish animus is multifaceted and multicausal, partly explainable by economic and social competition, class bias, nationalist forms of exclusion, or rhetorical hyperbole. But what he called "the secret soul" (568) of anti-Semitism was, in a word, "Christophobia," which for Maritain was "the spiritual essence of the demoniacal racism of our pagan world" (570).

Maritain elucidated how the divine eschatological "Mystery of Israel," whose worldly mission as a "witness people" served both as the irritant of conscience and the goad toward emancipation (572), was attacked by anti-Semites who sought to avenge themselves "for the pangs of its history": the pain and suffering that Christian ideals demand. Jacques Maudaule, cited by Poliakov in the passage on the *causa specifica* of anti-Semitism, aptly summed up Maritain's argument: "There is a mystery of anti-Semitism that complements the mystery of Israel; it is the reverse, if you will, of the election of Israel, and in the last analysis is a religious problem" (*Harvest of Hate*, 299). The mystical passion of Christ was

Maritain's model for the suffering of humanity. Following Pascal, who maintained that "Jesus Christ is in agony until the end of the world," Maritain argued that "Christ suffers in every innocent man who is persecuted. His agony is heard in the cries of so many human beings humiliated and tortured, in the suffering of all those images and likenesses of God treated worse than beasts. He has taken all these things upon Himself, He has suffered every wound" (570, 572). The Holocaust, which Maritain was aware was unfolding at the time of his writing, therefore constituted what he called the "passion of Israel" (572).

But "Israel's passion" was not the mystical passion of Christ and the Church; it was explicitly *not* "a co-redemptive passion" capable of "the eternal salvation of souls" (572). Rather, it was the carnal, temporal torture of God's people, who were eternally yoked as suffering servants testifying to God's call: "To persecute the house of Israel is to persecute Christ, not in His mystical body as when the Church is persecuted," wrote Maritain, "but in His fleshly lineage and in His forgetful people whom He ceaselessly loves and calls" (572). Maritain mobilized this argument not only to spur Jewish-Christian reconciliation, but unequivocally to castigate the perpetrators of as well as the bystanders to anti-Semitism. "It is impossible to compromise with anti-Semitism," he insisted, for "it carries in itself, as in a living germ, all the spiritual evil of Nazism. Anti-Semitism is the moral Fifth Column in the Christian conscience" (566).

While Maritain was clearly calling for a united front of Jews and Christians, his argument also makes evident the risk in Freud's, Samuel's, and Poliakov's claim that the *causa specifica* of anti-Semitism is Christophobia. Ultimately, it constitutes a Christianizing of Jewish persecution. Jewish persecution is recognized only in light of the Christian supercessionist metanarrative that reinscribes Jews within the dramaturgy of the Christian salvation story where their role is at best witnesses to the truth of Christianity.

But if this is the risk of the formula that anti-Semitism is Christophobia, unpacking Poliakov's references to Freud, Samuel, and Maritain also indicates that this was the site of an important Judaeo-Christian dialogue that was beginning to emerge as the crisis of European Jewry deepened. Here Freud, the "godless Jew," Samuel, "the Zionist who thinks," and Maritain, the Catholic intellectual, proffered three permutations on a theme that opened the discussion of what Jews and Judaism shared with the Christian culture that was killing them in the name of its most sacred values.

NOTES

1. Take, for example, Paul R. Bartrop and Steven Leonard Jacobs, *Fifty Key Thinkers on the Holocaust and Genocide* (New York: Routledge, 2011), which does not even list Poliakov among its celebrated pantheon.

2. Léon Poliakov, *Bréviaire de la haine: Le IIIe Reich et les juifs* (Paris: Calmann-Lévy, 1951), translated as *Harvest of Hate: The Nazi Program for the Destruction of the Jews of Europe* (New York: Schocken Books, 1979). All subsequent page numbers are to the English-language version.

3. My citation is from the interview with Elisabeth Weber in *Questioning Judaism* (Stanford, CA: Stanford University Press, 2004), 87.

4. The biographical information on Poliakov comes either from his interviews with Georges Elia Sarfati, *L'envers du destin* (Paris: Éditions de Fallois, 1989), 9 (hereafter cited in text as *ED*); or from Poliakov's *Mémoires* (Paris: Jacques Grancher, 1999) (hereafter cited in text as *M*).

5. On the influx of Jewish immigrants in this period, see Vicky Caron, *Uneasy Asylum: France and the Jewish Refugee Crisis, 1933–1942* (Stanford, CA: Stanford University Press, 1999).

6. For an overview on the Vichy period, see Julian Jackson, *France: The Dark Years, 1940–1944* (Oxford: Oxford University Press, 2001). For the experience of Jews under the German occupation, see Michael Marrus and Robert Paxton, *Vichy France and the Jews* (Stanford, CA: Stanford University Press, 1981); Susan Zuccotti, *The Holocaust, the French, and the Jews* (New York: HarperCollins, 1993); Richard Weisberg, *Vichy Law and the Holocaust in France* (New York: New York University Press, 1996); Renée Poznanski, *Jews in France during World War II*, trans. Nathan Bracher (Hanover, NH: Brandeis University Press, 2001).

7. On the general experience of the French POWs, see Yves Durand's excellent *La captivité: Histoire des prisonniers de guerre français, 1939–1945* (Paris: Fédération nationale des combattants prisonniers de guerre et combattants d'Algérie, Tunisie, Maroc, 1982). See also Sarah Fishman, *We Will Wait: Wives of French Prisoners of War* (New Haven, CT: Yale University Press, 1991). For a more global account of POWs, see Bob Moore and Kent Fedorowich, *Prisoners of War and Their Captors in World War II* (Oxford: Berg, 1996).

8. On Kojeve's Hegel seminar, see Vincent Descombes, *Modern French Philosophy*, trans L. Scott-Fox and J. M. Harding (Cambridge: Cambridge University Press, 1980); Jacques d'Hondt, *Hegel et Hégélianisme* (Paris: Presses universitaires de France, 1982); Michael S. Roth, *Knowing and History: Appropriations of Hegel in Twentieth-Century France* (Ithaca, NY: Cornell University Press, 1988); Judith Butler, *Subjects of Desire: Hegelian Reflections in Twentieth-Century France* (New York:

Columbia University Press, 1988); and Ethan Kleinberg, *Generation Existential: Heidegger's Philosophy in France, 1927–1961* (Ithaca, NY: Cornell University Press, 2005), 49–110.

9. On the importance of Jacob Gordin, see Léon Askénazi, "Philosophie et revelation biblique: La demarche de Jacob Gordin," in *Pardès: Revue européenne d'Études et de Culture juives*, no. 23 (1997): 71–77.

10. On the UGIF, see Richard Cohen, *The Burden of Conscience: French Jewish Leadership during the Holocaust* (Bloomington: Indiana University Press, 1987).

11. In the revised edition of his *Mémoires*, Poliakov itemized his profound differences with Braudel over the questions of anti-Semitism, Jewish identity, religion, and the State of Israel, which Poliakov suggested hampered his career. See *Mémoires*, 257–58n11. On the *Annales* school and Braudel's reign over it in the postwar period, see Peter Burke, *The French Historical Revolution: The "Annales" School, 1929–1989* (Stanford, CA: Stanford University Press, 1990), 32–64.

12. A. Latreille, *Le Monde*, October 16, 1952; P. Grappin, *Politique étrangère*, no. 4 (1951); J. Gallois, *L'Observateur*, July 12, 1951.

13. Jacques Maritain, *Social Research* 23 (Summer 1956); R. H. S. Crossman, *New Statesman*, July 28, 1956.

14. Hannah Arendt, "The History of the Great Crime," *Commentary* 13 (March 1952): 300–304.

15. Poliakov had already developed this argument in his documentary reader, the first book he produced as head of the CDJC, *La condition des juifs en France sous l'occupation italienne* (Paris: Éditions du Centre, 1946). For a more recent work that has problematized the role of Italy and the Jews, see Robert Wistrich and Sergio DellaPergola, eds., *Fascist Antisemitism and the Italian Jews* (Jerusalem: Vidal Sassoon International Center for the Study of Antisemitism, 1995).

16. This has been contentious terrain in both the scholarship and in public discussions of the Holocaust, including most famously Raul Hilberg's depiction in *The Destruction of European Jews*, and especially in the response to Arendt's *Eichmann in Jerusalem*. See Isaiah Trunk, *Judenrat: The Jewish Councils in Eastern Europe under Nazi Occupation* (New York: Macmillan, 1972). For a more recent intervention in this discussion, see Zygmunt Bauman, "Soliciting the Co-operation of the Victims," in *Modernity and the Holocaust* (Ithaca, NY: Cornell University Press, 2000 [1989]), 117–50.

17. See Poliakov's discussion on page 132. On the historiography, see Omer Bartov, "German Soldiers and the Holocaust: Historiography, Research and Implications," in *The Holocaust: Origins, Implementation, Aftermath*, ed. Omer Bartov (London: Routledge, 2000), 162–84.

18. On Poliakov's prescience in dealing with these topics, see Abraham Edelheit, "Historiography of the Holocaust," in *Encyclopedia of the Holocaust*, ed. Israel Gutman (New York: Macmillan, 2000), 666–72, quote on 667. Poliakov discusses the Jewish resistance in chapter 9 and the Nazis' plans for "inferior peoples" in chapter 11.

19. *Harvest of Hate*, 48–49; see also 52–53. Michael Marrus and Robert Paxton would gain far greater acclaim for helping to rupture the Gaullist myth with the publication of *Vichy France and the Jews* (Stanford, CA: Stanford, 1995 [1981]).

20. See Poliakov, *Harvest of Hate*, 127–32, 209, 215, 247.

21. Daniel Jonah Goldhagen, *Hitler's Willing Executioners* (New York: Knopf, 1996); Christopher R. Browning, *Ordinary Men: Reserve Police Battalion 101 and the Final Solution in Poland* (New York: HarperCollins, 1992). For their debate, see Daniel Jonah Goldhagen, "The Paradigm Challenged," *Tikkun* (May–June 1988), and Christopher R. Browning, "Ordinary Germans or Ordinary Men? A Reply to the Critics," in *The Holocaust and History: The Known, the Unknown, the Disputed, and the Reexamined*, ed. Michael Berenbaum and Abraham J. Peck (Bloomington: Indiana University Press, 1998).

22. A.M.P., "Mort de l'historien Léon Poliakov," *Le Figaro*, December 9, 1997.

23. Christian Delacampagne, "Léon Poliakov: Un spécialiste de l'analyse de l'antisémitisme," *Le Monde*, December 10, 1997, 24.

24. A.S., *L'Humanité*, December 9, 1997. Elaborating on Poliakov's role as a witness, Patrick Girard placed him side by side with two other titans of the testimonial literature written in French, Claude Roy and David Rousset, who also died around the same time. See Patrick Girard, "Léon Poliakov, Claude Roy, David Rousset: Adieu à la passion de la vérité," *L'Événement du Jour*, December 18/24, 1997, 25.

25. "L. Poliakov, 87, Historian of Anti-Semitism," *New York Times*, December 10, 1997, 25. Poliakov would publish a book on the trial of Eichmann, *Le procès de Jérusalem: Jugements, documents* (Paris: CDJC-Calmann-Lévy, 1963). Along with presenting the documentation from the trial, Poliakov wrote a long introduction (eighty-five pages) and then, in the section titled "Judgments," he wrote an introduction to all of the various components of the case.

26. See Saul Friedländer, *Nazi Germany and the Jews*, vol. 1, *The Years of Persecution, 1933–1939* (New York: HarperCollins, 1997), chapter 3 and *Nazi Germany and the Jews*, vol. 2, *1939–1945: The Years of Extermination* (New York: HarperCollins, 2007). Friedländer sees his conception of "redemptive antisemitism" as a way to transcend the binaries of much of the scholarship focused around the polarities of Christian anti-Judaism versus modern anti-Semitism; Hitler's charisma against bureaucracy; and "ordinary men" opposed to "ordinary Germans." See Saul Friedländer, "The Extermination of the European Jews in Historiography: Fifty Years Later," in Bartov, *The Holocaust*, 79–91.

27. Norman Cohn, *Warrant for Genocide: The Myth of the Jewish World Conspiracy and the Protocols of the Elders of Zion* (Middlesex, UK: Penguin, 1967). This argument was put forward as early as Joshua Trachtenburg's *The Devil and the Jews: The Medieval Conception of the Jew and Its Relation to Modern Anti-Semitism* (New Haven, CT: Yale University Press, 1943).

28. Jeffrey Herf, *The Jewish Enemy* (Cambridge, MA: Harvard University Press, 2006).

29. Weber, *Questioning Judaism*, 94.

30. I am suggesting that here Poliakov anticipates Karl Schleunes, Ian Kershaw, and Saul Friedländer by suggesting that the twisted road to Auschwitz was built by "redemptive antisemitism," but it was paved by indifference.

31. The original title for Poliakov's book was *Génocide: Une contribution à l'étude de la haine pure.* See *Mémoires*, 284.

32. For this reason, Pierre Boutang, writing in the reconstituted journal of the Action française, *Aspects de la France*, remarked that Poliakov erred with his "ambiguous and unpleasant" title. See Pierre Boutang, *Aspects de la France*, June 29, 1951.

33. This communication is cited in the annex to Poliakov's *Mémoires*, 284.

34. This letter is reprinted in full in ibid., 287.

35. The exchange between Mauriac and Poliakov is contained in ibid., 288.

36. Sigmund Freud, "Analysis of a Phobia in a Five-Year-Old Boy" (1909), in *The Standard Edition of the Complete Psychological Works of Sigmund Freud*, ed. James Strachey et al. (London: Hogarth, 1955), 36. See also Jay Geller, "The Godfather of Psychoanalysis: Circumcision, Antisemitism, Homosexuality and Freud's 'Fighting Jew,'" *Journal of the American Academy of Religion* 67, no. 2 (June 1999): 355–85, quote on 357.

37. Geller, "The Godfather of Psychoanalysis." 357. The literature on Freud's Jewishness is fairly extensive. It includes the racial interpretation of Charles Maylan, *Freuds Tragischer Komplex: Eine Analyse der Psychoanalyse* (Munich: E. Reinhardt, 1929); David Bakan's interpretation of a hidden Jewish essence to Freud that connects him to the Jewish mystical tradition, *Sigmund Freud and the Jewish Mystical Tradition* (Princeton, NJ: Van Nostrand, 1958); the argument for Freud's cultural Jewishness in John Murray Cuddihy, *The Ordeal of Civility* (New York: Basic Books, 1974); following Freud's first biographer Ernest Jones, the interpretation of Peter Gay that Freud was a "godless Jew" in *A Godless Jew: Freud, Atheism, and the Making of Psychoanalysis* (New Haven, CT: Yale University Press; Cincinnati: Hebrew Union College Press, 1987); a more nuanced interpretation of the religious influences on Freud in Emanuel Rice, *Freud and Moses: The Long Journey Home* (Albany: SUNY Press, 1990). The most important recent interpretations of Freud's Jewishness along with Geller's are Yosef Hayim Yerushalmi, *Freud's Moses: Judaism Terminable and Interminable* (New Haven, CT: Yale University Press, 1991); and among Sander Gilman's many publications on the topic, see *Freud, Race, and Gender* (Princeton, NJ: Princeton University Press, 1993) and *The Case of Sigmund Freud: Medicine and Identity in the Fin-de-Siècle* (Baltimore: Johns Hopkins University Press, 1993); and Daniel Boyarin, *Unheroic Conduct: The Rise of Heterosexuality and the Invention of the Jewish Man* (Berkeley: University of California Press, 1997), 189–270.

38. See "Thoughts for the Times on War and Death" (1915), *Group Psychology and the Analysis of the Ego* (1921), and *Civilization and Its Discontents* (1930).

39. Freud, *Moses and Monetheism*, in *Standard Edition* 23:91–92. Emphasis added.

40. There are now a slew of writers who have complicated this interpretation, beginning with Jules Isaac, and then Poliakov, but now including Rosemary Ruether, Roy Eckardt, Friedrich Heer, Franklin Littell, Malcom Hay, John Gager, James

Carroll, Robert Michael, Dora Begen, and Susannah Heschel, among others who have looked at the close affiliations of the Christian churches and Hitlerism.

41. See Geller, "Godfather," 358, for the double binds of Freud's situation as the summation of the new historiography on him.

42. See Jay Geller, "*Atheist* Jew or Atheist *Jew*: Freud's Jewish Question and Ours," *Modern Judaism* 26, no. 1 (February 2006): 1–14.

43. Boyarin explores how Jews like Freud and Theodor Herzl found symbolic means to assimilate to the dominant norms of central European culture. See Boyarin, *Unheroic Conduct*, 226: "The ambivalence underlying wishes for Jewish assimilation, like other performances of colonial mimicry, is deeply embedded in issues of both gender and sexuality."

44. Samuel explicitly denies the influence of Freud's *Moses* in a footnote, insisting that the shared viewpoint is an expression of the fact that "an understanding of the truth is now in the air." See Maurice Samuel, *The Great Hatred* (New York: Knopf, 1948 [1940]), 140. All references are to the 1948 edition and cited parenthetically hereafter.

45. Milton Hindus, ed., *The Worlds of Maurice Samuel: Selected Writings* (Philadelphia: Jewish Publication Society of America, 1977), 236.

46. Louis Fisher, *Men and Politics* (New York: Duell, Sloan and Pearce, 1941), 243.

47. Ilan Stavans, "Thinking Aloud: The Education of Maurice Samuel," *Pakn Treger*, no. 49 (Fall 2005): 15–23.

48. While there are examples of the use of "Judeo-Christian" provided in the Oxford English Dictionary from 1899 and 1910, it was only in 1939 that the term was first used in the contemporary sense of a shared tradition of ethical values. According to Arthur A. Cohen, *The Myth of the Judeo-Christian Tradition* (New York: Harper and Row, 1957), "It was only in the late nineteenth century in Germany that the Judeo-Christian tradition, as such, was first defined. It was introduced by German Protestant scholarship to account for the findings developed by the Higher Criticism of the Old Testament and achieved considerable currency as a polemical term in that period. There, quite clearly, the negative significance of the expression became primary. The emphasis fell not to the communality of the word 'tradition' but to the accented stress of the hyphen. The Jewish was Latinized and abbreviated into 'Judeo' to indicate a dimension, albeit a pivotal dimension, of the explicit Christian experience" (xviii). As such, Solomon Schechter called it "Higher Anti-Semitism." For more on the emergence of the construct "Judeo-Christian," see Mark Silk, "Notes on the Judeo-Christian Tradition in America," *American Quarterly* 36, no. 1 (Spring 1984): 65–85. See also Jonathan Sarna, *American Judaism: A History* (New Haven, CT: Yale University Press, 2004), 266–267.

49. This is similar to the argument that was made by Franz Rosenzweig in *The Star of Redemption*, trans. William Hallo (Notre Dame, IN: University of Notre Dame Press, 1970), 413–17.

50. Emmanuel Levinas, "Reflections on the Philosophy of Hitlerism," trans. Seán Hand, *Critical Inquiry* 17, no. 1 (Autumn 1990): 62–71.

51. On Maritain's shifting position in the interwar period, see Richard Crane, "Surviving Maurras: Jacques Maritain's Jewish Question," in *Naming Race, Naming Racisms*, ed. Jonathan Judaken (New York: Routledge, 2009), 51–77. For Maritain's lifelong stance on the Jewish question, see Richard Crane, *Passion of Israel: Jacques Maritain, Catholic Conscience, and the Holocaust* (Scranton, PA: University of Scranton Press, 2010).

52. Jacques Maritain, "On Anti-Semitism," *Christianity and Crisis* (October 6, 1941), reprinted in Jacques Maritain and Raïssa Maritain, *Oeuvres complètes*, vol. 8 (Paris: Éditions universitaires Fribourg Suisse and Éditions Saint-Paul, 1989), 564–77, quotation from 566. The Maritain citations are to this article and cited parenthetically hereafter.

10

André Neher

A Post-Shoah Prophetic Vocation

EDWARD K. KAPLAN

We do not introduce our masters. I simply want to convey to
him, on behalf of everyone, our gratitude for having been,
during the German occupation and immediately after, one of
the few who had the courage and the competence to reinvent,
if I may say so, principles that are now, twenty years later, taken
for granted, and especially the fact that it is possible to
approach Jewish thinking without losing substance, and at the
very level of thought.
—Léon Askenazi, addressing André Neher, in *La conscience
juive face à l'histoire: Le pardon*

This chapter traces the inception of André Neher's significant role in the
renewal of French Jewish intellectual and spiritual life after the Shoah.
Born in 1914 in Obernai, in the Bas Rhin region of France, he was educated as both a secular intellectual and a religiously observant Jew. (His
family moved to Strasbourg, which became French in 1918.) In 1936, aged
twenty-two, he began to teach German language and literature at the
Collège de Sarrebourg while also pursuing yeshiva studies in Montreux,
Switzerland.[1] Mobilized in 1939, Neher made a crucial life decision when
the Vichy government removed him from teaching on December 2, 1940.
Shocked at the indifference of his colleagues, he resolved to specialize in
Judaic studies after the war. After publishing articles on German literature and Judaic topics in the early 1940s, and teaching Jewish children at
the École d'Orsay outside of Paris, in 1947 he defended his *doctorat d'état*
dissertation on the prophet Amos at the University of Strasbourg.
(Neher's *thèse complémentaire*, "Les douze prophètes dans le Talmud," is
also dated 1947; that year he also married Renée Bernheim, who became

his close collaborator.) Neher published his dissertation on Amos in 1950, with the prestigious philosophy publisher J. Vrin. Five years later, in 1955, he was promoted to *professeur de littérature juive* at the University of Strasbourg. This prestigious academic post provided Neher with the authority to interpret sacred sources in a manner faithful both to Jewish tradition and to contemporary philosophical and ethical thought. I focus on how he thereafter combined sober philological scholarship and stirring interpretation, with the goal of making Jewish tradition relevant to his day. Put another way, André Neher sought to reconcile the often dissimilar ideals of academic scholarship, Jewish piety, and prophetic witness. Key to my concerns, therefore, is how Neher thus sought to repudiate the negativity of the Shoah and the French norm of assimilation by interpreting traditional Judaism in a manner congenial to French secular culture. To that end, he was a principal founder of the Colloques des intellectuels juifs de langue française (Colloquia of French-Speaking Jewish Intellectuals), inaugurated in 1957, and which continue today. At these annual conferences Neher became an eminent voice through his biblical lessons, along with the Talmudic lessons of Emmanuel Levinas.

Early Writings

After Neher abandoned his career as teacher of German literature, his initial writings on Judaism combine resistance to the Shoah and a scholarly methodology congruent with spiritual values. Neher wrote his earliest manifesto with his brother Richard, a dense, personal essay entitled "Transcendance et immanence" (Transcendence and immanence), printed as a pamphlet by Éditions Yechouroun in Lyon in the first trimester of 1946; the preface announced that the essay was conceived "en pleine guerre" and was inspired by their recently deceased father, Albert Neher, a traditional Jew who taught them the Bible.

At the time, the publication of "Transcendance et immanence" was judged by many dedicated Jews to be "an event in the world of Jewish thought; these twenty-five pages created a new orientation for Jewish Studies" in France.[2] The authors' insistence on the historicity of Judaism and the relevance of religion was seen as a rebuttal of Jean-Paul Sartre's famous analysis, both psychological and ideological, "Portrait of the Anti-Semite,"[3] part of which first appeared in the December 1945 issue of *Les Temps modernes*. Late the following year, the enlarged book, entitled *Réflexions sur la question juive* (Reflections on the Jewish question), was published by a small press.[4]

Sartre's phenomenology of the Other quickly became the normative conceptual model of Jewish identity after the occupation and the return of survivors.[5] However, for traditionally educated Jews, the price paid for Sartre's support was too steep. Famously, Sartre was said to define Jewish identity as originating in the gaze of the Other, often conditioned by anti-Semitic stereotypes.

André and Richard Neher's 1946 essay opposed the view that Judaism had no history and that a Jew derived his or her identity from the anti-Semite. This work of filial piety intended to give meaning to the future after the atrocious events. Quoting their father's last writing of June 1944, the brothers defined the goal of philosophy as to enable people to act: "It's about locating the problem, clarifying the methodological givens, and only then, to approach the answer."[6] The patriarch Abraham became the Nehers' model for postwar French Jewish thinkers.

Essentially, the Nehers sought to reconcile the religious and the secular dimensions of human experience, not by absorbing one into the other, but through "contiguity," that is, preserving boundaries for the sake of shared ethical action:

> The mission for the children of Abraham, Isaac, and Jacob, of students of Moses and of the Prophets, is to seek the absolute in the contingent, the extraordinary in the ordinary, the divine in the earthly, therefore not to surpass the physical, but to render it metaphysical, in such a way as not to demonstrate the identity of the two terms—what is easy to conceive, but impossible—but to demonstrate their contiguity—which is difficult to conceive, but possible. Possible, because the [Jewish] condition, instead of being a passion, is an effort. Indeed, where there is effort, there is a need for law, equilibrium, continuity.[7]

This essay was a preliminary map of André Neher's doctoral dissertation and his subsequent interpretations of biblical categories of thinking. The definitions are subtle and sometimes confusing, but here is the essential message:

> [Biblical time as] fusion, coexistence, rootedness, extension, *chain*. . . .
> Consulting the time of *history*; it is fragmented, and we must turn our back to the future to find it only in the past. . . . But with Biblical Time, history is a *chain*. Not the past, but a *covenant*, a *contract*. Not the present, but a *commitment*, an *effort*. Not the future, but a *mission*.[8]

André Neher launched his postwar academic career with this activist conception of Judaic studies. But first he had to earn his French university credentials. Following the customary strategy, he began by publishing articles related to his dissertation. Most relevant here are "Fonction du prophète dans la société hébraïque" (The prophet's role in Hebrew society) in the *Revue d'Histoire et de Philosophie religieuses* (1948–49) and "Aspects actuels des études bibliques" (Present trends in biblical studies) in the Protestant journal *Études évangéliques* (January–March 1950).

Neher defined himself within the university system by his title and by his scholarly stance. In "Aspects actuels des études bibliques" he launched a frontal attack against the still dominant ideology of Julius Wellhausen and his historical-critical method. (Neher signed this paper "Chargé de cours d'Histoire du Judaïsme à la Faculté des Lettres de Strasbourg," basically, assistant professor without tenure.) He audaciously defended the sociological approaches of Max Weber (1864–1920) and, to his credit, the little-known David Koigen (1877–1933) (Abraham Heschel's mentor in Berlin).[9]

Both Koigen and Weber demonstrated what Neher considered to be the fundamental role of the covenant, the *berith*, in Israelite religion and society: "The first religious charter of the people of Israel, the Torah of Moses, was struck at the confluence of the *berith* [the covenant] and of Levitism. . . . [According to David Koigen], the liberation movement that in Egypt moved the people of Israel out of slavery, determined to an extraordinary extent the victory of the religious social contract of the covenant."[10] The conclusion of the earlier article, "Fonction du prophète" (1948–49), is even more explicit: "In Greece and in Rome, the oppressed, half-breeds, and slaves, were repressed above and beyond the limits of the social edifice. . . . In Israel, the common people actively participated in the national existence, through the voice of the prophets."[11] The final sentence restates the author's ethical and religious ideal without ambiguity or pedantry: "the reintroduction of the humble person (the 'little man') in the grand drama of human society.[12]

It remains for us to analyze—or, more realistically, to characterize briefly—the books that consolidated André Neher's reputation—for better and for worse—between 1950 and 1955. The book that earned him a professorship at Strasbourg was of course the doctoral thesis, *Amos: Contribution à l'étude du prophétisme*, published in 1950 by the Librarie Philosophique J. Vrin. (It was reproduced verbatim, with a new preface and bibliographical additions, in 1981.)

Neher's dedication page points to its deeper purpose, to confront his excruciating solidarity with victims of the war: "TO THE MEMORY OF MY FATHER who with my mother made our household glow . . . with goodness, with wisdom[,] with faith in the Bible of which he wrote commentaries"; and, with the names of five men, "TO THE MEMORY OF my friends, classmates, students . . . executed by the Germans or died in deportation."

The ideological battles within the budding field of French Judaic scholarship emerge clearly from book reviews. I can only suggest how three subsequent books, in addition to numerous articles and essays of a popular or scholarly nature, complete Neher's definition of modern biblical Judaism. In 1956, Neher reached his widest readership in *Moïse et la vocation juive* (Moses and the Jewish calling), published in 1956 by Éditions du Seuil (but surely completed by 1955), a lively, popular book of 192 pages with abundant illustrations in its wide-ranging series, Microcosme (Maîtres spirituels).

Returning to 1951, the year after the academic study of Amos appeared, Neher published a small inspirational book, *Notes sur Qohelet (L'Ecclésiaste)*, Editions de Minuit, 110 pages, "sous le patronage de l'Union des étudiants juifs de France" (sponsored by the Union of French Jewish Students); and in 1955, he extended the Amos book with the more academic study *L'essence du prophétisme*, Presses universitaires de France, 359 pages, in the Collection Épiméthée (directed by the philosopher Jean Hyppolite). These books anticipate the direction of Neher's life's work: defining the essence of prophecy and the universal vocation of Judaism and the Jewish people.

By 1955, Neher had not only earned a professorship in Jewish thought at a distinguished secular university but also contributed to religious publishing programs beyond any narrow Jewish designation. (In fact, there were not yet any dedicated Jewish publishers in France.) Neher's choice of identity models for his contemporaries is significant: from Abraham, Isaac, and Jacob, through Amos, and then to back to Moses. For Neher, Jewish tradition provided not only a way of thinking, but a way of life.

A Committed Jewish Academic

From "Transcendence and Immanence" on, therefore, Neher was explicit about his heterogeneous or eclectic methodology, about his moral and theological commitments. He was writing to define biblical Judaism as a model of restoring and renewing French Jewish life, awareness of God joined with ethical responsibility.

In his *avant-propos* and introduction to *Amos*, Neher explained its "subjective" foundation: first, family and community—he dedicated the book to his deceased father and to classmates, friends, and students murdered by the Nazis. He also presented himself autobiographically as a role model, explaining his conversion from an academic career in German literature, in which Judaism played an ancillary role, to Judaic scholar and teacher. During the war he abandoned his dissertation project, "Germany in the Works of Heinrich Heine"; as he explained: "From then on, the goal of my work became clear in the method that I thought would introduce a type of historical theology which would not exclude either scientific certainty or philosophical inquiry."[13]

Neher spells out his method and presuppositions even more explicitly by rejecting the individualism of existentialists such as Karl Jaspers and Gabriel Marcel, the radical solitude of Kierkegaard, and even Martin Buber and Franz Rosenzweig. (He does quote Benjamin Fondane with approval.)[14] Neher, for his part, seeks to define a more authentic Jewish exegetical tradition, one that joins the individual and the community; to that end, he seeks to "rehabilitate the school of Jewish exegesis of the Middle Ages. . . . It is less about a school whose representatives would be united by one identical doctrine, than about bringing together thinkers engaged in a common attitude: the awareness being connected to the Biblical text by a sort of existential continuity. . . . These thinkers are very sensitive to the clearly sociological dimension of the Biblical style, as it reveals a *doing* [faire] rather than a *done* [fait]."[15] In other words, Neher puts forward scholarship as commitment, as prophetic witness, as activism.

Two major reviews responded to this confession of faith in two radically different ways—though both recognized and appreciated, to different degrees, the author's passionate manner of thinking and writing.

The earliest review came from France's most eminent Judaic scholar, the Hungarian-born Georges Vajda (1908–81; he immigrated to Paris in 1927). Vajda's judgment of Neher's academic study of Amos was stormy and uncompromising with regard to details, but fair in defining his own professional standards. Representing the rigors of scientific philology, the prevailing approach to Bible study, Vajda defended the fortress of academic criticism, with some irony, from the very first sentence:

> This work is superficially brilliant. [Cet ouvrage se présente des dehors très brillants.] The author has a definite gift for literary analysis and a philosophical knowledge for which he should be commended. His multifaceted style, his "warm and captivating eloquence," can clearly lead the reader to these glories. However, since we are dealing with a doctoral dissertation defended at a Faculty formerly renowned for its Oriental Studies, we must be forgiven for reviewing this book first as a work of philology and history, without taking into account the option of faith that underlies the author's thinking (see Foreword), nor the value of edification that he can have in certain circles foreign to scholarly research.[16]

Vajda's categories do not admit nuance or compromise with the strictest disciplinary frontiers. His examination of details in Neher's thesis mercilessly goes on for seven tightly printed pages to denounce "a confused mass of arbitrariness and bias, of distortions of texts and of homiletical developments entirely without serious foundation."[17] Biblical scholars can judge Vajda's expert opinions; for us, his abusive rhetoric implies a more interesting ideological debate.[18] Here is Vajda on some of Neher's details: "pure verbiage" (108); "free and fanciful" (110); "the three pages of declamation following this deplorable absurdity vanish in smoke"

(110); "after so many absurdities and Sophistries" (110); "once again, exege-sis turns into a sermon " (111); "brilliant pages that are, however, hard to take seriously" (111); "this means nothing at all, despite the nonsense of the note j" (111). Vajda's conclusion is more positive, as his final sen-tences express this regret that the author had expended his genuine literary talent to work in a false genre, an impossible marriage of inspi-rational literature and autonomous research: "The study of M. Neher is a midrash. Considered as such, it merits some interest. But its real contri-bution to historical and philological exegesis is almost negligible."[19] Here is the positive lesson I would draw: Neher indeed strives to develop "un genre faux," an impossible alliance of faith, biblical solidarity, and critical philosophy.

And this is exactly what French Jews needed so soon after the war, according to Neher: connection with Jewish religious and ethical tradi-tions, historical continuity. André Neher's leadership in the Colloques des intellectuels juifs de langue française would become his primary vehi-cle—in addition to his writings—for such a program of revival, both Jewish and interfaith, as well as with secular thinkers of all backgrounds.

To conclude, I cite two reviews that were particularly sensitive to the possibilities of a modern French Judaism inspired by Neher's model of committed, activist exegesis of the Hebrew prophets. One is the brief review by Robert Aron in the October 1951 issue of *La Nef*, titled "La pesanteur et l'histoire" (Gravity and history), a word play on Simone Weil's notorious book of 1950, *La pesanteur et la grâce* (Gravity and grace). (Robert Aron had recently founded the *Revue des Études juives*, in which Vajda chastised Neher.) Sympathetically polemic, Robert Aron appreciated Neher's attachment to God and to Jewish tradition as a chal-lenge to Simone Weil's negativity.

The most substantial of review of Neher's *Amos* and, I would argue, the most authoritative, is that by the Protestant philosopher Paul Ricoeur entitled "Aux frontières de la philosophie" (At the limits of philosophy), in the section entitled "Le prophétisme" (prophecy), which appeared in the November 1952 issue of *Esprit*, the progressive personalist journal founded in 1931 by Emmanuel Mounier.[20] In addition to his brilliant summary of the structure and content of the book, Ricoeur appreciated Neher's demonstration of the universality of Jewish prophetic inspiration, which does not compromise its particularism.

Essential was Neher's insight that Amos's universalism reflects the covenant with Noah (Genesis 9–10).[21] Ricoeur goes on to cite *Amos* to underline the "compenetration" of the ethical and the religious: "*The omnipresence of God and the omnipresence of the neighbor [le prochain]* are the foundations of the prophet's metaphysical conception . . . [Ricoeur quotes Neher's suspension points] God's presence and the presence of the neighbor interpenetrate; their simultaneity constitutes the absolute demand and there can be no others' (264)."[22] Inspired by Neher, Ricoeur ends with an invitation and a challenge: "The question is to know if and how it is possible to philosophize this chosenness from this covenant, from this eschatology, in short, to know if reflection born of the Greeks can break away from its own particularism to accept the universality buried in another particularism: that of the people Israel."[23] Ricoeur acknowledges the gulf separating Athens and Jerusalem, but he hopes, with André Neher, that the Hebrew Bible will provide common ground and inspire shared hope.

NOTES

1. See the complete bibliography and biographical sketch in *Mélanges André Neher*, preface by Eliane Amado Lévy-Valensi, Théo Dreyfus, Jean Halpérin, and Freddy Raphaël (Paris: Librairie d'Amérique et d'Orient Adrien-Masonneuve, 1975). See the recent volume edited by David Banon, *Héritages d'André Neher* (Paris: Éditions de l'Éclat, 2011). The Neher archives are stored at the Hebrew University in Jerusalem. For further biographical details, see Sandrine Szwarc, "André Neher, philosophe," *Archives juives* 42 (2008): 140–45. For invaluable background, see Sandrine Szwarc, *Les intellectuels juifs de 1945 à nos jours* (Paris: Le Bord de l'Eau, 2013), and Johanna Lehr, *La Thora dans la cité: L'emergence d'un nouveau judaïsme religieux après la Seconde Guerre mondiale* (Paris: Le Bord de l'Eau, 2013).

2. See Paul Zylbermann, "Évocation d'André Neher," http://judaisme.sdv.fr/perso /neher/zylberm.htm. See also David Banon, "André Neher: Du souffle prophétique à l'humanisme maharalien," *Pardès: Revue européenne d'Études et de Culture juives* 23 (1997): 207–15. In January 2012, a conference inaugurated the Chaire André Neher at the Centre communautaire de Paris as part of the Institut Elie Wiesel.

3. See the special issue of *October 87* devoted to Sartre's book; Denis Hollier, "Introduction," *October 87* (Winter 1999): 3.

4. Sartre gave a widely publicized lecture at the Alliance israélite universelle on June 3, 1947; see Emmanuel Levinas, "Existentialism and Antisemitism," *October 87* (Winter 1999): 27–31; published partially in the *Cahiers de l'Alliance*, June 27, 1947, 33–46.

5. As often happens with intellectual trends, Sartre's viewpoint, as liberating as it might have seemed for many Jews, became a cliché after it had inspired thinkers such as Frantz Fanon and Albert Memmi, until Alain Finkielkraut reexamined its presuppositions in his autobiographical work, *Le juif imaginaire*, in 1983. By then the Sartrian paradigm was no longer valid, starting with the November 1967 press conference of General Charles de Gaulle after the Six-Day War.

6. "Transcendance et immanence," republished in Neher, *L'existence juive* (Paris: Le Seuil, 1962), 13.

7. Ibid., 15–16.

8. Ibid., 18.

9. See Martina Urban, "Religion of Reason Revised: David Koigen on the Jewish Ethos," *Journal of Jewish Thought and Philosophy* 16, no. 1 (2008): 59–89. See the chapter on Koigen in Edward K. Kaplan and Samuel Dresner, *Abraham Joshua Heschel, Prophetic Witness* (New Haven, CT: Yale University Press, 1998).

10. André Neher, "Aspects actuels des études bibliques," *Études évangéliques* (January–March 1950): 45.

11. André Neher, "La Fonction du prophète dans la société hébraïque," *Revue d'Histoire et de Philosophie religieuses* no. 1 (1948–1949): 42.

12. Ibid., the final sentence.

13. André Neher, *Amos* (Paris: Vrin, 1980), xvii.

14. Ibid., xvii–xix.

15. Ibid., xvii.

16. Georges Vajda, *Revue des Études juives* 110 (July 1949–December 1950): 107 (107-14).

17. Ibid.; the following references in parentheses are from the same article.

18. In the 1981 edition of his *Amos*, Neher himself admitted to "quelques défauts juveniles," vii–xi.

19. Vajda, *Revue des Études juives*, 114, the final sentences.

20. It is strange and sad that Neher, who had been criticized for the careless bibliography of his thesis, made an incorrect reference in the 1981 re-edition of *Amos*; the "Mise au jour bibliographique" erroneously notes: "Ricoeur, Paul, 'Limites de la philosophie,' à propos d'André Neher, *Esprit*, mars 1951.'" The correct essay on Neher appears in the November 1952 issue of *Esprit*.

21. Paul Ricoeur, "'C'est dans la portée noadihique de la *berith* que réside l'universalisme d'Amos," *Esprit* (November 1952) 62: 763.

22. Ibid., 764–65.

23. Ibid., 765, the final sentences.

11

René Cassin and the Alliance Israélite Universelle

A Republican in Post-Holocaust France

JAY WINTER

This chapter contextualizes the claim that French Jews emerged from World War II with a sense of disenchantment with the republican tradition by presenting the opposite case, that of a man whose republican commitment was unshakable and indeed deepened by the war and the Shoah. René Cassin, jurist, international statesman, and one of the authors of the Universal Declaration of Human Rights, never lost his faith in the republican project at home and abroad. From 1940 on, he worked to revitalize that tradition, not to discard or refashion it.[1]

I will bypass the story of his wartime role as the jurist of France libre between 1940 and 1944, and his mediation of the return to the republican legal order after the Liberation. Instead I will focus on his work on behalf of the Alliance israélite universelle (AIU, or the Alliance), of which he was president from 1943 until his death thirty-three years later.

How did he get there? It was not through a lifelong commitment to Jewish beliefs and practices. Born in Bayonne in 1887, he had a Jewish education to satisfy his mother, and then, like his father, left religious practice behind. He was severely wounded in 1914 and married a Catholic woman, Simone Yzombard, in 1917. From 1940, he had a liaison with a second Catholic woman, Ghislaine Bru, a film actress with whom he fell in love in London during the Blitz. They married in 1975, when he was eighty-eight years old, just three months before his death.

Until the 1930s, René Cassin was an assimilated Jewish republican whose Jewishness was of secondary importance to him. From the 1930s on, and even more so after the defeat of 1940, he became a republican Jew, with a commitment to the Jewish cause as a central element of his commitment to universal rights. In 1948, René Cassin himself noted that it was a year of great achievements for him, including in terms of the *pilot-age* of the Universal Declaration of Human Rights through the General Assembly of the United Nations; it was passed without dissent (though with seven abstentions) on December 10, 1948. In that same year he was elected to the Academy of Moral and Political Sciences, and thereby became a member of L'Institut de France. He received many letters of congratulation on this honor. One was from an admirer who rejoiced in the honor Cassin had brought to the Jewish people. Cassin protested that this "immense praise" was gratifying though unjustified. Cassin went on: "I will say only that I have been given virtues that I do not have. In particular my loyalty to Judaism is quite specific, for I do not attend synagogue frequently. Only since the persecution of 1933 have I stood in solidarity among the persecuted. But if one day they became the persecutors, I will no longer be with them."[2] Cassin's commitment to France libre and to human rights brought him to a position of prominence within French and world Jewry, and not the other way around. Once installed as a major Jewish leader, Cassin spent the last thirty years of his life as the president of the most important secular Jewish institution in France, the Alliance israélite universelle. He had little idea of what would follow when de Gaulle asked him to be its president in 1943.[3] But through this position, he became a major Jewish figure both in France and in the world of transnational Jewish politics.

The Alliance

The AIU was founded in 1860 by a group of French Jews dedicated to Jewish emancipation within the wide crescent of French influence and control from Morocco to Persia. The AIU ran an archipelago of schools in which students, Jews or non-Jews, were educated in French. It was the prerogative of the Central Committee of the AIU, and not de Gaulle, to name him president, but the Central Committee had been forced into a kind of hibernation.[4] In 1943, in extraordinary times, and for his own political reasons, de Gaulle filled the vacancy with an incontestable choice, a Jew with impeccable credentials and unqualified loyalty to him.

This act achieved several objectives. The AIU represented a part of republican culture which was still very much alive, despite the break with Vichy. At the beginning of 1942, Cassin had gone on a mission for France libre and visited Middle Eastern and French organizations, prominent among which were the AIU and its schools.[5] For de Gaulle, who was incensed at steps taken by British authorities that seemed to threaten French hegemony in the Levant, Alliance schools were evidence of long-standing French interests in Syria, Lebanon, and Palestine, and the more they were tied in with France libre, the better. They were one of the pillars of French influence, and de Gaulle defended these schools in the same manner as he defended the Alliance française, of which 69 of 108 committees had sided with London rather than with Vichy.

In March 1943, the revival of the leadership of the AIU was a gambit in the conflict opposing de Gaulle and Henri Giraud. The heart of the work of the AIU was in North Africa, then under the authority of General Giraud. He had confirmed Vichy's abrogation of the Loi Crémieux, under which the status of Jews in Algeria as full French citizens had been established in 1870. De Gaulle promised to restore it. In this context, to take control of the AIU was to consolidate de Gaulle's position as leader of France libre. Who could object to the nomination of Cassin? He was commissioner—minister—of national education and justice on the French National Committee. As such, he represented France in the Inter-Allied Educational Conference, and he had made great efforts to preserve those elements of the university world not under the control of Vichy.

Cassin accepted the presidency of the AIU with gusto. He decided to form a small committee of the AIU, which met in London on April 3, 1943. Two months later, he installed the office of the AIU in Algiers, in rue Bab-el-Oued. The next step toward the restoration of its normal life was after the liberation of Paris. There, the provisional executive committee of the AIU met in its old headquarters on rue Labruyère, in the ninth arrondissement, on September 11, 1944.[6]

Cassin remained president of the AIU for thirty-three years. This was the one post among the many he occupied in which he served without interruption for the longest time. He was vice president of the Conseil d'État for sixteen years; French delegate to the League of Nations for fourteen years; and honorary president of the Union fédérale (UF) for longer, but he played no direct part in the work of the organization after the 1950s.

The parallel period of commitment to the UF and the AIU was no accident. Both were dedicated to healing the wounds of war and to affirming the dignity of those who suffered, not only during war but long afterward. It is not surprising, therefore, that the only active post he kept until the day he died was the presidency of the AIU.

Cassin was no figurehead. As president, he attended to the great questions as well as to the small matters of everyday life. He wrote condolence notes to the widows of deceased colleagues; he wrote hundreds of letters soliciting funds for Alliance projects; he was a font of nominations for honors due, and frequently received by, his colleagues in the Alliance. To take but one example, he personally wrote in support of the nomination for the Légion d'honneur of Emmanuel Levinas, and he personally bestowed the Chevalier de la Légion d'honneur on him.[7] He supported applications for naturalization by Alliance teachers. He attended the evening meetings of the Central Committee religiously, following the daily rigors of his work in the Conseil d'État. He met visiting dignitaries and journalists, and his elbow must have been sore from the all too frequent efforts he made to raise his glass to salute the latest in an endless queue of honorable colleagues who came to pay their respects or to ask for his assistance.

When he became president of the AIU in 1943, the Alliance was split in two. The head office in Paris had effectively been brought to an end. Its library had been seized and transported to Germany; it would be recovered and reconstructed piecemeal between 1946 and 1950.[8] The Central Committee of the Alliance ceased to function as such, and the core administrative staff, carrying their archives with them, moved successively to Lyon, to Marseille, and then to the small market town of Felletin in the department of the Creuse, where many Jewish children were hidden on farms and in other institutions.

The domestic life of the Alliance was virtually at a standstill. Danger lurked everywhere, since the offices of a Jewish organization were ready-made targets for roundups of deportees. In addition, the creation of the *Union générale des israélites de France* (UGIF) in November 1941 as a portmanteau organization for French Jews presented the threat of confiscation of Alliance funds.

Fortunately, the Alliance was still alive. Outside of France, the work of its network of schools extended from Morocco to Iran. They continued to function, even at the worst moments, thanks to the dedication and care of their teachers and administrative personnel. In addition, the Service des oeuvres françaises à l'étranger (SOFE) continued to support AIU schools financially, despite the fact that this service operated within the French Foreign Ministry. Ironically, Vichy supported the AIU while France libre slowly took it over.[9] Nevertheless, the organization faced an unprecedented financial crisis. It was necessary to draw up an accounting of the damage caused by the war, to bring the Alliance out of the shadows of wartime fear and poverty, to breathe new life into it, and to turn to the problems of the postwar world.

The provisional Central Committee was small but distinguished. Alongside Cassin, Louis Kahn, inspecteur général des constructions navales, and Bernard Mélamède, later inspecteur général de l'économie nationale, served as provisional vice presidents of the AIU. Their role was clearly limited to planning for the postwar challenges the institution would face. The daily work of the AIU was the responsibility of others. Central to the AIU was Jules Braunschvig, born in 1908, from an Alsatian family that made a fortune in Tangiers and then moved between North Africa and the mainland after 1914. He was active in the Alliance before the war and spent four years in a prisoner of war camp in northern Germany. His direct knowledge of the Maghreb was essential to the Alliance. Eugène Weill was the organization's tireless secretary, constantly in touch with Cassin about Alliance business large and small. Marcel Franco was a Turkish-born graduate of one of the Alliance's schools whose marriage to an American brought him to New York, where he was an essential interlocutor with the American Jewish community. Cassin had, from 1947 on, the assistance of André Chouraqui, a young Algerian lawyer, poet, and man of letters for whom Cassin had great esteem. He served as Cassin's personal emissary and became something like an adopted nephew, protected by Cassin when others in the Alliance doubted his usefulness to the organization.[10] With Cassin's backing, Chouraqui occupied an unusual position in the AIU, working to build the organization's international ties six months of the year, and on his "travaux personnels relatives aux matières hébraïques et judaïques" (personal work on Hebrew and Jewish subjects) for the remainder.[11] He translated the Bible into French. He was a difficult colleague, however, a bit arrogant and aloof, despite his evident talents. Finally, there was the philosopher Emmanuel Levinas, who, like Braunschvig, had returned from a prisoner of war camp, and who ran the école normale of the

Alliance, training the organization's teachers in Paris before dispatch-
ing them abroad.[12] Together these individuals formed an inner circle of
the Alliance and gave it a cosmopolitan and varied outlook: secular,
republican, and Jewish in equal measure.

The AIU's schools were a rich and complex mixture of thriving institutions and those which were barely surviving. A lot depended on
personalities. The center of the Alliance's network was in North Africa,
and there its Moroccan program was the most important. Its forty-seven
schools provided education for approximately 15,000 students who were
looked after by 180 teachers and 160 assistant teachers. The school in
Casablanca had 300 pupils studying trades including ironwork, wood-
work, tailoring, leatherwork, and electricity. There were forty pupils
in Fez, fifty in Rabat, thirty-six in Marrakech, and the beginnings of
an agricultural school in Meknes. Ruben Tajouri was the head of the
Alliance's Moroccan operation. He was evidently a very able administrator and enjoyed the trust of everyone concerned.[13]

Seventy percent of all students educated in Alliance schools after
World War II were Moroccan. Between 1956 and 1964, when France relin-
quished its formal protectorate in Morocco, the population attending
Alliance schools dropped by half, as a substantial part of the Jewish

Students in the schools of the Alliance israélite universelle, 1952–1971

	1952–1953	1963–1964	1968	1971
Egypt	427	—	—	—
Israel	3,997	5,253	4,828	5,044
Lebanon	1,260	1,301	1,109	—
Morocco	24,788	13,525	8,054	7,652
Syria	386	447	431	480
Libya	100	—	—	—
Tunisia	3,355	3,797	1,366	147
Iran	—	5,933	5,158	4,034
Total	34,313	30,256	20,946	17,357
Percentage in Morocco	72%	48%	38%	44%

Sources: AIU, AM Présidence 005b, Budget pour 1952, May 28, 1952; André Chouraqui, L'Alliance israélite
universelle, Annexe 4, 498–506; AIU, Jewish Virtual Library, www.jewishvirtuallibrary.org/jsource/judaica
/ejud_0002_0001_0_00834.html; AIU, AM Présidence 013a, Cassin au Comité de Liaison des amis de l'AIU,
January 3, 1971.

community immigrated to Israel. The number fell further in the later 1960s and early 1970s, though Alliance schools in Israel contributed to the assimilation of Moroccan Jews who settled there. Until the 1970s, there were significant numbers of schools and students in Tunisia too, and though the total attending Alliance schools remained stable in the first postwar decade, the situation was troubled. There, personal conflicts and administrative muddles produced less impressive reports and results. Deep animosities divided teachers in schools elsewhere too.

In monthly meetings of the Alliance's Central Committee in Paris, Cassin immediately took time to get into the details of school affairs. He dealt with questions as to the training of the Alliance's teachers in Casablanca and in its École normale israëlite orientale in Paris, directed by Levinas. Cassin showed here his interest in teaching and in the education of elites, also displayed in another postwar institution he helped to create, the École nationale d'administration (ENA). In 1950, forty-two boys and thirty-eight girls were in training in the École normale israëlite orientale.[14] In 1952, he declared in Levinas's presence that this college "did not maintain the level of instruction it should attain, and students felt isolated." He urged Levinas to do something about it.[15] He explored problems of parity between teachers' pay in the Alliance schools and in other schools, as well as provisions for pensions for retired teachers and administrators abroad. He received reports for his approval on the organization of the teaching day. In Isfahan, the day was divided into classes on "reading in Persian, writing in Persian, dictation in Persian, arithmetic, Hebrew, writing style, gymnastics, music," all in French.[16] He oversaw repairs and building plans for the Alliance's schools. He read of squabbles among administrators and teachers in Isfahan, who personally wrote to him, defending themselves vigorously and hurling calumny at their accusers.[17] He scrutinized the financial accounts time and again, alongside educational matters of all kinds. In short, in 1944, Cassin entered a still-robust transnational educational project filled with life, evident even in its most ferocious internal conflicts.

It was a unique institution, with a record of which anyone would be proud. In June 1951, he provided this profile to the secretary-general of UNESCO, yet another of Cassin's creations: the AIU ran 130 primary, secondary, technical, and agricultural schools serving 52,000 students in Muslim countries from Morocco to Persia. "The Alliance is unique and one of the greatest educational enterprises in the world." Alliance schools, he pointed out, were open to children of all religions, and the organization "has long-standing and the most cordial ties with all the sovereigns and governments of Muslim countries and enjoys a first-rate moral reputation in these countries."[18]

While the institution had survived the war, its financial future was much more uncertain. There were three primary sources of support for these schools. The first was local authority and national subventions; the second was the central funds of the Alliance; the third was the contribution of the families of the pupils and the local Jewish community. For example, roughly one-sixth of the cost of the Alliance's schools in Tunisia was provided by the Tunisian state; thus financial worries about where the rest would come from were endemic. To lead the Alliance was to be a fund-raiser, along with many other things. From 1945 on, fortunately, there was a new way of assuring the financial stability of the schools: American philanthropy. We will turn later to the international diplomatic efforts Cassin led to help make certain that this new flow of funds continued efficiently and generously in the first decade after the war.

There were two other national sources of both fixed and recurrent expenditure which were of considerable significance to the Alliance. The first was the aid given by the French Foreign Office to the support of French-language education outside, that is to say outside metropolitan France. This assistance had gone on during the war, as we have already noted, and continued throughout Cassin's long presidency. The second was funding for Alliance schools in Israel through the Israeli Ministry of Education and urban local authorities supervising schools. This too was a source of real importance to the Alliance, though it required considerable diplomatic skill to secure and define. The diplomatic problem was twofold: how to preserve its teaching in French, and how to preserve its independence with respect to the state in which the schools operated.

The first problem was resolved without much difficulty. The new Israeli Ministry of Education had an understandable interest in building up the primary and secondary school systems of the state and their commitment to Hebrew as the mandatory language of instruction. Here some French-language instruction could be and was interpolated into the new system in which the Alliance's Israeli schools operated.

Of greater importance was the need to keep the Alliance free from the charge that it was an agent of the Israeli state. That charge threatened the entire edifice of educational provision it had so carefully constructed over three generations. The Alliance had to affirm and reaffirm its commitment to the education of Jews as good citizens of their states outside of Israel. Again, we shall return later to this matter, which clearly shaped the Alliance's attitude to Zionism.

The AIU was not only a network of schools. The words "Alliance israélite universelle" are a French translation of a Hebrew expression that means "all Jews are brothers." Cassin took on the presidency of the AIU in part to speak for his murdered brothers, to protect and transmit their heritage. Once more his mission was to heal the wounds of war.

At the outset of his career as president of the Alliance, he wrote to a British colleague, S. D. Temkin, the British secretary of the Anglo-Jewish Association, about the daunting task ahead of him: "As to French Jewry, it will be more difficult to recover from the terrible blows it suffered. We do not know on which personalities we will be able to count to take charge of its destiny and to raise it up from the abyss in which Hitler sank it. We know nothing about its former leadership. The only point we can state clearly is that, as you have mentioned, the desire to see the activities of the AIU in Paris revived has already been achieved."[19]

The mission Cassin took on, with the complete support of the Central Committee, was larger than education alone. The first step after the Liberation had been to ask for reports on the state of the Alliance's schools from each of its directors, but as early as November 29, 1944, he created a Commission for External Affairs as well as a new center of documentation to aid the Alliance in its future work and to provide evidence for war crimes trials to come.[20] There was much work to do in the field of public relations and propaganda in order to dispel the clouds of hatred Vichy and the Nazis had generated during the war. Here was the charge: education, engagement in the defense of Jewish rights, and public outreach.

In a way, this assignment was not very remote from that of the prewar period. And yet the Commission for External Affairs recognized that the

Shoah had changed everything, and in particular, it gave a new meaning to the defense of human rights. Here is its language:

> The Commission believes that, under the circumstances, it must revise its foreign policy. The Alliance must fight against anti-Semitism and to safe-guard the rights of Jews in France, as well as in other countries.
>
> But on the other hand, the Commission's position is that the defense of the rights and the interests of Jews in France must be placed in the hands of lay associations and committees of lawyers who do not separate Jews from other victims of the enemy and his collaborators.
>
> The role of the Alliance is to ensure that the rights of Jews are not sacrificed.[21]

Here is the Alliance at the very moment René Cassin put his mark on it. To him, the defense of anyone's human rights anywhere was at the core of the defense of Jewish rights. Cassin's achievement was to show that the universalist objectives of the founders of the Alliance at that moment, just after the Holocaust, lay precisely in the field of human rights. From the time he assumed the presidency, everything the Alliance did was intended to be a step toward a new rights regime.[22]

This is how Cassin reinterpreted the emancipation motif of the founders of the Alliance. To them education was the first step toward freedom. Cassin concurred, but his generation faced another emancipatory task, that of freeing men and women from the depredations of what he termed the Leviathan state. The potential for destruction of such a state was so evident in 1945 that emancipation meant limiting the power of the state—any state—to abuse the rights of its own citizens or those of other countries.

By making the Alliance into a carrier of the message of human rights after 1945, Cassin was clearly extending the vision of its founders into another period of history. But he managed through his work for the Alliance to give a new coloration to his own form of Jewish identity: that of a French Jew, a patriot, a soldier, a Resistance leader, a man whose Jewishness was defined less by the injunctions of the Torah than by the emancipatory messages of the French Revolution, of Abbé Henri Grégoire and of the Universal Declaration of Human Rights of 1789 and 1793. The Polish historian Isaac Deutscher liked to call himself a "non-Jewish

Jew."[23] Cassin's personality is better captured in seeing him as a secular Jewish universalist, a man whose Jewishness was not initially at the core of his personal identity; it was made so by racists and killers.

In June 1947, Cassin chaired Jean-Paul Sartre's lecture titled "Reflections on the Jewish Question," given under the sponsorship of the AIU. In his introduction, Cassin observed that the catastrophe of the war, "which led to the extermination of two-thirds of European Jewry, can provoke among the survivors two attitudes: one toward forgetting, and which is normal, or the vow not to forget, to uncover the sources of the disaster, which is a more dignified response. Jean-Paul Sartre has chosen the second attitude."[24] Cassin did not endorse Sartre's view that it was the anti-Semite who defined the Jew; Cassin himself also rejected the view that the synagogue defined his own Jewishness.[25] In sum, Cassin was a man who listened to the prophets more than to the rabbis, and thereby stood in a line of Jewish-born freethinkers from Spinoza to Marx and Freud, who drew inspiration from but who lived primarily outside the Jewish tradition.

Cassin devoted his energy and passion to the Alliance, and in doing so, he realized one of his ambitions. As president of the AIU, he became a Jewish statesman at the very moment he was catapulted into work for the nascent United Nations and its Human Rights Commission. There was too an element of great pride in his standing as president of the Alliance. In effect, he was the foreign minister of Francophone Jewry, speaking for a persecuted and endangered population in Europe, North Africa, the Middle East, and beyond. In 1944, when his presidency effectively began, he was finally able to operate on the level of world affairs where he had hoped in vain de Gaulle would place him in 1941 in France libre. Three years later, he took on a new role as spokesman for an institution embedded in the republican tradition in France and abroad.

As president of the Alliance, he could affirm the significance of French language and culture as the carriers of the message of universal freedom. The schools of the Alliance, after all, were there to hand the torch of emancipation to whomever sought it. He was a French cultural patriot and proud of it, assuming "en toute sérénité," as he liked to say, that France's *mission civilisatrice* was to bring progress and enlightenment to the world at large. The schools of the AIU were carriers of excellence and gateways outside of France for Jews and others to the kind of citizenship the Revolution had brought to the Jews of France. The schools were emblems of French culture abroad, and deserved the financial and diplomatic support the French state provided for them. He defended the interests of Francophone Jews in North Africa and in the Middle East, protected in part from the worst of the Shoah. After 1943, he had a constituency, a Jewish world to represent, and he did so in Paris, in Casablanca, in New York, and in Jerusalem. The war made him a Jewish statesman.

In the aftermath of World War II, the balance of numbers and power in the Jewish world moved westward, over the Atlantic to New York. There the World Jewish Congress (WJC), founded in Geneva in 1936, exercised considerable authority in the coordination of international efforts to reconstruct Jewish life after the Shoah. The driving force of this organization was Nahum Goldmann, a German-educated, Lithuanian-born firebrand who had been the Jewish Agency's representative at the League of Nations in the 1930s. He probably met Cassin there. The Jewish Agency was the chief instrument of Jewish immigration to Palestine and, after 1948, to Israel. Goldmann was a Zionist in a way Cassin never was. For Goldmann, Jews had to learn Hebrew, not French,[26] though, like Cassin, he never believed that all Jews had to immigrate to Israel.

Goldmann's base of operations was New York, where he acted both as president of the WJC and, after 1956, as president of the World Zionist Federation. In October 1951, as chairman of the Jewish Agency, Goldmann helped found the Conference on Jewish Material Claims against Germany, arising out of a long-term reparations agreement he negotiated secretly with Konrad Adenauer for payments to Jews in Israel and elsewhere. "Elsewhere" included France and North Africa, opening up an important conduit for financial aid for the Alliance.

Alongside the claims conference, there was the "Joint," the American Joint Distribution Committee (JDC), which provided funds for Jews in need and for the restoration of Jewish educational life, including that undertaken by the AIU. In 1950, the Joint allocated $250,000 for use by the Alliance "in such a way as to bring about the largest possible enrolment of Jewish children in the schools, and the best type of service."[27] From 1949, the JDC provided social and educational support earmarked for the Jews of Morocco. In 1952, for example, the Joint provided 95 million francs to the Alliance, covering two-thirds of the deficit registered for that year.[28]

In the first postwar decade, those who held the purse strings Cassin needed to pry open for the Alliance were either American or working in New York. In the elegant surroundings of the suite he inhabited as a French delegate to the United Nations, in the Waldorf Astoria or the Biltmore Hotel, Cassin entertained the elite of world Jewry and joined them in their efforts to repair some of the damage done to the Jewish people as a whole during the war. His standing as a Jewish statesman came not only out of the Alliance, but also out of his years as a leader of France libre, as well as his position as vice president of the Conseil d'État. He had many friends in high places, including Eleanor Roosevelt.

Here is where his work as president of the Alliance intersected most clearly with his commitment to the human rights instruments of the newly founded United Nations. Cassin was able to make the case for international aid for the Alliance, as one of the oldest Jewish organizations engaged in education as the pathway to emancipation. It mattered not one iota that the Jews of North Africa and the Middle East had been spared the worst of the persecution. They had been sentenced to death by the Nazis just as he had been. Persecution of Jews anywhere was an affront to human rights everywhere. To provide North African Jews with the education they needed to live productive lives as full citizens of their countries was an even more essential task than ever. When he spoke on behalf of the Alliance, Cassin did so with the confidence of a man whose various commitments formed one integrated whole.

This period of Cassin's life was hectic and fruitful, but not always easy. He secured Joint funding of the Centre de documentation juive contemporaine, founded in 1943 and instrumental in collecting and preserving evidence of Nazi persecution used in later war crimes trials.[29] He helped set up a portmanteau group to represent French, British, and American Jewish opinion in the UN and in UNESCO. This body, the Consultative Council of Jewish Organizations (CCJO), acted as an international Jewish NGO. Not surprisingly, it spoke out strongly in favor of the implementation of enforcement mechanisms for the international human rights regime which Cassin had done so much to foster. In September 1951, the CCJO presented to the UN a memorandum supporting the right of individual petition and calling for the creation of a UN attorney general for human rights;[30] both measures were part of Cassin's program. The CCJO was also able to benefit from funds provided by the claims conference both in Israel and in France, thereby channeling German reparations money into the AIU, among other beneficiaries.[31]

The independence of the CCJO from Zionist organizations at times drew down the wrath of Goldmann, intent on orchestrating Jewish international efforts on his own. In 1955, Goldmann went incognito to Morocco to negotiate with the king in secret, and established his own network there, cutting right across already existing Alliance lines of communication established for years.[32] He was an Israeli official whose interests overlapped but did not coincide with Cassin's. As Chouraqui put it to Cassin, "Nahum is only interested in the North African problem from the broader perspective of Arab-Israeli relations."[33]

There was never the slightest doubt what Goldmann was up to. He wore one hat as an Israeli statesman, chairing the Jewish Agency, and another as a spokesman for international Jewry. Cassin's outlook was different. He wanted to make it possible for the work of the Alliance to continue, not to bring it to an end by mass emigration from Morocco or elsewhere. To Goldmann, such emigration was a good in and of itself; Cassin thought otherwise, though he believed that everyone had a right to emigrate. Cassin was a French statesman sympathetic to Zionism. Goldmann was a Zionist sympathetic to the needs of Diaspora Jews.

The problems facing Moroccan Jews were a constant preoccupation of Cassin in these years. Funding Alliance schools was a perennial headache. Braunschvig was the Alliance man on the spot, and he wrote time and again about the financial tightrope walk the organization faced. There were other issues at stake aside from financial ones. Chouraqui provided an expert report on the legal situation of Moroccan Jews, giving Cassin the chapter and verse he needed not only to protest against the limitations Moroccan Jews faced in the exercise of their citizenship, but also to secure the continued support of the king and the political elite for the work of the Alliance in Morocco.[34] If the Alliance were undermined, they argued, there would be fewer reasons for Moroccan Jews to stay in the country their ancestors had lived in for centuries. Until 1956, this was a persuasive argument, but it lost purchase in the subsequent decade when Jewish migration to Israel accelerated.[35]

Cassin's presidency of the Alliance spanned a period when French Jews, under the impact of the Shoah, became more and more sympathetic to Zionism. The prewar Alliance had been active in Palestine, but its leadership was either neutral or hesitant about Zionism, seeing it as a potential destabilizing element in their work. By the mid-1940s, French Jewish opinion had changed, and the Alliance changed with it.

Cassin, the AIU, France, and Israel

In late 1944, Edmond Fleg, Louis Kahn, and Maurice Leven drafted a statement of the Alliance's principles which was signed by Cassin, among others, as well as by the chief rabbis of France and Paris, and by Léon Meiss, president of the Consistoire.[36] Here, the secular and religious leaders of French Jewry restated the mission of the Alliance. Leven wrote:

> [The essential aim of the Alliance] was to liberate Jews from oppression and to develop among them the sense of their dignity. . . . To raise up the population of Jews downcast by centuries of oppression, both in the eyes of the world and in their own eyes, the Alliance israélite universelle opened schools in the Mediterranean basin and in the Near and Middle East.
>
> There, from Morocco to Persia, in spite of the abominable policy of Vichy and the disarray the war brought about, there was not a single day during the whole course of the war that the 100 schools of the Alliance closed their doors to its more than 50,000 students.
>
> Surviving the worst moments in its history, the Alliance, in the spirit of the new United Nations, asks its members to dedicate themselves to the service of the conscience of humanity.

To this end, the Alliance demanded for those Jews who could not return to their homes after the ravages of the war and the Shoah "the right to enter Palestine":[37] "The Alliance, while committed to the complete incorporation of Jews in the countries where they live, has never ceased to participate in the mutual Jewish effort in favor of the Holy Land. . . . For them it is more than a refuge; it is a center of spiritual warmth, the only one in which they are awaited impatiently, and from which, perhaps one day, the truths of Israel will shine forth once more."[38]

On the international level, the Alliance did everything it could to foster the case for partition and the creation of the State of Israel. On June 9, 1947, Cassin himself authored and sent to the secretary-general of the

UN, Trygve Lie, a "Memorandum of the AIU on the Palestinian Problem," which put the case for Jewish statehood in unequivocal terms. After the Holocaust, expediting Jewish immigration to Palestine "is the first duty of the international community." The reason was clear: "The survivors of Israel in Central and Eastern Europe desire, by a large majority, to build a new life in Palestine." To the Alliance, "this is a right humanity cannot refuse them." "The Alliance believes," he wrote, "that today the Jewish community in Palestine aspires to a change in its status, permitting an independence merited by their work and their creative spirit. We believe that the democratic spirit of the Near East can only but prosper through the influence of Jewish accomplishments in Palestine."[39]

The Alliance schools in Palestine were caught in the crossfire in the 1948 war. In Tel Aviv, the AIU school was located between present-day Tel Aviv and Jaffa. As soon as partition was announced, the school was under repeated gun and artillery fire. One teacher was badly wounded. Refugees poured in from surrounding homes. The school's director wrote to Paris, "Our school today is in the front line."[40] Alliance schools in Beirut were damaged at the same time. One of the first schools established by the Alliance in 1870 was in Mikve-Israel, in the southern suburbs of Tel Aviv. It was a pillar of the Zionist project. In the war of 1948, over 200 of its graduates were killed.

Once the State of Israel was established, the question of the future of the Alliance's schools within the new state rose to the top of the Alliance's agenda. Aside from Mikve-Israel, the Alliance ran schools in Haifa, Safed, Tiberius, Tel Aviv, and Jerusalem. All were funded by the French government, and now needed to come to an understanding with the new government of Israel.[41]

Cassin engaged in years of negotiation on the future of these schools and on their character within the framework of educational provision of the new state. French financial support made sense only if French were the language of instruction at least in part in these schools. The priorities of the Israeli Ministry of Education were different, however. First, there was the replacement of "teaching in French by teaching French" in a country that needed to teach Hebrew, Arabic, and increasingly English to its rapidly growing population of immigrants. Second, there was the need to place the curriculum and timetable of instruction of Alliance schools within that stipulated by the Ministry of Education.

The key issue was funding. And here Cassin played a crucial role, in large part due to the close rapport he had developed in New York and elsewhere with the first Israeli foreign minister, Moshe Sharett. In a visit to Israel, Cassin secured agreement from Sharett that Alliance schools would have a special status in Israel, since they contributed to "the gigantic task of the settling of new immigrants and the expansion of the national economy."[42] Ultimately, the Israeli Foreign Ministry approved a measure under which it undertook to pay one-third of the costs of salaries of Alliance teachers.

Over time, the Alliance schools merged with the Israeli school system. This was inevitable, not only given the political realities of the new state, but also because of the financially precarious position of the Alliance in light of its responsibilities throughout the Mediterranean basin. Alliance schools were important in the integration of North African immigrants in the 1950s and 1960s. What remains to this day is a commitment to social service and human rights in Israeli schools linked to the Alliance. There is a school for the deaf in Jerusalem as well as three schools in Mikve-Israel Youth Village. There are Alliance high schools in Tel Aviv and Haifa and two in Jerusalem, one named after Jules Braunschvig and the other after René Cassin.

From 1948 on, the critical question was how the Alliance could contribute to Israeli education while maintaining its independent stance in the educational system of those Muslim lands in which its schools were located. The answer was not at all clear. Alliance schools in many countries were targets for anti-Israeli agitation. On August 10, 1949, the director of the Alliance school in Damascus wrote to Cassin about a grenade attack in the court of a synagogue in Damascus in which twelve people were killed.[43]

The position of Moroccan Jews was similarly precarious. In May 1948, the sultan of Morocco issued a proclamation enjoining Morocco's 250,000 Jews "to avoid all attachments with the new Jewish state."[44] The Alliance spoke out forcefully against this statement and demanded protection for Moroccan Jews. The French resident general, Alphonse Juin, was surprised by their firm stance, which arose, said Eugène Weill, the secretary of the Central Committee and Cassin's right-hand man, because the Alliance "was concerned not only with education but also with the protection of Jews."[45]

This was Cassin's position throughout the postwar years, and to further it, he used his role as French delegate to the UN Human Rights Commission to great advantage. It was not only that he had access to leaders who could pass messages on to higher authorities. It was also that he could speak with an independent voice, one unconstrained by instructions from his government on this matter. One illustration among many is a letter he wrote to Sharett on June 13, 1952, labeled "urgent and personal." In it he asked Sharett to reconsider Israel's provisional acceptance of a UN General Assembly extraordinary session on Tunisia, then at the beginning of a nasty two-year war for independence. The substance of Cassin's advice is less relevant than the language he used in giving it. He asked his friend Sharett "to consider his vigilant friendship as a source of his pleading not only for the cause of France but for the indivisible cause, in my eyes, of France, Israel and North African Jewry, of which I believe I am one of the responsible trustees. . . . The Jews of Africa can say nothing. . . . They are muzzled by legitimate fear. . . . Their terror of massacres prevents them from speaking out. Moroccan and Tunisian peasants know that it is only the presence of France which enables them to live and remain protected from thieving and bloody indigenous masters."

He begged Sharett not to play into the hands of those "who, to hasten the immigration to Israel of 400,000 North African Jews, orchestrate fatalism and panic, without even hesitating before the prospect of pogroms."[46]

This is a revealing document in that it shows the two essential facets of Cassin's Jewish stance at this time. The first is as protector of North African Jewry in the face of violence directed at them in the midst of the upheavals imbedded in the struggle for decolonization. The second is as an interlocutor between France and Israel, and as someone who could point out in no uncertain terms the importance of French protection for Jews not only in Tunisia or Morocco, but in Lebanon and Syria too.

It is clear that insinuations that Cassin and other Jews on French delegations were really Israeli representatives were without the slightest foundation. Cassin had interests and commitments that diverged from those of Sharett and the rest of the leadership of Israel.

Cassin was a Diaspora Zionist, a man who believed that Jews who wished to live a collective life in Palestine should be free to do so. He was not among them, but in the postwar years he shared their aspirations and did what he could to help realize them. Others on the Central Committee of the Alliance made aliyah; both Braunschvig and Chouraqui ended their days in Jerusalem. Cassin never considered it but defended the rights of those who wanted to join them. He was not one of those who suffered a sense of disenchantment with the republican tradition in the aftermath of the war. He worked to revitalize that tradition, not to discard or refashion it.[47]

In 1960, the French government joined in the chorus of praise for the work of the AIU, then celebrating its centenary in Paris, in New York, and from Morocco to Iran.[48] The Alliance and its president could reflect with pride on this substantial achievement, maintained despite the catastrophe of World War II.

From that point on, though, the Alliance's position vis-à-vis the French government changed, and not always for the better. The problem was clear: how to maintain the work of Alliance schools in countries severing their ties with France. The trouble in doing so was both financial and human. The ending of the French protectorate in Morocco meant the nationalization of Alliance schools. Their independent character could not be maintained, though in the case of Morocco their status was reconfigured, under the designation Ittihad-Maroc, to enable their work to go on.[49] Even then complex problems remained; there was, for example, the question of pensions for Alliance teachers in the Maghreb who were living in retirement in France. Who would pay their pensions, and at what levels? In Algeria, the choices were starker still. The end of French rule in 1962, after eight years of civil war, meant the end of a way of life for the French population of Algeria, who immigrated massively to France. Among them, tens of thousands of Algerian Jews had an additional reason to leave, either for France or for Israel. The Alliance did not run schools in Algeria, since the French educational system was installed there, but its commitment to defending Jews wherever they were persecuted required action in the wake of the Algerian war of independence. Cassin was well placed to patrol the corridors of power to this end, and his repeated statements on the need to defend Jews in peril or those in need of assistance were consistent with long-standing Alliance practice.

The shift of French policy toward Israel and the Arab world leading to de Gaulle's famous press conference of 1967 is a story beyond the scope of this chapter. Suffice it to say that Cassin took de Gaulle to task in public for his insulting remarks about a stiff-necked and domineering people. My own view is that de Gaulle was actually referring to himself in these terms, and believed naively that Jews should be flattered by the comparison. Cassin did not see it that way, but he never broke with de Gaulle. The shared world of France libre and the impeccable record de Gaulle personally had of immunity from the anti-Semitism rife within France libre itself accounts for the continuation of their relationship, *malgré tout*.

Cassin's Jewish life, born in the period when he was a French delegate to the League of Nations, came into its own during World War II largely because de Gaulle asked him to lead the AIU out of the dark years of the war. Cassin's family suffered during the Shoah: twenty-six relatives—men, women, and children, from age two to eighty-eight—were deported, never to return. His family suffered from *spoliation*, but were protected from *aryanization* by friends and colleagues who handed back considerable family assets, derived from the wine business in Marseille and elsewhere, virtually intact. But what the war did was to provide an institutional focus for Cassin's *ahavat Israel*, his love for the people of Israel, which was manifest in a host of ways in the second half of his very long life. Through the Alliance, and through the international negotiations he carried on for and alongside it, he became one of the most prominent Jewish statesmen of the twentieth century. His name is forever celebrated as the spokesman for the Jewish secular tradition of human rights. That tradition was deepened by and during World War II, and despite the predicaments presented by Israeli policy in the years after 1967, Cassin remained committed both to Israel and to human rights.

How he might have reacted to subsequent events is a moot question. Should Jews become oppressors, he said in 1948, he would not be with them. There is nothing at all in the record of his life which indicated that he would have tolerated Israeli violation of human rights, though there is also nothing in the record to indicate that he placed Palestinian rights on the same level as the Jewish right of return after 1945. He saw the Palestinian cause as being that of victims of war, those who should find appropriate reparation, but he never placed their predicament in the same category as the Jewish right to self-determination. In this he was a man of his generation, with a Eurocentric view of rights and a tendency to shy away from the problems of torture in Algeria and conflict on the West Bank.

A child of republican France and its empire, a child of the Dreyfus affair, *un ancient combatant de la grande guerre*, and one of the founders of the French veterans' movement, René Cassin made human rights his life's mission. He was a militant Jewish pacifist, a stalwart friend of Israel, a Zionist rooted in France, whose last dream was to have his remains moved to the Panthéon. That indeed occurred in 1987, on the centenary of his birth. He remains to this day the only Jew honored in this way, a proud figure of the republican tradition, his commitment to which withstood the shock of war, occupation, collaboration, and Shoah. Whatever degree of disenchantment there was among French Jews in this period, René Cassin never even remotely embraced it.

NOTES

1. For the opposite view, see Muriel Pichon, *Les français juifs, 1914–1950: Récit d'un désenchantement* (Toulouse: Presses universitaires du Mirail, 2009).

2. AIU, Paris, AM Présidence 001e, Cassin to Sam Lévy, directeur des Cahiers Sfaradis, in Neuilly, April 12, 1948.

3. AIU, Central Committee, Minutes, 1941–46, September 11, 1944.

4. AIU, AM Présidence 006a, for the rules governing the election of the president of the AIU.

5. François-Joachim Beer, "René Cassin et le judaïsme," in *La pensée et l'action* (Paris: Éditions F. Lalou, 1972), 283; André Chouraqui, "René Cassin devant l'aventure d'Israël," *Les Nouveaux Cahiers* 45 (1976): 21.

6. AIU, Central Committee, Minutes, October 18, 1943, René Massigli, commissioner for foreign affairs, "expressly recognized the legal existence of the Central Committee and that the Central Committee of Algiers was authorized to manage its moral and material interests." See also the Chouraqui archive in Jerusalem: Cassin, "L'Alliance pendant la guerre et le retour à Paris en 1944," Central Committee, Minutes, September 11, 1944.

7. AIU, AM Présidence 007C, circular of April 11, 1956.

8. Jean-Claude Kuperminc, "La reconstruction de la bibliothèque de l'Alliance israélite universelle, 1945–1955," *Archives juives* 34, no. 1 (2001): 103.

9. Laurent Grison, "L'Alliance israélite universelle dans les années noires," *Archives juives* 34 (2001): 9–22.

10. AIU, AM Présidence 007a, Chouraqui to Cassin, February 26, 1954.

11. Chouraqui archives, Jerusalem, Cassin to Chouraqui, October 14, 1947; AIU, AM Présidence 005a, Cassin to Chouraqui, May 23, 1952; AM Présidence 030, Chouraqui to Cassin, August 21, 1957.

12. AIU, Central Committee, Minutes, May 25, 1945.

13. AIU, AM Présidence 001C, Report by J. Rudnansky, April 29, 1946.

14. AIU, AM Présidence 003a, Central Committee, October 4, 1950.

15. AIU, AM Présidence 005a, Commission des écoles, May 13, 1952.

16. AIU, AM Présidence 001b, Isfahan, emploi du temps, 1944–45.

17. AIU, AM Présidence 001b, letters and telegrams, January 1945.

18. AIU, AM Présidence 005a, Cassin to J. Torres-Bodet, director-general of UNESCO, June 8, 1951.

19. René Cassin to S. D. Temkin, September 25, 1944, Anglo Jewish Association papers, AJ37/6/6/5/2, Parkes Library, University of Southampton. Thanks are due to Maud Mandel for drawing my attention to this source.

20. AIU, AM Présidence 005a, Cassin note, June 5, 1952.

21. AIU, AM Présidence 001A, Commission des affaires extérieures, November 29 and December 9, 1944.

22. On this period in the history of the AIU, see Catherine Nicault, "L'Alliance au lendemain de la Seconde Guerre mondiale: Ruptures et continuités idéologiques," *Archives juives* 34, no. 1 (2001): 23–53.

23. Isaac Deutscher, *The Non-Jewish Jew and Other Essays* (Oxford: Oxford University Press, 1968).

24. "Conférence de Jean-Paul Sartre," *Cahiers de l'Alliance israélite universelle* (May–June 1947): 3. I am grateful to Samuel Moyn for drawing my attention to this text.

25. Jean-Paul Sartre, *Réflexions sur la question juive* (Paris: P. Morihien, 1946).

26. Joseph Frankel, "Dr Nahum Goldmann," *Canadian Jewish Chronicle,* July 9, 1954, 6.

27. AIU, AM Présidence 003a, Joseph Schwartz to Cassin, August 16, 1950.

28. AIU, AM Présidence 005b, budget for 1952, May 28, 1952.

29. AIU, AM Présidence 005a, Cassin to Jacob Blaustein, March 7, 1952.

30. AIU, AM Présidence 004b, Moses Moskowitz, Memorandum on human rights, September 15, 1951.

31. AIU, AM Présidence 005a, Memorandum on Israeli-German negotiations, March 16, 1952.

32. AIU, AM Présidence 007b, Braunschvig to Weill, April 4, 1955.

33. AIU, AM Présidence 007a, Chouraqui to Cassin, September 3, 1956.

34. André Chouraqui, *La condition juridique de l'Israélite marocain*, preface by René Cassin (Paris: Presses du Livre français, 1950).

35. Yaron Tsur, "L'AIU et le judaïsme marocain en 1949: L'émergence d'une nouvelle démarche politique," *Archives juives* 34, no. 1 (2001): 54–73.

36. On the drafting of this document, see Nicault, "L'Alliance au lendemain de la Seconde Guerre mondiale," 29. Her interpretation is that Fleg and Kahn drafted the

text and Leven edited it. My hunch is that Leven did more than edit it, but I defer to Nicault's expertise on this point.

37. AIU, AM Présidence 001b, "Une déclaration de l'Alliance israélite universelle," November 11, 1944.

38. Ibid.; on this declaration, see Chouraqui, "René Cassin devant l'aventure d'Israël," *Les Nouveaux Cahiers* 45 (1976): 22; and for the full text, see *Cahiers de l'Alliance israélite universelle* (June–July 1947).

39. AIU, AM Présidence 030, René Cassin, "Memorandum de l'AIU sur le problème palestinien," June 9, 1947.

40. AIU, AM Présidence 030, A. Silver to Cassin December 3, 1947.

41. AIU, AM Présidence 030, "Memorandum relatif aux oeuvres françaises en Terre-Sainte présenté à la Commission spéciale des Nations Unies pour la Palestine," July 27, 1947. There is here a full list of Alliance schools and student numbers in each.

42. AIU, AM Présidence 030, Sharett to Cassin, May 10, 1950.

43. AIU, AM Présidence 002a, Rahmani to Cassin, August 10, 1949.

44. Tsur, "L'AIU et le judaïsme morrocain en 1949," 54.

45. Israel State Archives, Ministry of Foreign Affairs, 2563/14, September 26, 1948, as cited in Tsur, "L'AIU et le judaïsme marocain en 1949," 55.

46. AIU, AM Présidence 010, Cassin to Sharett, June 13, 1952.

47. For the opposite view, see Pichon, *Les français juifs*.

48. In the basement of the International Institute for the Rights of Man in Strasbourg, among Cassin's books and papers, there is a book on the tribes of Israel personally dedicated to Cassin by Yitzhah Ben Tsvi, president of the State of Israel. Cassin received the book on this occasion.

49. AIU, AM Présidence 015, Cassin to Léon Benzaquen, June 13, 1972.

ABOUT THE CONTRIBUTORS

LUCILLE CAIRNS is Chair in French at Durham University, UK. She is the author of *Marie Cardinal: Motherhood and Creativity* (1992); *Privileged Pariahdom: Homosexuality in the Novels of Dominique Fernandez* (1996); *Lesbian Desire in Post-1968 French Literature* (2002); *Sapphism on Screen: Lesbian Desire in French and Francophone Cinema* (2006); and *Postwar Jewish Women's Writing in French* (2011). She is also the editor of *Gay and Lesbian Cultures in France* (2002) and coeditor of "Jewish Identities in Contemporary Europe," *Jewish Culture and History* 14, nos. 2–3 (August–November 2013). She is currently researching French Jewish writers' literary representations of Israel for a monograph entitled *Francophone Jewish Writers Dwelling in/on Israel*, to be published in 2018.

BRUNO CHAOUAT is Professor of French and Jewish Studies at the University of Minnesota. His most recent book is entitled *L'ombre pour la proie: Petites apocalypses de la vie quotidienne* (2012). He is finishing the manuscript of a book to be titled *Is Theory Good for the Jews? French Responses to the New Antisemitism.*

DANIELLA DORON is lecturer in Studies at the Australian Centre for Jewish Civilization at Monash University. She is the author of "'A Drama of Faith and Family': Familialism, Nationalism, and Ethnicity among Jews in Postwar France," *Journal of Jewish Identities* 4, no 2 (2011): 1–27, and the book *Jewish Youth and Identity in Postwar France*, forthcoming with Indiana University Press in August 2015. She is currently researching a new project on the emigration of Jewish children from Europe to the United States from the late nineteenth century to the post–World War II period.

SAMUEL GHILES-MEILHAC teaches modern Jewish history at Sciences-Po Paris and international relations at the Rouen Business School. He is the author of *Le CRIF 1943 à nos jours: De la Résistance juive à la tentation du lobby* (2011). He is currently writing a biography of Theo Klein.

SEÁN HAND is Professor of French Studies and Head of the School of Modern Languages and Cultures at the University of Warwick, UK. He is the author of *Michel Leiris: Writing the Self* (2002), *Alter Ego: The Critical Writings of Michel Leiris* (2004), and *Emmanuel Levinas* (2008); and the editor of *The Levinas Reader* (1989) and *Facing the Other: The Ethics of Emmanuel Levinas* (1996). He is currently preparing a book about surviving atrocity and disaster in contemporary French and Francophone culture.

JONATHAN JUDAKEN is the Spence L. Wilson Chair in the Humanities at Rhodes College. He is the author of *Jean-Paul Sartre and the Jewish Question* (2006), editor of *Race after Sartre* (2008) and *Naming Race, Naming Racisms* (2009), and coeditor (with Robert Bernasconi) of *Situating Existentialism* (2012). He is currently working on a monograph entitled *Critical Theories of Anti-Semitism* that examines the major theories and theorists of anti-Semitism.

EDWARD K. KAPLAN is Kaiserman Professor in the Humanities at Brandeis University. He has published books on Jules Michelet, Baudelaire, and Abraham Joshua Heschel, in addition to articles on Martin Buber, Thomas Merton, Howard Thurman, and Heschel. He is currently researching the Colloques des intellectuels juifs de langue française.

STEVEN T. KATZ is the Slater Professor of Jewish and Holocaust Studies at Boston University and Founding Director of the Elie Wiesel Center for Jewish Studies. His publications include *Post-Holocaust Dialogues: Critical Studies in Modern Jewish Thought* (1983) and *The Holocaust in Historical Context,* vol. 1 (1994). Recent edited volumes include *The Cambridge History of Judaism,* vol. 4: *The Late Roman-Rabbinic Period* (2006); *The Impact of the Holocaust on Jewish Theology* (2007); and *Comparative Mysticism: An Anthology of Original Sources* (2012). He founded and continues to edit the journal *Modern Judaism.*

LISA MOSES LEFF is Associate Professor of History at American University. She is the author of *Sacred Bonds of Solidarity: The Rise of Jewish Internationalism in Nineteenth-Century France* (2006) and is currently completing a book on French Jewish archives after World War II.

MAUD MANDEL is Director of the Program of Judaic Studies and Associate Professor of History and Judaic Studies at Brown University. She is the author of *In the Aftermath of Genocide: Armenians and Jews in Twentieth-Century France* (2003) and *Muslims and Jews in France: History of a Conflict* (2014). She is currently researching a book on the impact of the Holocaust and the birth of Israel on the Jewish Diaspora.

SUSAN RUBIN SULEIMAN is the C. Douglas Dillon Professor of the Civilization of France and Professor of Comparative Literature at Harvard University. Her books include *Authoritarian Fictions: The Ideological Novel as a Literary Genre* (1983), *Subversive Intent: Gender, Politics, and the Avant-Garde* (1990), *Risking Who One Is: Encounters with Contemporary Art and Literature* (1994), *Crises of Memory and the Second World War* (2006), the memoir *Budapest Diary: In Search of the Motherbook* (1996), and several edited volumes, including most recently *After Testimony: The Ethics and Aesthetics of Holocaust Narrative for the Future* (with Jakob Lothe and James Phelan, 2012). She is currently writing a book on Irène Némirovsky, her daughters, and problems of Jewish identity in France before and after World War II.

DAVID WEINBERG is Professor Emeritus at Bowling Green State University and Wayne State University. From 1993 through 2013, he served as Director of the Cohn-Haddow Center for Judaic Studies and Professor of History at Wayne State University in Detroit. Dr. Weinberg is the author of *A Community on Trial: The Jews of Paris in the 1930s* (1977) and *Between Tradition and Modernity: Haim Zhitlowski, Simon Dubnow, Ahad Ha-Am, and the Shaping of Modern Jewish Identity* (1995). He is presently preparing a study of the reconstruction of Jewish life in western Europe after World War II.

JAY WINTER is the Charles J. Stille Professor of History at Yale University. His books include *Sites of Memory, Sites of Mourning: The Great War in European Cultural History* (1995), *Remembering War: The Great War between History and Memory in the 20th Century* (2006), *The Legacy of the Great War: Ninety Years On* (2009), and, with Antoine Prost, *René Cassin* (2011). He has edited the three-volume *Cambridge History of the First World War* (2013).

INDEX

1950s, 20, 22
1960s, 20
1970s, 20

Academy of Moral and Political Sciences, 204
Adorno, Theodor, 160
Agricultural growth, 16
Agriculture, 17
Air France, 16
Algeria, 22, 47, 48, 131, 223; and Algerian immigration, 41, 47; Algerian Jews, 46, 48, 49, 53n6, 56n48, 57n55, 205, 207, 221 (*see also* North African Jews); Algerian terrorists, 23n3; Algerian War of Independence, 2, 22, 41, 52, 122, 131, 136n9, 221. *See also* Decolonization, and era of
Aliyah, 23n3, 24n14, 32, 57n54, 154, 221
Alliance française, 205
Alliance israélite universelle (AIU), 5, 6, 7, 15, 53n5, 64, 65, 73, 74, 79, 80, 82, 91, 201n4, 203, 204, 205, 206, 207, 208, 209, 211, 213–18, 221, 222, 223n2, 223n4, 223n6, 223n7, 223n8, 223n9, 223n10, 224n11, 224n12, 224n13, 224n14, 224n15, 224n16, 224n17, 224n18, 224n20, 224n21, 224n22, 224n24
Allied powers in World War II, 4, 11, 16, 18, 19, 75, 78, 85, 110n2, 113n37. *See also* United States of America
American armed forces, 19, 61. *See also* Allied powers in World War II; United States of America

American Jewish Committee (AJC), 5, 28, 29, 32, 33, 35
American Jewish Joint Distribution Committee (American Joint Distribution Committee; AJDC; JDC; "The Joint"), 5, 7, 9, 28, 29, 30, 33, 35, 37n3, 37n4, 41, 44, 47, 53n15, 56n39, 57n54, 57n59, 63, 68, 70n10, 89, 91, 112n28, 113n34, 141, 214, 215
American Jewry, 21, 32, 36, 183
Anglo-Saxon dominance, 17
Anti-Semitism, 21, 22, 25n30, 29, 32, 35, 38, 44, 55n29, 62, 63, 70n10, 103, 104, 108, 130, 156, 157, 159, 169, 170, 176, 177, 178, 179, 180, 181, 183–86, 188n11, 189n26, 212, 222. *See also* Persecution; Vichy regime: persecution of Jews
Arab-Israeli War, 22
Arendt, Hannah, 76, 157, 167n7, 175, 176, 188n14
Ariel, Joseph, 68. *See also* Fisher, Joseph
Aron, Raymond, 138n34, 169, 179
Artists, and postmemory, 20
Artwork, 6, 98
Asch, Sholem, 185
Ashkenazi, Léon, 14
Assimilation, and the French Republic, 1, 2, 3, 4, 6, 14, 15, 38, 39, 49, 56n48, 56n51, 58, 143, 191n43, 194, 209
Assimilationism, 34, 55n30, 157
Association des enfants cachés, 118–19
Association des fils et filles des déportés juifs de France (Association of the Sons and Daughters of Jews Deported from France), 21